Frontiers, Plantations, and Walled Cities

Frontiers, Plantations, and Walled Cities

Essays on Society, Culture, and Politics in the Hispanic Caribbean, 1800–1945

Luis Martínez-Fernández

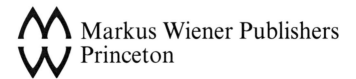

Markus Wiener Publishers
Princeton

For information, write to
Markus Wiener Publishers
231 Nassau Street, Princeton, NJ 08542
www.markuswiener.com

Library of Congress Cataloging-in-Publication Data

Martínez-Fernández, Luis, 1960-
  Frontiers, plantations, and walled cities : essays on society, culture, and politics in the Hispanic Caribbean, 1800-1945 / Luis Martínez-Fernández.
  p. cm.
  Includes bibliographical references.
  ISBN 978-1-55876-511-5 (hardcover : alk. paper)
  ISBN 978-1-55876-512-2 (pbk. : alk. paper)
  1. Caribbean Area—History. 2. Caribbean Area—Social life and customs.
3. Caribbean Area—Politics and government. 4. Frontier and pioneer life—
Caribbean Area. 5. Plantation life—Caribbean Area—History. 6. Cuba—History.
7. Puerto Rico—History. 8. Dominican Republic—History. 9. Caribbean Area—
Relations—United States. 10. United States—Relations—Caribbean Area. I. Title.
  F2176.M37 2011
  972.9'04—dc22
    2010025360

Markus Wiener Publishers books are printed in the United States of America on acid-free paper and meet the guidelines for permanence and durability of the Committee on Production Guidelines for Book Longevity of the Council on Library Resources.

For Luis Alberto,
my firstborn son,
with love and admiration

Contents

Acknowledgments

I wish to express my gratitude to Markus Wiener for inviting me to compile and edit this collection of previously published articles, and to Janet Stern, senior editor at Markus Wiener Publishers, and Molan Goldstein, for their special care in the editing of this book. I also want to thank all the colleagues and friends who over the past few years have commented on and made recommendations to improve these articles. Finally, I wish to thank the editors of *New West Indian Guide*, *Cuban Studies*, *The Journal of Ecclesiastical History*, *Diplomatic History*, *Magazine of History*, and *Revista Mexicana del Caribe* for granting me permission to reprint the articles in this book.

Introduction

This book is a compilation of seven articles that were previously published in different scholarly journals and an edited book over the past few years. They appear here in revised and updated form. Some of them were published in European and Latin American journals with limited circulation in the United States. Together, these works represent the variety of topics that I approached over several years of research on the nineteenth-century Hispanic Caribbean (Cuba, Puerto Rico, and the Dominican Republic), including aspects of economic history, foreign relations, gender, slavery, politics, religion, and culture. The fact that my research on the region and period led to so many different topics is a reflection of my belief that human phenomena are interrelated and that historical developments should be viewed not in isolation but rather in connection to a broader web of realities and circumstances. My earlier work on politics and foreign relations, for example, pointed to new avenues of social and cultural history research in areas such as religion and gender relations. The historical forces that pushed a segment of the Cuban planter elite to embrace annexation to the United States, I realized, were the same forces that opened the doors to Protestant missions in Cuba, eventually turning the island into the Latin American country with the largest Protestant presence. Likewise, decades of foreign meddling and intervention in the precariously independent Dominican Republic helped shape a political culture of regionalism and *caudillismo* that produced a succession of authoritarian rulers, culminating with the brutal dictatorship of Rafael Leónidas Trujillo (1930–1961). Meanwhile, Puerto Rico's coffee boom of the last third of the nineteenth century brought the island's commerce closer to Spanish and European markets, and by extension, its elites developed a political culture dominated by autonomist aspirations, parliamentary solutions, and lobbying practices.

Despite the enormous potential for regional and comparative approaches to the history of the Caribbean, and more specifically the Hispanic Caribbean, very few scholars have produced works that transcend the traditional island-by-island approach. A handful of pioneering works produced in the second half of the 1980s, while not systematically comparative, began to point in the direction of regional and comparative possibilities for a less fractionalized view of the region. During the 1990s, some of my work, along with that of a few other historians, further established the Hispanic Caribbean as a regional unit of study and generated a modest body of comparative and regional studies.[1]

This volume reflects the regional and comparative approach that has characterized most of my research on the Hispanic Caribbean. Four chapters are explicitly comparative, and include two or more components of the Caribbean. The other three (one on women in Cuba, one on *caudillismo* in the Dominican Republic, and one on U.S. intervention in Puerto Rico) are implicitly comparative, informed by a deeper understanding of the region and the broader Atlantic context.

The opening chapter, "The Frontier and the Plantation," compares different Caribbean and Cuban socioeconomic habitats to seek explanations for regional cultural differences stemming from diverse economic activities and the habitats' relations with the outside world. Chapter 2 looks at the distinct ways in which Cuba and Puerto Rico responded to the growing worldwide demand for sugar during the mid-nineteenth century. It compares the islands' planter classes, their ability to expand and incorporate the latest sugar-making technology, the islands' commercial networks, the composition of their respective labor forces, and the way in which each island responded to an expanding worldwide demand for sugar. The third chapter, "Life in a 'Male City,'" studies the manifold social restrictions and forms of discrimination imposed on white, nineteenth-century Havana women. It explains their causes by examining the city's socioeconomic makeup stemming from the coexisting realities of class, patriarchy, slavery and Catholicism. Chapter 4 recreates and explains early Protestant activities in four particular locations: Havana and Matanzas, both in Cuba; Ponce, Puerto Rico's most politically, culturally, and economically vibrant municipality; and the small island of Vieques, off Puerto Rico's eastern coast. This chapter identifies four very different types of Protestant communities and seeks to explain their differences based on a number of variables, including location, demographics, social structure, and geopolitical realities. The following chapter, on *caudillos* and annexationism in the Dominican Republic, studies these phenomena, partially as a result of the republic's endemic vulnerability to foreign meddling and intervention and the rivalry among empires seeking to gain preponderance and control over the struggling republic. Under such circumstances, various Dominican strongmen embraced either annexationist or nationalist positions. Chapter 6 analyzes the context, actual annexation, and aftermath of the process whereby the United States acquired Puerto Rico in 1898. It also looks at the ways in which the population, its traditional political leaders, and the economy responded to the transition from Spanish rule to U.S. colonial domination. Lastly, chapter 7 seeks to answer the intriguing question of why the three insular components of the Hispanic Caribbean developed such disparate political cultures and followed markedly different political trajectories, despite being neighboring islands with similar historical experiences.

The works included in this volume actually go beyond the geographic limits of the Hispanic Caribbean. The Caribbean since the 1500s was the testing ground of what centuries later has come to be known as globalization. In the aftermath of the swift conquest of the larger Antilles, the region became deeply integrated within the brewing global system created by the European naval powers. Demographically decimated as a result of the initial clashes between natives and conquistadors, Cuba, Puerto Rico, and Santo Domingo were essentially built from scratch to satisfy European economic, military, and geopolitical needs. The settlers, enslaved labor force, agricultural know-how and machinery, language, legal system, religion, and much more were all imported—and soon thereafter were transformed through miscegenation and creolization. The works included in this book do not look at the Hispanic Caribbean as an isolated region but rather within the broader Atlantic, upon whose commercial powers it became dependent in official commerce, navigation, smuggling, military defense, and many other regards.

The Frontier and the Plantation: Two Competing Keys to Cuban and Caribbean Culture

Black Race: Guinea Blacks in Cuba, published by M. Pujadas. Barcelona: Montaner y Simón (ca. 1845).

Cuban demography, society, and culture and the various, often conflictive, definitions of national identity derived from them are the result of a series of intense historical processes unfolding over the past 500 years. I will enumerate just eight of them: (1) A population of approximately 110,000 natives was decimated by disease, war, and enslavement to the point of virtual extinction within three decades of the island's conquest by Spain.[1] (2) A total of around 700,000 African slaves were imported to Cuba between the early 1500s and the late 1800s; a large proportion of them endured the rigors of plantation slavery.[2] (3) A parallel, sustained European, mostly Spanish, immigration flowed into the island throughout the same period, producing a white majority by the second half of the nineteenth century.[3] (4) Between 1847 and the early 1870s, an estimated 125,000 Chinese workers arrived in Cuba as indentured servants; they endured conditions not too dissimilar from those of slavery and suffered appalling death rates.[4] (5) During the Cuban wars of independence between 1868 and 1898, an estimated 300,000 Cubans perished as a result of the wars and internment in concentration camps; another 100,000 were forced into exile, mostly to the United States.[5] (6) After 1898, the island received a massive influx of Spanish immigrants, over 400,000 between 1904 and 1916; about half of them remained permanently on the island.[6] (7) The sugar booms of the 1910s and 1920s attracted a quarter of a million workers from Haiti and Jamaica.[7] (8) Since 1959, more than a million Cubans have left their homeland, fleeing the Castro regime. Today, as in 1898, roughly one-tenth of the Cuban population resides in the United States. If V. S. Naipaul's statement is true that the

---

A version of this chapter was originally published in Spanish as "La frontera y la plantación: Reflexiones sobre dos claves para empezar a entender las culturas cubana y caribeña," in Josef Opatrný and Consuelo Naranjo Orovio, eds., *Visitando la isla: Temas de historia de Cuba* (Madrid/Frankfurt: AHILA/Iberoamericana/Vervuert, 2002): 149–59.

Caribbean is made up of manufactured societies, shaped and reshaped by the pressures and demands of empires, it is nowhere truer than in Cuba.[8] Another useful metaphor in understanding Cuba's troubled history is that of an open wound that begins to heal and form scar, only to be opened over and over again, like the gaping wound leading to Prometheus's liver.

Given its dramatic and violent history of depopulation, forced immigrations, and recurrent massive exile, Cuba's cultural essence has been the subject of much debate. Conflicting definitions of nationhood have surfaced and resurfaced. Cuba has been characterized as the most African—with the exception of Haiti—of the hemisphere's societies. It has been described as the most Spanish of all New World countries—Spaniards certainly appear to be more at home in Cuba than elsewhere in the Americas. Cuba has also been described as the most Americanized—meaning more like the United States—than any other Latin American nation, even after five decades of anti-American revolution. Although there are very few Chinese and Jews left in Cuba, at an earlier point, Cuba was among the most Chinese and Jewish nations of Latin America. And finally, Cuba is often portrayed and defined as a mulatto nation, culturally as well as racially. But Cuba is also none of the above; in the words of Carlos Franqui: "Cuba is not Indian. Cuba is not White. Is neither black nor yellow. Cuba is mulatto, mixed, whitish black, and tobacco-hued."[9]

The very legitimate coexistence of such disparate characterizations of Cuba and the Cuban people raises further questions, such as should one speak of a single definition of Cuban nationality or of several coexisting ones; to what extent have creolization and syncretism produced a cohesive, culturally homogeneous Cuba; and to what extent do these processes remain incomplete, even after five decades of a revolutionary government's attempts to eradicate racial, social, and regional inequalities? I do not pretend to be able to sort out these questions, certainly not within the context of this chapter. What I will do, instead, is discuss the complexities of these and related questions and survey two overarching keys that scholars have used to decipher Caribbean and Cuban national culture: the interpretative frameworks of the frontier and the plantation. Perhaps the first person to systematically compare these two keys was Dominican sociologist Pedro Francisco Bonó, who in an 1881 essay linked different regions and agricultural products of the Dominican Republic with contrasting social, political, and economic realities. Decades later, Cuban anthropologist Fernando Ortiz contrasted these models in his masterful *Cuban Counterpoint* (1940). Sugar and tobacco, Ortiz concluded, were the protagonists of Cuba's history, each of them the creator of a particular culture diametrically opposed to the other.[10]

Needless to say, culture and race are not synonymous, although they would appear to be, given how much of the discussion dealing with national identity in Cuba and the Caribbean treats such categories. Ortiz warned of the dangers of "studying the human factors of Cuba through race." "To understand the Cuban soul," the Cuban scholar stated, "one should study not races but cultures instead."[11] Race, of course, is more easily determined and quantifiable. We know with some precision, for example, how many slaves were imported to Cuba, St. Domingue, or Jamaica. We even have a pretty good idea of the ethnic and regional origins of these slaves, and how they changed over time.[12] We can also determine the current racial composition of say, Puerto Rico or the U.S. Virgin Islands. Now, culture is another matter. The development of the distinctive cultures of the Caribbean has responded to a multitude of factors beyond patterns of race, which scholars have weighed studiously over the years. Among these factors are the timing of the colonies' settlement, the timing of the development of the plantation complex, the cultural package—baggage, if you will—brought by colonizers from their respective metropolises, the religious and legal institutions that framed each particular colonizing enterprise, and the way in which slavery was abolished.[13]

It is easily recognizable that the particular historical trajectories of the Hispanic Caribbean have produced populations in Cuba, Puerto Rico, and the Dominican Republic with larger proportions of European ancestry than in Francophone or Anglophone islands such as Martinique or Barbados. In the middle decades of the nineteenth century, for example, while the rest of the Caribbean exhibited black-to-white ratios of around 10:1, the proportion of whites in the three components of the Hispanic Caribbean ranged between 30 and 60 percent.[14] What remains unclear and subject to debate is the relative cultural Africanness of the various insular components of the Caribbean. Is Cuba, as some have argued, an essentially African country?

Ortiz was among the first scholars to recognize the centrality of African contributions to what eventually crystallized as Cuban national culture. That which stands as most authentically and essentially Cuban, Ortiz asserted, is the Afro-Cuban contribution.[15] More recently, Antonio Benítez Rojo built upon on these conclusions, stating that African cultural influences in Cuba—racially one of the least African nations of the Caribbean—are stronger than in almost any other Caribbean island: "Cuban religious beliefs, music, dance, painting, literature, and folklore show an African influence unequaled in any other Antillean nation except Haiti." He underscored culture's independence from race, adding that in Cuba "even those who can trace back their four grandparents to European provinces know that their cultural mother, their great mother, originates in Africa."[16] Likewise, regarding neighboring Puerto Rico, sociologist José Luis González forcefully sustained the thesis that the island's pre-plantation, Afro-*mestizo* population constituted Puerto Rico's first and therefore foundational storey. González's assertions in his *El país de los cuatro pisos* challenged those of Sidney W. Mintz, who characterized the cultural contributions of Puerto Rico's population of color as "subtle, interwoven, and reworked," while maintaining that Puerto Rico, and by extension most of the Caribbean, were profoundly "westernized."[17]

Are these conflicting characterizations based on the study of particular geographic pockets within the islands, or are they true for the islands in their entirety? Is Puerto Rico less or more culturally African than Cuba? If so, why, given that both countries had similar historical trajectories? Why is Cuba's Oriente more strongly Africanized than the western province of Pinar del Río?

While racial miscegenation has served as a useful metaphor for the more elusive process of cultural syncretism—Nicolás Guillén's poem "Balada de los dos abuelos" comes to mind—the extent of miscegenation seldom parallels the process of syncretism in any given insular component of the Caribbean.[18] Haiti and Barbados have a similar racial composition, whereby more than 90 percent of the population is black, yet the encounter of cultures has produced very different results, with Haiti being an essentially African country and Barbados being a heavily Westernized society, sometimes referred to as Little England or the Britain of the Caribbean. The political cultures of these nations, for example, differ greatly. While Haiti exhibits a personalistic, authoritarian, and violent political culture, similar to that of several African countries, Barbados's political culture derives from the British Westminster model. On the other hand, the three Caribbean nations where mulattoes constitute larger proportions of the population—the Dominican Republic, Puerto Rico, and Cuba, in that order—are not the societies with the most syncretic cultures. Linguistically, for example, none of these islands produced Creole languages the likes of those that emerged in the French and British colonies, where markedly lower rates of miscegenation prevailed.[19] The Spanish spoken by Cuban *guajiros* or Dominican city dwellers may not be pure Castilian Spanish, but it is much closer to it than the English spoken in St. Vincent or Dominica is to the "Queen's English."

I am not certain whether or not cultural anthropologists would agree with the following assertion, but I see culture, in its broadest definition, as the history that we inherit. As a historian, furthermore, I see that inheriting of history as a dynamic process subjected to manifold forces that continuously shape it. This definition of culture includes, of course, more than the three usual suspects at their material level: music, food, and dress. Although certainly relevant, these three elements are superficial aspects of culture. What a particular group of people eats is important, but I propose that far more revealing than the actual food items is the web of rituals and meanings attached to their preparation and consumption. I am pointing at questions that look deep into a culture's underlying assumptions: Does one usually eat alone or in a group? Does lunch last fifteen minutes or two hours? Who pays when the check arrives? Do the men or the oldest person in the group pay, or does someone take out a calculator to split the tab in equal parts to the nearest cent? Similar questions could be raised about music and its consumption. Is the music meant to be enjoyed individually, as through an iPod? Or is it meant to be enjoyed in a communal, participatory fashion, along the lines of call and response, the way much of the Caribbean's African-derived music is created and enjoyed?[20]

I wish to expand on the notion of culture as inherited history by elaborating on a couple of concrete examples from Cuban culture. Anyone familiar with the Cuban populations of Miami, San Juan, and Union City, New Jersey, the three largest Cuban enclaves outside of Cuba will recognize the fact that many Cuban men like to wear, in an ostentatious fashion, a profusion of gold jewelry: thick gold chains with large medallions of the Virgin of La Caridad del Cobre, bulky gold watches—*relojazos*—and diamond-studded rings. This cultural trait has profound roots and multiple social meanings: it is not simply a fashion statement. For one, in a society whose history has been scarred by the profound disruptions outlined at the beginning of this chapter, jewelry stands as the most compact and mobile form of wealth. For another, since in Cuba almost every generation has produced its own elite, gold jewelry has served as a visible marker of hierarchy and economic accomplishment. Furthermore, the propensity for male physical adornment must be understood within a nineteenth-century colonial context in which it developed: one marked by heavily male populations both in Havana and in the island's sugar plantations.

As I stated above, this chapter does not pretend to define the essence of Cuban culture or to solve the many mysteries of syncretism and cultural diffusion among Cubans and other peoples of the Caribbean; rather it seeks to categorize broadly some of the most salient theoretical frameworks that have been applied to the region with varying degrees of success over the past few decades. As a group, while applied with different terminology by different scholars, these competing perspectives can be categorized into one of the two overarching types: the frontier or the plantation.

The Frontier

The frontier category combines a wide body of interpretative perspectives that have been successfully applied over the years under different rubrics, among them tobacco peasant culture, settlement colonies, squatter societies, reconstituted peasantries, leather economy, Windward Passage–type cultures, the counter-plantation, and maroon cultures.[21] What they all share in common is the recognition of a culture that crystallizes beyond from the grip of the colonial state and the sugar plantation complex. While not strictly a frontier product, the tobacco that produced the culture that Ortiz contrasted to that of sugar encompasses many of the defining characteristics of the frontier model. While far from being the idealized world portrayed by Ortiz, tobacco cultivation in Cuba's west developed at a distance from, and with relative independence from, the long arm of the colonial state and the insatiable demands of sugar. In Ortiz's view, tobacco engendered all that was good in Cuban culture: free labor, small landholdings, democracy, liberalism, national pride. Six decades before, Bonó had reached similar conclusions about the impact of tobacco in Dominican political culture. According to him, tobacco was "the true father of the nation . . . the foundation of our infant democracy. . . [and] the most serious obstacle to the possible development of an oligarchy."[22]

More recently, Benítez Rojo contributed to the frontier model, but rather than finding the source of Cuban nationality in a "frontier" product like tobacco, he recognized its origins in the early colonial Windward Passage societies of the Caribbean of which Cuba's Oriente was an integral part. In his words, Cuban Creole culture was the product of "enterprising people, *mestizos* and *mulatos* in large measure who, because they lived far from the cities, stayed outside of the orbit of the colonial bureaucracy, the military fortifications, and the Church's watchful eye."[23] José Luis González offered a parallel model for the origins of Puerto Rican culture, one which he argued, was essentially Afro-*mestizo* and pre-plantation.[24] Sociologist Ángel G. Quintero Rivera later expanded this focus to include religious practices, musical syn-

cretisms, and other cultural manifestations developing in the hinter-
lands. More recently, in a stimulating essay on the quintessentially
Puerto Rican art of *bregar*—a negotiated form of conflict avoidance—
Arcadio Díaz Quiñones finds the origins of the custom in "old con-
cealing practices," essential to the survival of maroons and others
subsisting beyond the reach of state, church, and plantation.[25]

Bonó, Ortiz, Benítez Rojo, González, Quintero Rivera, and others
who have resorted to the frontier model agree on the fact that the frontier setting was more conducive to social fluidity and egalitarianism
and provided greater possibilities for cultural syncretism and racial miscegenation. Taken one step further, their arguments establish that such
characteristics produced the conditions for the early emergence of liberal ideologies and nationalism.[26] Even if eventually overshadowed or
absorbed by the sugar plantation complex, the salient characteristics
of pre-plantation frontier societies were preserved and continued to influence national culture in subsequent centuries. This bedrock of pre-
plantation culture, H. Hoetink argued, preserved the socio-racial
continuum of the frontier, most notably in the Hispanic Caribbean.[27]

The Plantation

The opposing interpretative complex is that of the plantation, with its
inseparable twin pillars: sugar and slavery. This model has a longer and
wider history among Caribbean intellectuals. One of the first scholars
to apply it systematically was Ramiro Guerra y Sánchez, whose *Azúcar
y población en las Antillas* was first published in 1927. Guerra viewed
the plantation as the region's most pervasive and insidious institution,
the source of the Caribbean's social, economic, and political ills.[28] Likewise, Ortiz associated "doña azúcar" with Cuba's historical misfor-
tunes: slavery, latifundia, social hierarchism, dependency, colonialism,
neocolonialism, and dictatorship. Sugar, Ortiz concluded, was essentially un-Cuban.[29] Since Ortiz, many other scholars have recognized the
evil legacies of sugar. Eric Williams enumerated the "concomitants of
sugar"; V. S. Naipaul poignantly stated that the epigraph of the
Caribbean's history could well be "Cane is bitter." "It is a brutal plant,"

he added, "tall and grass-like, with rough, razor-edged blades." W. R. Aykroyd expounded on the "sweet malefactor"; and George Beckford, Sidney W. Mintz, and filmmaker León Ichazo have also elaborated on the societal scars of the plantation in contemporary Caribbean societies.[30]

Indeed, the social ills associated with the plantation have demonstrated a lasting propensity to ratoon like cane stalks shortly after the harvest. There are virtually no sugar plantations left in Puerto Rico, where seventy years ago a large proportion of arable land was covered with sugarcane. Still, many of the social values and underlying assumptions about power, kinship, and social class associated with the plantation remain firmly in place. In Cuba, fifty years of revolution against the legacies of the plantation have not eradicated most of the evils of the "sweet malefactor." Although sugar production has fallen dramatically since the 1990s, and it is no longer Cuba's main revenue generator, whips, powdered wigs, and colonial militia rifles continue to haunt the sugar island as ghosts from a bygone era.

While there may be some disagreement about the centrality of the plantation in the formation of Caribbean culture and society, most scholars tend to see the plantation context as the least conducive to syncretism and most likely to perpetuate segregation of the races and their respective cultural contributions. Benítez Rojo, for one, recognized the plantation as the context that most exacerbated the tensions between the dwellers of the baracoon and the dwellers of the big house and that "hampered the consolidation of a national culture and national consciousness." Both González and Miguel Barnet have recognized the plantation as producing two distinct cultures: one pertaining to the master class, the other the product of the enslaved and laboring masses.[31] The resulting cultural bifurcation produced societies that remained unintegrated socially, culturally, and politically.

Barnet has made the unsubstantiated claim that as a result of the Cuban Revolution's triumph, "the entire culture that grew out of sugar, our popular traditional culture, as well as expressive forms arising from associated economic systems, were embraced together by our people in a natural and spontaneous movement." There is much truth to his premise of a Cuba socially and culturally divided by the legacies of the plantation. Barnet, in a sense, was also right when he argued that the revolution led to a sense of national integration, with the culture of the popular classes becoming dominant. Where he erred is when he suggested that this integration was the result of the government's measures; it was rather the result of a massive exile process in which the heirs of the culture of the master class were overrepresented.[32] The question remains: was the revolution led by the heirs of the master class or was it fueled by the heirs of the enslaved masses? Further yet, was the revolution led by the heirs of the culture of the frontier?

I will not attempt to answer these questions now, but to conclude I will draw attention to two moments in the history of the Cuban Revolution that I think shed much light. In 1970, Castro's government implemented a program to produce a record ten-million-ton sugar harvest. It failed, but in the process, as Benítez Rojo has reminded us, the island functioned like a virtual plantation. Modern-day slave quarters were erected, and like their ancestors two centuries before, part of the labor force went maroon.[33] The second moment was 1997 when a massive repatriation effort was orchestrated by the Cuban government to relocate tens of thousands of Orientales, heirs of the frontier culture, because they had become a nuisance in Havana, the metropolis that sugar built. Habanero humor immediately picked up on the irony, and jokes began to circulate that the repatriation must include the two most famous Orientales: El Comandante and his brother Raúl.

While much of what happens today on both sides of the Florida Straits reminds us of the pervasiveness of the sugar plantation, I believe that the keys to Cuban culture (the frontier and the plantation or, if you prefer, tobacco and sugar) are not mutually exclusive but rather two sides of a people whose collective liver, like Prometheus's, seems condemned to perpetually feed the ravenous appetite of a hungry eagle. Rather than the children of either don tabaco or doña azúcar, all Cubans, wherever they are and wherever their ancestors came from, are heirs of an Ortizian counterpoint in which the oppositions of the plantation and the frontier coincide and collided.

CHAPTER 2

The Sweet and the Bitter: Cuba and Puerto Rico's Responses to the Mid-Nineteenth-Century Sugar Challenge

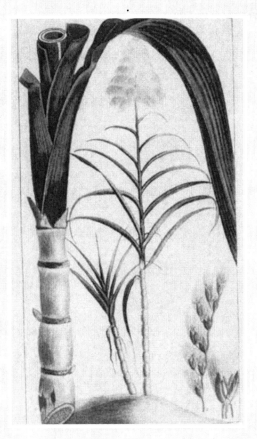

Botanical print of sugarcane (*Saccharum officinarum*), introduced to the Caribbean in 1493.

The 1840s and 1850s were decades of intensified international market demands on the economies of Cuba and Puerto Rico—in fact, on all sugar-exporting countries. Sugar consumption increased tremendously in Great Britain and the United States as new, lower tariffs for the sweetener were set. As Sidney W. Mintz aptly put it: "A rarity in 1650, a luxury in 1750, sugar had been transformed into a virtual necessity by 1850."[1] Increased demand for sugar—an apparently favorable development for sugar producers—was, however, only half the story. The supply of cane sugar from a variety of regions and beet sugar from western and central Europe also increased exponentially during the period, with world beet sugar production jumping from 60,857 metric tons in 1845 to 351,602 metric tons in 1860. Sugar prices thus fell or, at best, remained stagnant during 1840–1856, shrinking the profit margins of sugar producers around the world.[2] Under such pressing circumstances, Caribbean sugar planters had to adjust to the new exigencies of the world market. The Cuban and Puerto Rican planter classes responded differently to these pressures, a reflection of their divergent circumstances, including different levels of capital resources and adaptability.

Cuba's Response

Cuban planters, as a whole, responded to the new realities of the world market by accepting the sugar challenge: in light of diminishing profit rates, they sought to expand sugar production. Cuba's economy continued to steer away from diversification and relative self-sufficiency to-

This chapter was originally published as "The Sweet and the Bitter: Cuban and Puerto Rican Responses to the Mid-Nineteenth-Century Sugar Challenge," *New West Indian Guide* 67:1–2 (May 1993): 47–67. Reprinted with permission.

ward sugar monoculture and dependency. By 1855, sugar and its by-products represented 84 percent of the island's exports, and by 1862, 58 percent of its entire agricultural production.[3] Other traditional staples like coffee, tobacco, and cotton suffered serious setbacks as land, labor, and capital previously dedicated to those crops were siphoned off to the insatiable world of sugar. The number of coffee farms, for example, fell from 2,067 in 1827 to 1,670 in 1846, and to 782 in 1862, a 62 percent drop in thirty-five years. By the late 1870s, less than 200 coffee estates remained. In contrast, the number of sugar estates grew considerably during the same period from 1,000 in 1827 to 1,422 in 1846 and to 1,650 in 1850. During the 1850s, their number actually declined a bit to 1,365, a reduction, however, that reflected concentration rather than contraction.[4] The Cuban economy accepted foreign dictates regarding not only how much sugar to produce but also what quality of sugar. The United States and Britain, with refining industries to protect, shut off their markets to Cuban semi-refined sugar and called upon the island to produce more and more of less and less: of a lesser quality, for a smaller number of markets.

By the end of the 1850s, Cuba was a full-fledged sugar island. Seventy percent of the island's agricultural production consisted of sugar, close to 50 percent of all slaves worked in sugar plantations, and more than 25 percent of its cultivated land was designated to sugarcane.[5] These transformations were apparent to contemporary observers. "There are no manufactures of any consequence; the mineral exports are not great; and, in fact, sugar is the one staple," wrote Richard Henry Dana, Jr. "All Cuba has but one neck—the worst wish of the tyrant." A year later, sociologist and botanist Ramón de la Sagra warned against the island's dependence on a single export crop and coined the term *agricultura de rapiña* (preying agriculture). The problem of monoculture was aggravated by the fact that sugar exports increasingly headed to a single market: the United States.[6]

To stay competitive and to meet international quantity and quality demands, Cuba's planter class embarked on expansion resting on two simultaneous, although seemingly contradictory, strategies: the mechanization of the sugar industry and the expansion of the servile labor force. New machines had for a long time been a symbol of status among Cuban planters. Their mouthpiece of the late eighteenth and early nineteenth centuries, Francisco de Arango y Parreño, had emphasized the necessity of integrating Europe's latest technology into the island's *ingenios*. Steam-powered engines made their debut in Cuba as early as 1796, and the island's first railroad was in place by 1837, years before it would appear in Spain, Cuba's de jure metropolis.

The mechanization of Cuba's sugar industry in the 1840s and 1850s did not, however, touch all aspects of sugar production and transportation. Despite some efforts to introduce steam-powered plows, planting and harvesting remained in their primitive forms as labor-intensive, brutalizing manual tasks. New technology, however, transformed most of the manufacturing stages of sugar production. Steam engines to power larger and more sophisticated cane grinders were commonplace in the 1840s and 1850s. Whereas in 1827 only 2.5 percent of the island's sugar mills were run by steam engines, in 1860 close to 70 percent used this type of energy. Some estimates put this proportion near 91 percent by the end of the 1850s.[7] This transition from muscular and hydraulic power to steam sharply increased the grinding capacity and speed of the average *ingenio*.

The next major step in sugar production, the crystallization of the *guarapo* (cane juice), now required improved mechanization in order to keep pace with the larger and faster outputs of the grinding phase. The major technological innovation of this phase was the vacuum pan, known in the region as *tacho al vacío* or *tren Derosne*. In 1844, Wenceslao de Villaurrutia introduced one such device in his *ingenio*, replacing the open-pans system (*trenes jamaiquinos*) in which boiling cane juice had to be manually transported through a succession of pans of different sizes. Because of their exorbitant price tags, however, Derosnes and similar crystallizing machines were slowly incorporated into sugar making. Only the largest and most financially sound—or the most daring—*ingenios* managed to acquire vacuum pans. By 1863, only 4 percent of Cuba's *ingenios* had them. Four years later, a total of seventy-five *tachos al vacío* were operating at a staggering average cost of $120,000.[8] The rest of the planters had no option but to multiply the number of open *trenes* in order to keep up with the increased grinding capacity achieved with steam.

The following step, the *purga* or separation of sugar crystals and molasses, was the next phase in the mechanization orgy of the midcentury. Bottlenecks now occurred in this slow and simple process. Traditionally, the *purga* was accomplished through a long process of filtration (lasting thirty to fifty days), which consisted of pouring saturated molasses into conical containers with a cloth-covered hole on the bottom. By force of gravity most of the molasses covering the crystals dripped out into special containers, leaving behind sugar crystals of various degrees of purity. This stage was revolutionized by yet another innovation of the industrial age: the centrifuge, a spinning device with a metallic screen that pushed excess molasses out of its inner drum, leaving dried sugar crystals in the inner chamber. Cuba's pioneer in the use of the centrifuge was Joaquín de Ayestarán in his *ingenio* La Amistad in 1850. These machines were popularized to such an extent that 116 of them were purchased in 1862 alone.[9]

Students of Cuban agrarian and social history have underscored the importance of yet another aspect of the industry's mechanization: railroads. According to Manuel Moreno Fraginals, construction of the Güines railroad (1837) marked "a fundamental milestone" in the rapid expansion of sugar in the 1840s and 1850s. In the same vein, Franklin W. Knight later concluded that railroads were instrumental in freeing sugar production from earlier constraints that limited the extension of single *ingenios*. Knight stressed that the introduction of locomotives reduced transportation expenses and liberated a considerable segment of a plantation's labor force, which could now be transferred to the production stages. Indicative of the railroad's importance is the use by Laird W. Bergad of the year 1837 as a periodization watershed in his book on sugar in Matanzas. Twenty-two years after the Güines locomotive puffed its first clouds of smoke, the Cuban railroad network consisted of 378 completed miles; another 184 miles remained under construction. By 1865, the network stretched along 754 miles.[10]

The mechanization of the Cuban sugar industry was not as simple as choosing models from the catalogues of the West Point Foundry or

Derosne and Cail. It required enormous amounts of money, which planters often did not have. Since the addition of new machines had to be coordinated with land acreage, the number of slaves, and the rest of the machines in the complex, one addition in any particular phase usually translated into the necessity of further investments in more machines, land, and slaves. Setting up a midsized sugar plantation in the 1850s required an original investment of between $300,000 and $350,000, with yearly injections of $40,000 for upkeep and renovation of the slave force.[11]

Because of the costs involved, only a small segment of the old Cuban planter class managed to reorganize and expand its sugar operations. Between 1838 and 1851, Francisco Pedroso y Herrera, Nicolás Peñalvar y Cárdenas, Ignacio Peñalvar y Angulo, Gonzalo de Herrera, Nicolás Martínez de Campos, and José Luis Alfonso and his brother José Eusebio Alfonso either set up new mechanized *ingenios* or reorganized the ones they had. Many other planters could not produce the cash or secure the credit required to buy expensive machinery and continued to struggle along with what they had for as long as they could. Between 1850 and 1860, 385 *ingenios* stopped operations, a 23 percent decrease. According to Moreno Fraginals, the incapacity to purchase vacuum pans ruined the old planter class.[12] One could also argue that it was precisely the disorderly, yet seemingly unavoidable, purchase of sugar-producing equipment that paved the road for their eventual ruin. Meanwhile, new capital from licit and illicit commercial enterprises moved in to accept the sugar challenge and establish fully mechanized sugar plantations.

Most planters wishing to mechanize also sought to reduce the industry's dependence on imported slave labor. The growing number of slaves and their majority status, first revealed by the census of 1841, were a constant source of anxiety among the propertied classes, which feared a St. Domingue–style racial war. Moreover, international pressures for the cessation of the slave trade sent clear signals to the Cuban plantocracy that they had better start looking for alternative sources of labor. In 1854, planter Cristóbal Madan estimated that the application of the latest technology could reduce labor demands by seventy-nine workers in a medium-sized 4,000-hogshead *ingenio*. He added that it was impossible "to enumerate the changes fostered by the exclusion of ignorant and barbaric hands, substituting them by a higher intelligence, one manifested in machines and inventions as well as direction and rational structuring of the work process."[13]

Since the mechanization of the sugar industry failed to touch the planting and harvesting of sugarcane, the process did not alleviate labor needs; on the contrary, it increased them. The voracious appetite of the flashy new mills had to be fed, thus requiring the expansion of the cultivated area and the addition of new planting and cutting hands to allow the costly machinery to operate at full capacity. Alternative sources to bonded labor, however, were not easily forthcoming. Immigrants from the Iberian Peninsula and the Canary Islands tended to avoid plantation labor, and by the 1850s the island's planter class gave up hopes of promoting white colonization after innumerable failures during the previous decade. Attempts were also made to reduce the dependence on black slavery by introducing indentured laborers from China. During the second half of the 1850s, some 37,000 Chinese workers arrived as contract laborers. An anonymous planter dramatized the labor crisis when he stated in *La Gaceta de la Habana* that he would welcome not only Asian laborers, but even "orangutans if these were susceptible to domestication."[14] Thus, a paradox arose whereby, on the one hand, the planter class embraced modernization, acquiring the latest available technology, while on the other, it remained deeply attached to slavery and other forms of servile labor.

The relationship between mechanization and slave labor has long been a subject of Cuban historiography. In the late 1940s, Raúl Cepero Bonilla put forth the thesis that the continuation of slavery was incompatible with the modernization of the sugar industry. He argued, rather dogmatically, that the enormous cost of slavery hindered the accumulation of capital necessary for successful mechanization and that slaves were not capable of operating complex machinery. Other Cuban historians have built upon Cepero Bonilla's interpretation, most notably Moreno Fraginals and Fe Iglesias García. Iglesias García has asserted that slavery was a drag to industrialization, and she estimated that slaves represented between 38 and 40 percent of an average mill's investments.[15]

Rebecca J. Scott challenged this "incompatibility" thesis, concluding that "during the 1860s and 1870s, when the 'contradictions' within Cuban slavery were in theory becoming most apparent, the major sugar areas were nonetheless holding on to most of their slaves." According to Scott, it was precisely in the most advanced and mechanized sugar regions where slavery persisted. More recent studies by Bergad emphasize both the viability and profitability of slavery well into the late 1860s. Actually, the Cuban planter class had no alternative but to mechanize and expand if it was to stay in business; this demanded more labor, and since alternative sources failed to provide it, the only reasonable response was to remain attached to slavery. Neither theoretical incompatibilities, which do not affect the course of history, nor slave resistance, which is oftentimes romanticized, brought about the institution's eventual demise.[16]

During the 1850s, following four years of sharply reduced slave importation after the conspiracy of La Escalera (1848), slave trading boomed once again. Increased demand and the slave population's inability to reproduce itself spurred the growth of the slave trade. According to estimates reported by the British judges of the Havana Mixed Commission for the Suppression of the Slave Trade, a total of 67,422 slaves were imported between 1849 and 1858. In October 6, 1855, British Consul-General Joseph T. Crawford reported: "This Island seems to be beset with slavers; they are swarming and what is worse, they appear to succeed in landing their Slaves eluding the vigilance of the Spanish authorities always." The high-water mark of slave importation was 1859–1861, when the Mixed Commission registered 58,705 smuggled slaves and ninety-four enslaving expeditions.[17]

Growing demand for labor and increasing legal difficulties faced by slave traders translated into higher slave prices. The average price for a *bozal* (African-born) jumped from between $300 and $350 in 1845 to between $1,000 and $1,500 in 1860.[18] Another indicator of Cuba's desperate demand for labor were recurrent attempts to siphon slaves from Puerto Rico and Brazil. According to the late Arturo Morales Carrión, a student of Puerto Rico's slave trade, the 1850 cholera epidemic in Cuba, which killed 30,000 slaves, spurred the flow of slaves from Puerto Rico to Cuba. Speculators were accused of buying up entire estates in Puerto Rico just to gain control over their bonded labor force for export to Cuba. This practice continued even after authorities in Puerto Rico imposed a seventy-five-peso export tax (per slave) in 1853. Harsher labor conditions in Cuba made the threat of being sold there one of the most effective disciplinary measures that a planter in Puerto Rico could use. In fact, Cuba was to the Puerto Rican slave what Mississippi and Alabama were to slaves in the Middle Atlantic region of the United States: hell.[19] In March 1854, Governor Fernando de Norzagaray effectively put a stop to the flow of slaves out of Puerto Rico. In the decree's preamble, he alluded to constant complaints by Puerto Rican planters. Cuba also imported slaves from Brazil, mostly from that country's depressed sugar regions of the Northeast.[20]

If planters' labor needs were the main stimulus behind slave trading, bribes and traders' profits ensured the continuation of the trade. Captain-General Leopoldo O'Donnell is said to have left Cuba in 1848 with a fortune of over half a million pesos derived from slave importation bribes. His successor, Federico Roncali, true to O'Donnell's precedent, charged bribes of fifty-one pesos per imported slave.[21] In an 1853 dispatch, British Consul Crawford reported on the extent of official corruption regarding the slave trade: "Spanish Officers are bribed; the Slave Traders interested commit their offences and repeat them with the most complete impunity; Commissions sent by the Chief Authority of the Island to investigate such offences are baffled, or corrupted, the Masters and Crews are not punished, the Vessels are allowed to escape." In one instance, the smugglers of 468 *bozales* to the southern coast of Cuba paid bribes amounting to 468 gold ounces to the port's commanding officer, 234 gold ounces to the captain of the port, and 200 gold ounces, each, to the port's collector and tide surveyor, a total of over a thousand gold ounces. Rumors circulated that Captain-General José de la Concha received one gold ounce (seventeen dollars) for each slave landing on Cuban shores and that in 1859 alone, these fees earned him 680,000 pesos.[22]

Despite this high rate of "taxation," slave traders reaped enormous profits. According to an 1860 report by the British consul-general, slavers could afford to lose four vessels to every successful expedition and still make a profit. In an 1861 report to Judge Truman Smith of the New York Mixed Commission, Robert W. Schufeldt estimated that a 500-slave expedition could net $236,500. He calculated costs to be $37,500 for the slaves, $7,000 for the ship, $19,000 for wages, and $100,000—the largest single category—for bribes. Later estimates stated that slaves costing only $40 worth of cheap liquor and rifles in Africa could be sold in Cuba for $600 or more. According to Hiram Fuller of the *New York Mirror*, an individual investor could buy $500 worth of stock in a slave trading company and expect a $10,000 return in a year or two.[23]

The mechanization and slave-trading frenzy of the 1840s and 1850s provided a means for social mobility that eventually led to the subordination of one elite by another. New machines and fresh slaves came at no small cost to Cuban planters. As a class, they soon found themselves indebted to the Spanish-born merchant class, which grew wealthy from speculation in slaves, credit, dry goods, and machines deemed necessary for the expansion of the sugar industry.

The Cuban sugar boom of the late 1700s and early 1800s stands as the deviant case of the Caribbean; it was the only such experience fueled by native capital and native managerial skill. On this matter, Knight has written: "The sugar revolution derived its greatest impetus from the entrepreneurial skills of the oldest families in Cuba. These families, having become rich in land and having access to public offices, found themselves strategically positioned to take every advantage of the early economic development."[24] Among the most prominent names of these old families stood those of Arango, Montalvo, Duarte, Peñalvar, Cárdenas, Herrera, Chacón, O'Reilly, Calvo de la Puerta, O'Farrill, Pedroso, and Nuñez del Castillo. Their sugar operations consisted of patriarchal, self-sufficient units, requiring little financing and unsophisticated technology. According to Moreno Fraginals, their magic numbers were one hundred slaves, producing 115 tons of sugar.[25] Growth beyond that was achieved simply by establishing additional *ingenios*.

Evidence suggests that by the late 1830s, the majority of Cuba's sugar planters lacked the capital needed to expand and reorganize their enterprises. "[T]here are many known cases," wrote one observer, "who while having estates worth 200,000 or 300,000 pesos cannot dispense 2,000."[26] Thus, for many planters willing to accept the expansion challenge, mechanization meant recourse to outside sources of credit. In a society where, with few exceptions, there were no real banks until the 1850s, merchants played the role of moneylenders by advancing cash and imported goods in exchange for the guarantee of the planters' next harvest. The recourse to this mechanism, known as *refacción*, represented the subordination of planters' interests to those of the mercantile class and eventually the takeover of landed wealth by the latter. Interest stipulated in *refacción* contracts ranged between 18 and 20 percent per year, a virtually confiscatory rate if compared with the going rate for credit in Europe of 4 to 5 percent. Aside from the income derived from interest, merchants were able to extract profits by forcing planters to buy overpriced hogsheads, by charging excessive sales commissions and storage fees, and by speculating with the sugar that they bought at an agreed-upon price before the harvest.[27]

Many contemporary observers and more recent students of the region's history have blamed these high rates of interest on a specific piece of sixteenth-century Spanish colonial legislation: *el privilegio de ingenios* (privilege of the sugar estates). This law protected sugar producers from having their land, slaves, and equipment seized for debt. Arango y Parreño was among the first Cubans to blame the ills of the island's sugar industry on the maligned *privilegio*. In a May 24, 1797, deposition to the Development Board, Arango y Parreño called for its abolition. He argued that the *privilegio* kept good lands in bad hands and that it favored not only those suffering misfortune but also "treacherous swindlers." Another critic implied that such laws favored the debtors as he recounted the anecdote of a merchant who was sentenced to forty years in prison for attempting to collect from a delinquent marquis.[28] In the middle decades of the nineteenth century, colonial administrators in Cuba and Puerto Rico stepped in to remedy some of the problems of the sugar industry by attacking the centuries-old *privilegio*.

On November 10, 1848, Captain-General Juan de la Pezuela promulgated a decree granting sugar planters in Puerto Rico the dubious right to renounce the *privilegio*. Four years later, a royal decree provided that *ingenios* established hence would no longer enjoy the *privilegio* and that all others would lose it by 1865. It is likely that in light of their pressing needs for credit, planters were willing to forfeit their *privilegio* as a precondition for credit.[29]

In summation, by accepting the expansion challenge, Cuban planters prepared the scenario for their downfall and demise. Having little capital to finance their industry's modernization, the most daring resorted to expensive sources of credit. Others simply backed away from expansion. By the end of the 1850s, the planter class had lost financial control over the sugar industry. With the *privilegio* gone or about to expire, the actual loss of property became a matter of time. The economic and financial crisis of 1857 accelerated this process. In that year alone, 250 bankruptcies were registered in Havana. Francisco López Segrera has concluded in his study of the Cuban economy that by 1860, Spanish commercial capital had gained almost complete control of the sugar business. According to Moreno Fraginals, by 1863, two-thirds of the Cuban sugar industry was mortgaged and consequently in the hands of the mostly foreign merchant class. At that point, 95 percent of the *ingenios* were mortgaged to some degree.[30]

The mechanization of the Cuban sugar industry and the consequent rise of slave importations, the two processes that sealed the fatal destiny of Cuban planters, were precisely the circumstances favoring the ascendancy of Spanish commercial capital. During the 1840s and the 1850s, the Peninsular segment of the population gradually moved into territory heretofore monopolized by the Creole elite.

Spaniards migrating to Cuba usually carved their niches in either the colonial bureaucracy, the Church, the military, or the commercial sector. Only on rare occasions did Spanish immigrants engage directly in agricultural ventures of their own, Basque immigrant Julián Zulueta being a notable exception to this. "I have not seen during the time I have been in this Island," wrote a visiting traveler, "a single Spaniard cultivating the soil."[31] Many Spaniards started out as *dependientes* (shop clerks) in commercial establishments, perhaps working for a so-called *tío* (distant relative, called uncle) or a *paisano* (fellow countryman). Through thrift, cunning, or deceit, or a combination of all three, some *dependientes* managed to amass small fortunes that eventually allowed them to set up their own commercial enterprises.

Made up mostly of Peninsulars, the commercial sector exploited and subordinated the planter class through a multitude of mechanisms. First, it advanced overpriced goods and cash at exorbitant rates of 18 to 20 percent. Second, it set the price at which sugar was received as payment. Third, it collected fees, commissions, and other charges for transporting, storing, and selling the sugar. As if this was not enough, some merchants refused to accept sugar not packed in the containers that they sold. Their hogsheads and barrels were, thus, forced upon indebted planters at prices far above their market value. An extreme practice by some merchants consisted of collecting the molasses that dripped from sugar hogsheads during storage. These dripping molasses were not credited to the planters at the time of shipping; rather they were retained by greedy merchants as an additional source of profit. For them, it was obvious: every drop counted.[32]

Rather than wait for drops of molasses to accumulate slowly, some merchants opted for quicker ways to make their fortunes. None was faster than trafficking in slaves. Roland T. Ely, a student of Cuba's nineteenth-century economy, concluded that a great many of the island's commercial fortunes were made through importing and selling slaves. Another student of nineteenth-century Cuban society, Robert L. Paquette, has asserted that slave trading was one of two ways in which newcomers became members of the elite—marrying into it being the other. Zulueta, a poor and illiterate Basque, started out as a *dependiente*, gradually moving up to become an independent merchant, and by 1844 a plantation owner as well. By 1857, Zulueta, who remained active in slave trading, became Havana's largest slave owner, with 1,475 slaves. To cite just another example, José Suárez Argudín arrived penniless from Asturias, Spain, and within a few years became one of the island's wealthiest men.[33]

Interestingly, contrary to the trend during the eighteenth and early nineteenth centuries whereby the new waves of Spanish immigrants soon became "Cubanized" through absorption into older Cuban clans, immigrants now tended to retain their Spanish identity and acted and saw themselves as superior, nonpermanent residents of the island. Spanish cultural clubs, such as el Casino Español, and participation in the infamous Volunteer Corps increasingly served to reinforce this sense of separateness during the later decades of the nineteenth century. The origins of this divide can, perhaps, be traced to the anti-Creole policies of Captain-General Miguel Tacón and to the midcentury ideological split over the controversy of the slave trade. This issue clearly marked the line separating the mostly Creole planter segment, opposed to the continuation of the slave trade, and the mostly foreign commercial sector, intimately linked to slave-trading activities.

Puerto Rico's Response

Puerto Rico responded differently to mid-nineteenth-century world market demands for tropical staples. Whereas Cuban planters attempted to remain competitive by increasing output through expansion and mechanization, in Puerto Rico planters fell victim to a sustained crisis marked by stagnation and decline. Between 1850 and 1859, Puerto Rico's sugar exports declined at an average yearly change rate of 26,317 quintals; the decade started with exports of 1,121,294 quintals and ended with exports of 884,443 quintals.[34] In light of this crisis, some of the capital backing sugar production was diverted to other agricultural ventures or commerce or simply faded away in the face of a prolonged crisis that reached its nadir in the 1870s.

A series of fundamental differences separated Cuba and Puerto Rico in terms of their economic history and their capacity to meet the sugar challenge. Above all, Puerto Rico's sugar boom, which started some fifty years later than Cuba's, was fueled, financed, and managed by foreign capital and immigrant entrepreneurs. Notably, while the origins of the Cuban sugar revolution are usually traced back to the British occupation of Havana in 1762–1763, an eleven-month period during which the port city received an influx of ten thousand slaves, the boom

in Puerto Rico is attributed to the measures of the 1815 Cédula de Gracias, which, among other things, promoted the immigration of foreign
capitalists. In short, while Cuba imported its labor force, Puerto Rico
began by importing its planter class.

A prosopographical analysis of Ponce's planter class by Francisco
A. Scarano has demonstrated that only between 28 and 30 percent of
the municipality's sugar planters were Puerto Rican in 1827–1845. As
he points out, even these percentages do not give a full picture because
the estates owned by Creoles were among the smallest. "By the middle
of the century," Scarano further concluded, "the privileged strata of
Ponce's society were primarily composed of first or second generation
immigrant families, while only a minority of the sugar estate owners
could trace their origins to the old elite of *hateros* and *estancieros*, the
patriarchical rural elite of the eighteenth century."[35]

One of the drawbacks of having a foreign-born elite leading Puerto
Rico's transition to an export economy was that the capital behind the
process was not firmly committed and remained highly mobile. French,
Spanish, or German planters could easily sell their land, slaves, and
equipment and retire back to Europe if pressed too hard, or they could
shift their capital resources into commerce, where most of the plantation capital originated. In contrast, the Cuban planter class had an additional incentive to face the sugar challenge. For them, holding on to
their land meant keeping an ancestral symbol of status and prestige;
their lands, linked in some instances to titles of nobility, had passed
from generation to generation and was deemed the most important
legacy they could hand to their heirs. Besides, Cuban sugar estates were
larger and could resist times of crisis better than their smaller counterparts in Puerto Rico.[36]

If Cuba's sugar boom was a revolution, Puerto Rico's was a revolt.
Puerto Rican expansion was shorter (through the 1820s and 1830s), lo-
calized, and was not as far-reaching in the regions it affected. As
pointed out earlier, during the 1840s the island's sugar industry began
to show signs of debilitation. The number of sugar estates dropped by
two-thirds from 1,552 in 1830 to 550 in 1860, while sugar output remained stagnant. Puerto Rico's newer planter class did not exhibit the

same staying power of its Cuban counterpart. Moreover, mechanization in Puerto Rico lagged decades behind, which meant that modernization to competitive levels required even larger investments. For example, as late as 1867, vacuum pans had not been adopted in Puerto Rico; that year there were seventy-five such units operating in Cuba. Three years later, only 120 (20 percent) of Puerto Rico's sugar estates used steam to run their mills.[37] Significantly, while Cuban planters were downgrading their sugar production to meet the quality standards of the U.S. market, Puerto Rico's sugar, with a higher content of molasses, was not deemed appropriate for the needs of the United States and other North Atlantic markets. Moreover, Puerto Rico was geographically more distant than Cuba from the United States, which made Puerto Rico's sugar less competitive when transportation expenses were added to the costs. Finally, chronic droughts and declining soil fertility affected the southern coast of Puerto Rico beginning in the 1840s.

Another significant contrast between Puerto Rico and Cuba was that large proportions of the arable land and labor force remained on the fringes of the smaller island's plantation economy. Sugar plantations had sprung up only in select pockets of Puerto Rico such as Ponce, Guayama, and Mayagüez, while most of the work force and tillable land remained allocated to minor crops and subsistence agriculture. In fact, it can be argued that Puerto Rico was not a plantation society. In the same sense, Cuba's Eastern Department was not a plantation society, although it harbored pockets of plantations in Santiago and Guantánamo. According to 1862 estimates, the amount of land used for minor crops (i.e., plantains, tubers, and corn) in Puerto Rico was about equivalent to that dedicated to the island's chief staples: sugar and coffee.[38]

Moreover, Puerto Rico had a massive population of independent or subordinate peasants who remained on the fringes of the plantation economy. In 1844, the British consul at San Juan described this segment of the island's population as follows: "the natives who are free surpass by far the slaves, many of them possess small plots in which they live, and since their needs are minimal, they only cultivate that which they find necessary to sustain themselves, they care little about improving their crops or their condition."[39] The availability of land had made this kind of lifestyle possible for centuries. According to Bergad, unoccupied lands were still plentiful in the first half of the nineteenth century, a circumstance that made labor-control difficult. The dual expansion of the state and staple agriculture, however, soon pushed this autonomous population into the frontier interior of the island.[40]

During the late 1830s and the 1840s, efforts were made to regiment the island's independent work force through anti-vagrancy laws and other coercive means. In June 1838, Governor Miguel López de Baños passed his notorious Bando contra la Vagancia (anti-vagrancy decree). Anti-vagrancy tribunals, called Juntas de Vagos y Amancebados, were established to punish those who preferred to subsist off legally vacant plots rather than become servile peons in export-oriented estates. The crown jewel of Puerto Rico's coercive labor legislation was Juan de la Pezuela's 1849 Ley de la Libreta. It stipulated that those without land or a profession either had to become tenants or had to search for employment under a landholder and carry with them their *libreta de jornalero* (journeyman's passbook) at all times. The *libretas* were used to make annotations about each *jornalero*'s work, wages, debts, and conduct. *Jornaleros* were also forced to remain in one particular municipality and to continue working for the same estate until their debts were cleared. To further control the mobility of the labor force, land owners commonly advanced overpriced goods to their workers from their own estate shops. British Consul Augustus Cowper praised the results of the *libreta*. "It has been in practice for fifteen years," he wrote in 1866, "and the results have been that every man, without distinction of color, has been forced to work; the productions of the soil have annually increased; and vagrancy, and the higher crimes are almost unknown."[41] The dual expansion of the state and the export economy eventually caught up with the people and the land of Puerto Rico's interior. As Fernando Picó has demonstrated in his studies of the Utuado municipality, the names of descendants of the town's founding families and its former local elite filled the rolls of the *jornalero* class.[42]

Perhaps the sharpest contrasts to be drawn between Cuba and Puerto Rico are those relating to slavery and racial patterns. In Puerto Rico, slavery never played the crucial role it did in Cuba. According to

Philip D. Curtin's estimates, a total of about 702,000 slaves arrived in Cuba, but only 77,000, close to only a tenth of that, were imported into the smaller island. Moreover, in Cuba the slave population reached its peak in 1841, with 436,500 or 43 percent of the population; in Puerto Rico it peaked around 1846, with 51,300 or less than 12 percent of the population. Patterns of change in the importation of slaves into Cuba and Puerto Rico further reveal divergent developments, since the crisis of the sugar industry in Puerto Rico had a considerable impact on the demand for slave labor. While an estimated 1,410 slaves entered Puerto Rico yearly between 1830 and 1845, during the following decade and a half only an average of 700 arrived each year, a decrease of upwards of 50 percent. Contrastingly, in Cuba, where the sugar industry continued to expand, yearly average imports of slaves increased from 10,014 during 1827–1847 to 10,546 during 1848–1860, a modest 5 percent increase.[43]

A series of factors explains the crisis of slavery in Puerto Rico. First, as suggested before, the island's economic reorientation away from sugar and toward coffee reduced the demand for slave labor. Second, those who continued to produce sugar were not always in the best position to invest in new slaves. Third, as demonstrated by José A. Curet, the low technological level of most sugar estates meant that bringing additional slaves to estates with fifty or more slaves produced only marginal returns.[44] These factors also help explain the loose attachment of planters in Puerto Rico to the continuation of the slave trade. In 1860, when slave imports were breaking records in Cuba, U.S. Consul Charles De Ronceray described the prevailing attitude in Puerto Rico in these terms: "the sentiments of the natives, including the planters[,] are opposed to the transportation of slaves from Africa and very little encouragement is therefore given to the slave trade either by the people or Government of the island notwithstanding the want of labor."[45]

The lesser importance of slavery was also reflected in Puerto Rico's racial patterns. The existence of large sectors of society at the margins of the state and the export economy during three centuries was conducive to the population's miscegenation. European visitors noted a high degree of racial mixture, a characteristic attributed to activities lying outside the sphere of the state and the official economy: piracy, smuggling, illegal immigrations, desertion, and *marronage*.[46] Census data for San Juan between 1823 and 1833 show that the proportion of free people of color in the city's different wards ranged between 38 and 59 percent of the population. By 1860, according to census figures, Puerto Rico's nonwhite free population was 241,015 out of a total of 583,308 inhabitants, or 41 percent. According to one abolitionist active in Puerto Rican politics, "there is no radical separation of the races in this country, and mulattoes constitute more than 50 percent of the population." Contrastingly, in Cuba, particularly in the Havana-Matanzas belt where plantations played such a central role, there was a far more defined separation of the races and a much stronger correlation between color and status. The Cuban census of 1841, for example, reflected a population consisting of 418,291 whites (41.5 percent), 490,305 blacks (48.7 percent), and 99,028 mulattoes (9.8 percent). Regarding Matanzas, specifically, the 1862 census reflected that 40 percent of the population was white, 46 percent was enslaved blacks, and only 6 percent was either free or *emancipado* of color.[47] Racism, the ideology used to sustain this kind of stratification and a close association between color and status, was also considerably stronger in Cuba than in Puerto Rico.

In conclusion, during the middle decades of the nineteenth century, world market demands put enormous pressures on the economies of the Spanish colonies of the Caribbean. Sugar planters were forced either to accept the sugar challenge by modernizing the industry and expanding slavery or to withdraw from the industry altogether. Despite belonging to the same geographical region, sharing similar climatic and geological conditions, and being subjects under the same empire, Cuba and Puerto Rico followed different economic paths. Conditions in Cuba were favorable for taking on the sugar challenge. Planters there resorted to expensive credit to modernize and expand sugar production. The result of this was that by 1863, two-thirds of the industry was in the hands of Spanish merchant-bankers, who held mortgages amounting to $200 million. Meanwhile, in Puerto Rico, the mostly foreign planter class had no choice but to continue operating at a reduced level or backing away and diversifying into other crops, coffee in particular. Both societies faced similar challenges, both responded to them as best they could, but in the end both foundered, each in its own particular way.

CHAPTER 3

Life in a "Male City": Cuban and Foreign Women in Nineteenth-Century Havana

Havana scene. Courting through bars.
Courtesy of the Ramiro Fernández Collection.

Throughout most of the nineteenth century, Cuba, and its capital of Havana in particular, remained trapped simultaneously between the two grips of colonialism and neocolonialism. The island remained a Spanish colony while enduring a neocolonial relationship with the United States. But this reality also placed Cuba between two worlds in another sense: a Hispanic one tied to tradition and hierarchy and an Anglo-American one heralding modernity. The island was also trapped between the contradictory structures of a slave-based system and the demands of agro-industrial capitalism. Nineteenth-century Cuba, thus, was neither Spanish nor North American; it was neither fully capitalist nor fully slave-based, neither black nor white.

The complex political, economic, and social realities of nineteenth-century Cuba produced a cultural web with a peculiar, and often contradictory, set of internal logics that regulated relations between the colonizers and the colonized, the rich and the poor, blacks and whites, and men and women. Often, these coexisting hierarchies reinforced each other, but on occasion they were contradictory. This chapter, which rests heavily on travelers' accounts written during the nineteenth century, seeks to explain the sources and meanings behind the practices and rituals of gender relations so carefully described yet woefully misunderstood by foreign visitors. It focuses on the social restrictions imposed on women residing in Havana and on how women from different racial, social, and ethnic backgrounds responded to them.[1]

An earlier version of this chapter was originally published as "Life in a 'Male City': Native and Foreign Elite Women in Nineteenth-Century Havana," *Cuban Studies* 25 (1995): 27–49. Reprinted by permission of the University of Pittsburg Press.

A "Male City"

Havana, with the phallic Morro Castle as its gatekeeper, was characterized by nineteenth-century travelers as a "male city," likened to the mythical "Rome of Romulus." "Where are the women and where are they to be found in Havana?" inquired one concerned visitor. According to another traveler, "the absence of the female form" constituted one of Havana's "most striking features."[2]

There were considerably fewer women than men in Havana, as well as on the island as a whole. According to the 1861 census, there were 149 men for every 100 women in Havana and its environs, while the ratio for the entire island was a less sharp 134:100. Although the overall gender imbalances were in some measure the result of slave-trading practices favoring males over females at a ratio of between 4:1 and 5:1, similarly striking gender imbalances were evident among whites, particularly those residing in Havana. On the island as a whole, the proportion of white males to white females grew steadily throughout the nineteenth century from 114 (1827) to 127 (1846) to 150 (1862) per 100.[3] The gender imbalance among whites was even sharper in Havana, the island's administrative-military-mercantile center to which the exclusively male population involved in such activities gravitated. Havana was also a city of immigrants and transients, most of whom were men. In 1861, according to census figures, there were 1.8 men for every woman among Havana's residents of European descent.[4]

Women in nineteenth-century Havana were not only a demographic minority; they were also subjected to seclusion, discrimination, limited options, and gross double standards of acceptable social behavior. The seemingly obsessive desire on the part of society to protect and seclude women of the upper classes appeared—was, in fact—stronger in Havana than possibly in any other Western society, colonial or metropolitan. In other societies, the United States among them, women faced similar forms of restriction, segregation, and exclusion but to a much lesser degree. What, then, accounted for Havana's more restrictive codes of female behavior? The answer to this question lies in the particular structure of its society: its slave base, its gender imbalance, its population of color constituting a majority, the strong correlation between color and class, its highly hierarchical social structure, and very limited opportunities for social mobility.[5]

Gender roles were thus intimately linked to demographic patterns, class, color, and restrictions on social mobility. Paradoxically, it was the women of the resident white upper and middle class who became the primary targets of seclusion and discrimination. Otherwise disempowered white Habaneras were, for example, forced to carry the burden of controlling access to society's white elite. As Verena Martínez-Alier concluded in her now classic *Marriage, Class, and Colour in Nineteenth-Century Cuba*: "the device through which the purity of the group was achieved was virginity, that is, female purity. By controlling the access to female sexuality, control was exercised over the acquisition of undesirable members of the group." Through seclusion, high regard for female virginity and chastity, and legislation obstructing interracial marriages, society "protected" white women and their race, and by extension their caste, from what was perceived as "racial pollution."[6]

Interestingly, the same central force that shaped the Cuban elite's political positions during the middle decades of the nineteenth century—fear of the black man—also shaped to a great extent the social rules regulating female behavior pertaining to virginity, courtship, and marriage. Some of the island's key midcentury political figures justified Cuba's annexation to the United States on racial and sexual terms. The annexationist editors of *La Verdad*, for example, referring to events in neighboring Venezuela, denounced "the most lamentable spectacle, the most repugnant liaisons to our instincts, the most shocking to our present state of civilization and public opinion, the most degrading and shameful to our race, marriages between white women and blacks, mulattoes, *zambos*, and *mestizos*."[7] Note that the editors' concern was not with miscegenation per se, a long-accepted way of dealing with Cuba's "racial problem," but specifically with men of color having sexual access to white women. Another contemporary observer hiding behind the title of "Yankee" but suspiciously familiar with Cuban ways referred to the seclusion of Havana's "ladies" (meaning white elite women) as a "necessity" to spare them the "risk of meeting blasphemous, *odorous*, and drunken negroes."[8] At one of the peaks of racial tension, stemming from a temporary suspension of laws interdicting interracial marriages in 1854, a critic of the suspension pointed out that this and other reforms had encouraged blacks to salute Havana's ladies and to pay them "compliments in impudent and audible commendations of their beauty." He added that such "insolence . . . carried alarm into the bosom of every family." Prison terms and other penalties were applied against men of color who dared approach white women in obscene or intolerably familiar ways.[9]

Clearly established social rules designed to both protect and subdue women contributed to keeping white Habaneras under seclusion. The prevailing etiquette did not allow "ladies" to walk on the streets, "not even two blocks." According to Mercedes de Santa Cruz y Montalvo, the countess of Merlín, even when crossing a narrow street to visit a neighbor, Havana's ladies dashed as "fearful doves that flee from the sound of the lumberjack's axe." Arriving in Cuba in 1848, the wife of Captain-General Federico Roncali sought to put an end to female seclusion by herself walking the streets of Havana. It was to no avail; her bold steps were not followed by other women of the local elite.[10]

Women of color and others not pretending to the title of lady, however, walked about as they pleased, sold fruits and other goods out in the open, and frequented places like cockpits which were completely barred to white women.[11] These privileges granted to Havana's women of color reflect a paradoxical situation resulting from the overlapping and somewhat conflicting logics of a slave-based and male-dominated society. The most evident paradox of these conflicting yet mutually reinforced power structures was that women of color, slave or free, appeared to enjoy greater liberties than women of the master class. Needless to say, Havana was still first and foremost a slave-based society and not a few black or mulatto women would have gladly given up the right to walk up and down Obispo or O'Reilly Street in exchange for the standard of living and privileges enjoyed by women of the elite.

Nonetheless, the highly visible "freedoms" enjoyed by black and mulatto Habaneras appear to have been a point of friction between women of different classes. The countess of Merlín, in her famous epistolary travelogue, scorned the almost snobbish pride with which Habaneras of color walked the streets, "cigar in mouth, almost naked with their round shining bare shoulders." The tone of the countess's comments reflects a degree of jealousy directed toward black women, who by virtue of their physical mobility and more revealing attires were made more visible, and therefore more accessible, to men of all races, including whites.[12] Other contemporaries also noted a degree of rivalry between secluded white Habaneras and their sable sisters and commented on the proud and jaunty air that the latter displayed while walking Havana's streets. One observer described black women walking nonchalantly, allowing their low-cut garments to "slip with picturesque negligence from their dusky shoulders." A midcentury moralist criticized Havana's women of color for seeking the status of white women by bleaching their skin and by luring "men of all classes."[13]

Foreign visitors often expressed their dismay at the sight of homebound white Habaneras clinging to the iron bars of their glassless windows from which they gazed at the forbidden outside world "like captives in durance."[14] An obviously amused visitor wrote that he had seen "[m]any a bright lustrous eye, and fairy-like foot . . . through the wires of her cheerful cage." Another traveler likened Havana to a "zoological garden, in which the insiders and the outsiders have changed places." Julia Ward Howe, a Bostonian feminist, found less to joke about and scorned the custom as a form of "Oriental imprisonment." Havana folklore had it that one North American visitor, on passing by, threw a few coins through an iron-barred window thinking that the sad-looking woman behind it was a convict and her home, the city jail.[15]

Never Out of Sight

While behind bars, Habaneras struggled to remain visible to those outside; custom could keep them from stepping outside but not from keeping their windows wide open. The compromise, thus, was to remain out of reach but not out of sight. A variety of contemporary sources attest that most windows were kept open and that the women came "freely . . . to the windows to chat with passers-by." According to one visitor

accustomed to Yankee privacy, wide open windows made it "nearly impossible to avoid glancing in upon domestic scenes that frequently exhibit the female portion of the family in déshabillé." According to
another observer, "one has the inspection of the interior arrangement
of all the front parlors of Havana, and can see what every lady wears,
and who is visiting her."[16] Passers-by complimented women with witty
piropos. Every night, after sundown, an army of bachelor Habaneros—
one visitor called them *lechuzos* (night owls)—proceeded to call on the
single, captive Habaneras, whom they courted "like monkeys" through
the iron-barred windows that extended from the floor to the ceiling of
their homes. According to the description by one keen observer of
Cuban social life, gentlemen callers positioned themselves at an angle
outside the windows to avoid being seen by their lover's family. Another
visitor hinted that iron bars failed to keep lovers from engaging in the
most intimate expressions of tenderness.[17]

Female travelers and long-term foreign residents of Havana faced
the dilemma of either complying with the roles and behavior expected
of white women or challenging them and facing the consequences. They
were for the most part shocked by the odious restrictions but also faced
considerable pressures to conform with the norms, particularly if they
were planning a long-term stay. According to one contemporary observer, foreign female travelers who challenged social mores by walking
the streets faced passing remarks, "annoyance and even insult," which
in the end forced most to comply.[18] A recorded incident described an
episode in which several men and boys chased a group of North American women while shouting insults at them.[19] Quite significantly, license
to harass women appeared to cut across class and color lines, as attested
by an incident in which "a couple of half-naked, horrible looking negroes" harassed Swedish visitor Fredrika Bremer.[20]

As one U.S. consul put it, his female compatriots would try walking
once or twice but would eventually conform to the restrictions and "be
quite miserable." Julia Ward Howe reported that even "the hardiest
American or English woman will scarcely venture out a second time
without the severe escort of husband or brother." In a humorous tone
she added that the North American woman, usually very jealous of her

own space and time alone in the United States, "suddenly becomes very fond of her husband" on whom, while in Cuba, she comes to depend as saving escort and bodyguard. As to the general rule of seclusion of Cuban women, she ended up rationalizing it by saying that in a place like Cuba where "the animal vigor of men is so large in proportion to their moral power . . . women must be glad to forgo their liberties" for their own protection.[21] Not all foreign women complied with Havana's strict norms about not walking in the streets. Rachel Wilson Moore and her friends, while recognizing that walking was not considered safe, stuck to what she called their "republican habits" and tried to ignore the stares and remarks that were thrown at them. Julia Louisa M. Woodruff, a visitor from New York, tired of being able to walk only up and down the halls of her hotel, decided to go shopping "after the American fashion." Her daring move attracted a storm of long and mean stares but she persisted.[22]

Wheels of Deliverance

For the otherwise imprisoned white Habaneras—at least for those whose families could afford it—there was an "Angel of deliverance": the *volanta*, a horse-drawn carriage. "Ladies" could move about freely throughout the streets of Havana only when riding on *volantas*, *quitrines*, and other carriages, whether these belonged to their families or were rented at a fixed fare. They were not, however, allowed to ride by themselves or to be accompanied by men, only by one or two female friends or relatives. Men rarely rode on *volantas*, preferring instead to walk or ride horses.[23] One North American traveler recounted an incident about a female compatriot of his who was momentarily left alone in her *volanta* by her male companion and was soon approached by a daring Habanero who "with the greatest familiarity [proceeded] to take a flower from her hand." The woman responded by smacking the man, who immediately left the scene shouting obscenities. Yet another instance of harassment included the gathering of a laughing and insulting mob provoked by the daring Woodruff going for a drive with a local male resident.[24]

Volantas were peculiar-looking carriages of Cuban invention that elicited obligatory comments, mostly mockery, from almost everyone facing one for the first time. This type of carriage consisted of a low-cut chaise-like body, sometimes ornamented with precious metal trimmings, resting on a pair of disproportionately large wheels measuring about six feet in diameter. *Volanta* cabins were set up for two passengers but a third seat, significantly called "el de la niña bonita," could be added for a third passenger. From the body of the *volanta* emerged two long shafts, sixteen to twenty feet long, attached to the sides of one or two small horses with their tails tightly braided and tied to the saddle or harness. In all, from the end of the wheels to the tip of the horse's nose, *volantas* measured about twenty-two feet.[25] On the horse sat the driver or postilion, usually a black slave or freedman dressed up in a most colorful livery consisting of a buckled top hat, a swallow-tailed scarlet coat trimmed with a generous dose of silver or gold braid, and leather jackboots with oversized spurs and silver buckles. One contemporary ridiculed the entire costume, describing it as "three parts jack boots and one part silver laced jacket."[26] The liveries of postilions working for some of the wealthiest families could cost several thousand pesos.

Most foreigners visiting the island were quick to criticize the ubiquitous *volanta* as strange-looking and impractical. One contemporary referred to it as comical, and another dubbed it a queer vehicle. Yet another observer described the *volanta* as the "oddest vehicle conceivable."[27] They failed, however, to understand that this peculiar Cuban invention reflected the needs and the structure of the society in which it was created. First and foremost, the *volanta* afforded mobility and visibility to the city's elite, particularly its women of marriageable age. At the same time, given the carriages' proportions and elevation from the road, *volantas* allowed a considerable distance between the female passengers and male pedestrians. Like the barred house windows, these vehicles kept the city's upper-class women out of reach but not out of sight.

Volantas also served to mark class boundaries in a society obsessed with maintaining distinctions between its classes. Such carriages, along with grand pianos and a coterie of domestic slaves, became the trade-marks of the elite. The wealthiest families were said to own a *volanta* for each marriageable daughter. Middle-class families would go out of their way to purchase one such vehicle, setting aside for this purpose the household's very first savings. One traveler remarked that middle-class Cubans "would sooner live on beans and cold water, dress in rags, and lie on straw . . . than go without a *volanta*."[28] Given the exorbitant cost of purchasing and maintaining a *volanta*, most middle-class families simply could not afford to own such vehicles. *Volantas* helped establish hierarchies within the elite as well. The richer the family, the more carriages it owned and the greater the extent of their ornamentation, including fancy woodwork and gold leaf, with postilions and horses dressed to match.

Given the narrowness of most streets inside the walled city of Havana, the length of the *volantas'* shafts appears senseless and cumbersome; this detail, however, secured a considerable separation between the passengers and the postilion and horses. The postilions' attire, which matched the gaudy ornamentation of the carriages and the horses, further established them as objects far removed from the human and individual qualities of those they served. Significantly, *volantas* as modes of urban transportation peaked precisely during the height of the slave trade and "Africanization" fear; they went out of style later during the process of gradual emancipation and lingered a bit longer in Matanzas, perhaps the island's most racially stratified town.[29]

The time of the *paseo* (evening carriage rides) in *volantas* was the daily high point for upper- and upper-middle-class Habaneras. According to one observer, most women spent their mornings and afternoons "killing time" in rocking chairs, fanning themselves in their *déshabillé* in anticipation of *paseo* time. "It is for their hour on the *paseo*," wrote the famed novelist Anthony Trollope, "that the ladies dress themselves." According to other accounts, young women preferred to go without food rather than skip the *paseo*.[30] During evening *paseos*, women of the upper classes displayed their charms and fancy clothing and elaborate coiffures from their *volantas* for the pleasure of the scores of gallant Habaneros who, either on foot or on horseback, saluted the ladies whom they passed by over and over again.[31] At *paseo* time, the covers of the *volantas* were pushed back to allow maximum visibility. Over the cabin's side panels were spread the folds of the occupant's skirts. According to one observer: "The full, flowing skirts of these ladies were spread carefully out at each side of the *volanta*, hanging nearly to the ground, and giving the vehicle, when viewed from the rear, the appearance of being furnished with wings." Another contemporary described a similar sight as "the most staring description that I ever witnessed."[32]

Volantas served another important function: they allowed white Habaneras to go shopping. So strict were the norms against walking on the streets that upper- and middle-class women shopped by using a curious predecessor to drive-by shopping or window service. As custom had it, "ladies" ordered their carriages halted in front of a given store, and then the shop's clerk would jump over the counter and proceed to walk outside carrying a handful of goods for the inspection of his prospective customers. Women tried on shoes and other items in their carriages parked outside the stores.[33] The fact that the entire transaction was carried out in the street and in what had to be a hurried manner must have put female customers at a disadvantage, given the haggling fashion in which purchases were usually made.[34] Women also had their carriages driven to the portals of the city's famous cafés, La Dominica and El Louvre, where they placed orders of ices and other refreshments to go from *mozos* serving the drive-by customers. Another shopping custom was to have merchants send articles for inspection to women's homes. Servants were used in these transactions, which could take an entire day of bargaining before a price was agreed upon.[35]

Church as Sanctuary

Another place allowing Habaneras some mobility and visibility was the interior of the city's churches. Churches were, in fact, the best place for foreign visitors and Havana residents to catch an unobstructed glimpse of the proverbial beauty of the elusive Habaneras. Several sources attest that they were indeed the only place to see white women.[36] Given its conservative stance on many other matters, it appears rather paradox-

ical that the Church was the one institution where white women found
freedom, comfort, and a space to call their own and where there were
no segregated spaces on the basis of gender or race. Canonical law, for
example, did not differentiate between male and female adultery as did
Spanish legislation and social custom.[37] A highly revealing episode in
mid-nineteenth-century Havana demonstrates these positions. In the
summer of 1852, the members of the all-male Real Archicofradía del
Santísimo Sacramento of the Church of Nuestra Señora de Guadalupe
wrote to Queen Isabella II, patron of the Catholic Church in Spain and
its possessions, requesting permission to erect railings to segregate the
sexes inside the church in order to "maintain the composure and deco-
rum required in the Lord's House . . . and to avoid the distractions with
which the common enemy would try to disturb devotion and concentration." Both the bishop of Havana and Captain-General Valentín
Cañedo had prohibited the use of the railings, the latter scorning it as
"a disagreeable distinction in the House of the Lord."[38]

Under the umbrella of the Church, women of the elite were also able
to take upon themselves the responsibilities of charitable work and raising funds for and taking care of the vestments of the images of virgins
and female saints.[39] Since it was considered sacrilegious for any man to
touch or even lay eyes on an undressed statue of a female saint or virgin, only women could fulfill the task of taking care of their vestments.
This exclusively feminine activity allowed some women to come together and establish yet another area of activity they could call their
own.

Church attendance was almost exclusively female; most accounts
agree that less than 10 percent of attendants to Havana's thirty-odd
churches were male and that most of the men seemed to be more interested in the devout Habaneras than in either mass or the saints that
lined the naves and side chapels. Julia Woodruff commented in her travelogue that she "could count on the fingers of one hand, all the males
that [she] had seen, during [her] whole stay in Cuba, engaged in any
voluntary act of devotion." Another observer remarked that men appeared to have "no religion at all."[40]

Male "worshippers" for the most part remained strategically positioned either behind the interior columns or preferably just outside the doors where they could catch "a glimpse of the pretty ankles ascending the steps of the volantes." According to one account, their actions and grins showed that they were "neither believers, nor ashamed of their unbelief." Another chronicler recounted that many of the men "merely come within the door, drop one knee, with their faces turned toward the principal altar, and utter a short, but scarcely audible prayer." Church authorities denounced the irreverent and disrespectful crowds of young men who habitually gathered outside the city's churches to see and talk to young women before and after mass.[41]

Despite the fact that church ceremonies were led by male priests, the church buildings were, indeed, the women's domain. There they were not only the overwhelming majority, but by most accounts they ran the show and were able to create spaces for themselves, establish communication networks, and move about freely. The fact that Havana churches had no pews facilitated mobility, as Habaneras were able to set up camp almost anywhere within the church. Those who could afford it were usually accompanied by servants of color who carried pieces of carpet and folding chairs for their mistresses' comfort and convenience. White women attended church dressed in black, their heads covered with black mantillas, while black and mulatto women wore white.[42]

Good Friday was the one day of the year when congregations spilled over to the streets; interestingly, it was also the only day when Havana's "ladies" were allowed to go out and walk in the streets. As one traveler put it, it was the "only day of the year when dainty Havanese female feet press the pavements." Referring to Holy Week in Matanzas, Woodruff wrote: "On this occasion alone, of the whole year, the entire population may be seen in the streets and on foot, without exception of class, color, sex, or age."[43] Women from the United States and Great Britain sojourning or residing in Havana, most of them Protestant, could find little comfort in the spaces that church ceremonies provided for Cuban women.

Several nineteenth-century travelers' accounts written by men include detailed, and somewhat lusty, descriptions of churchgoers of the opposite sex "whose graceful, voluptuous figures, bent down before their shrines." One visitor referred to the sight of a church filled with "pretty women" as a "source of amusement"; another described it as "a beautiful sight": "their necks and arms bare, and often resplendent with jewels; their dark glossy hair ornamented with pearls or flowers, and their exquisitely wrought fans, inlaid with gold and precious stones, 'glittering in their hands like so many butterflies.'"[44] Another traveler described female behavior inside the church as irreverent and somewhat disorderly:

> She kneels, but in the course of a few minutes sits. An ill-bred person would say, squats. Tired with the course of the ceremonial, she at length reclines. In the middle of the service the floor is strewn with a choice assortment of ladies' dress-goods with the ladies inside of them. At certain places in the ceremonial, it is necessary for everybody to place themselves again in a kneeling posture, and there is a general struggle to attain this end. To see two or three hundred women scrambling at once from a reclining to a kneeling position has a tendency for the moment to destroy the solemn feeling one should have under the circumstances.[45]

Still another observer described church as a rendezvous place of "gayety, and flirtation" where women communicated using the "telegraphic fan."[46]

Yet another public place where white Habaneras were allowed to be seen was in special upper balconies inside the city's theaters. There they sat "in full dress, décolletées, without hats." Although highly visible, these box sections were separated by gates and zealously guarded by older women and armed guards. Along with the glances and fan signals, handwritten notes passed back and forth between the balconies and the exclusively male pit section. Here again, Havana's women settled for being out of reach but within sight.

Beauty, Charm, and Indolence

Descriptions of Habaneras, of course, varied from observer to observer, but nearly all foreigners agreed on their "exotic beauty," "endearing charm," and "dignified grace." Most descriptions highlighted the Habaneras' lustrous dark eyes that "swim in melting lustre, and sparkle in expressive glances" and abundant jet black hair; "well formed," "fully developed," "magnificent busts" that seem "to expand from year to year"; and feet so tiny that "they do not afford a sufficient support to the body." Of the much celebrated Habaneras' feet, one visitor said that they were so small that it appeared they were "evidently never intended by nature to walk on."[49]

Visitors and residents alike commented on the fleeting nature of Cuban women's beauty. Women aged twelve to fourteen were considered marriageable, those in their late teens and early twenties in their prime, and those thirty or older ranked as "old."[50] The short-lived beauty of the Habaneras was referred to by contemporaries as the "beauty of the devil," lasting only as long as "the freshness of youth." At least some women accepted these notions, as exemplified by a fifteen-year-old's confession to a foreign visitor of "her sorrow at getting so old."[51]

Most contemporary accounts presented unflattering portraits of the Habaneras' intellectual capacities and aspirations. One traveler observed that Cuban women were civilized only in appearance and that even the very rich were illiterate. Another contemporary noted that they had "no intellectual resort." A woman traveler quizzed several Habaneras and concluded that they were quite ignorant about matters that she deemed essential knowledge.[52] A well-traveled foreign visitor, who had mostly good things to say about Cuba and its people, stated that during his sojourn on the island he "rarely ever saw a lady sitting quietly reading a book."[53] It is significant to note that the two best-known Cuban women writers of the nineteenth century, Gertudis Gómez de Avellaneda and the countess of Merlín, developed as writers not in Cuba but in Spain and France, respectively. One attempt by Gómez de Avellaneda to establish a women's magazine in Havana failed after the publication of only twelve biweekly issues of *Álbum Cubano de lo Bueno y lo Bello*.[54]

Habaneras were usually described as vain and overtly coquettish beings who wasted their time gossiping, sitting in rocking chairs, dancing, playing cards, and engaging in frivolous conversations and activities.[55] White Cuban women were also fond of wearing excessive amounts of whitening makeup (*cascarilla*), a paste made of pulverized egg shells mixed with egg whites that produced a clownlike effect meant to contrast sharply with dark eyes and hair. A credible source estimates that 40,000 pounds of *cascarilla* were produced annually on the island. One female visitor said that in Matanzas, not coincidentally a highly racially stratified region of the island, women were particularly fond of *cascarilla*, which they abused "to a degree that is positively ghastly."[56]

The marked emphasis on makeup, fine clothing, elaborate coiffures (some of which included live fireflies), and other attention-catching aspects of the Habaneras' appearance and behavior paralleled those of other slave-based societies.[57] The ideal of the Southern belle in the United States emerged under demographic and social circumstances similar to those of nineteenth-century Cuba. In both Cuba and the American South, white women of the upper classes struggled to look their best as they faced the competition of women of color for the sexual attention of white men. Slavery as an institution ultimately based on force made women of color, as a caste, especially vulnerable to the sexual desires of those belonging, de facto or potentially, to the master class. In the other direction, not a few black or mulatto women saw sexual liaisons with white men, even outside of marriage, as means of upward social mobility for themselves and their children.[58] Whatever the motivation, liaisons between white men and black and mulatto women were not uncommon. The opposite was of course socially unacceptable and quite rare.

Law and custom severely limited the educational options of Habaneras of all races. According to statistics from the 1830s, the proportion of white boys of school age receiving an education was twice that for white girls. By mid-century, there were 238 boys in school for every 100 girls. Access to education was also disproportionately higher for boys of color than for girls of color; within this group, there were two and a half times as many boys in school as there were girls. Educational opportunities for women were also of lesser quality, focused on such domestic and manual crafts as sewing and embroidery, and included considerably less contact hours; while boys had five to six daily hours of instruction, girls received only one.[59]

Like most aspects of Cuban life, education was also segregated. As one observer noted, it was a means to avoid mischief for the girls' own sake. "The Spanish mind is firmly fixed in the idea," he concluded, "that when the male and female of the human species are thrown together, there is sure to be mischief of some kind concocted."[60] Many families preferred to hire tutors to instruct their daughters in the safety of their homes rather than send them to school. Colonial education was thus yet another area in which discrimination and segregation were justified in terms of protection for women but ended up limiting their options and full integration into society.

Higher education for women was, to be sure, out of the question. Julia Ward Howe was scandalized by the fact that in Cuba women were not allowed to attend the university or most public places or to engage in intellectual activities of any sort. When she and a group of friends inquired about visiting the University of Havana, the professor in charge, through an intermediary, responded that he "would be happy to show the establishment to the ladies on Sunday" when the all-male student body would be gone. Not satisfied with the answer, they asked "Why?" The forthcoming response was: "For your own sake."[61] According to another contemporary North American observer, Cuban women knew nothing about "coöperative kitchens, or the Sorosis, or [their] inalienable right to serve on committees, edit newspapers, and lecture." "There never was a woman's rights convention in this happy land," he continued, "or a Dorcas society, or even a crusade."[62]

To conclude, of all the major cities in the West, Havana placed the strictest social restrictions on the female portion of its population. A combination of several demographic, social, and cultural factors explain why white Habaneras faced seclusion, segregation, and other restrictions to a higher extent than women elsewhere in the hemisphere.

The places in which Habaneras could move about freely, express themselves, and retain a degree of visibility were few: behind the barred windows of their homes, in *volantas*, inside churches, at the opera boxes. In such settings, they strove to establish communication with one another and with the opposite sex. Foreign observers, whether female or male, were struck by the social limitations that women in Cuba endured and were amused by their creative responses to those constraints. Outsiders failed, however, to understand both the restrictions and women's responses in their broader contexts of slavery, patriarchy, colonialism, and neocolonialism. That did not keep them from criticizing Cuba's social mores and prescribing "better" ways of doing things. Still, such recommendations would not have worked in the racially stratified context of Havana, where the restrictions on women of the ruling class served as a constant visual reminder of the separation between elite white society and the people of color they dominated.

Crypto-Protestants and Pseudo-Catholics in the Nineteenth-Century Hispanic Caribbean

Ossuary, Havana Colón Cemetery, 1890.
Courtesy of the Ramiro Fernández Collection.

This chapter seeks to reconstruct and examine the experiences of the thousands of Protestants who struggled tenaciously to retain or hide their faith in the context of colonial Cuba and Puerto Rico before the declaration of religious tolerance in 1869 and before the establishment of the region's first Protestant churches: the Anglican congregation of Ponce, organized in 1869; the Episcopal mission of Havana, started in 1871, and later extended to Matanzas; and the Anglican congregation of Vieques, a small island located eight miles off the coast of Puerto Rico, organized in 1880.[1]

Protestants residing in the Hispanic Caribbean constituted a very small minority. Their presence, however, had a far larger significance given that they emerged as a result of newly established trade and migration links between the Spanish colonies of the Caribbean and the commercial powers of the North Atlantic. The Protestants' experiences in Cuba and Puerto Rico during the first seven decades of the nineteenth century serve as a window to the tense and conflictive coexistence of rigid Spanish colonial rule and growing commercial ties within the Atlantic world that rested on the principles of economic liberalism. The sugar industry, with its demands of imported capital and technology, foreign markets, and foreign labor, was at the heart of this problematic coexistence of colonial domination under Catholic Spain and dependence on the Protestant commercial powers of the North Atlantic. It was not coincidental that the very first nuclei of Protestant communities to emerge in the region (Ponce, Havana, Matanzas, and Vieques) resulted from the sugar industry's need for foreign investors, merchants, technicians, field hands, and sailing crews. Havana and

Matanzas were the undisputed epicenters of Cuba's nineteenth-century sugar revolution. Ponce was Puerto Rico's biggest and most successful sugar-producing jurisdiction, while Vieques experienced a dramatic sugar boom during the last third of the century.

Since Protestant religious activities were outside the margin of the law—it was illegal for non-Catholics to reside in the Spanish colonies, let alone practice their faiths—reconstructing them from the historical record remains a challenging task. The methods and sources of social history so successfully applied by historians studying other historically marginalized groups allow us, however, to provide a face and a voice to Cuba and Puerto Rico's otherwise anonymous early Protestants. Ironically, the very documents so carefully gathered and kept by those seeking to silence this religious minority more than a century ago are the ones that today allow us to reconstruct the experiences, behavior, and values of the region's first Protestants.[2]

Immigrants, Transients, and the Emergence of Protestantism

Needless to say, Protestantism was not indigenous to Cuba or Puerto Rico; it originally emerged in the region as the result of immigration from the Protestant North Atlantic and the non-Hispanic Caribbean beginning in the first decades of the nineteenth century. The different origins and social status of the region's immigrants and transient foreigners help explain the distinct character and orientation of the first Protestant communities that formed in Ponce, Havana, Matanzas, and Vieques. The different Protestant groups' class composition and their relations with other segments of society are critical factors for the understanding of the Protestants' beliefs and religious behavior. The class variable helps explain, for example, the different Protestant responses to official Catholic exclusivism. While some Protestants responded by pursuing crypto-Protestantism—that is, by maintaining a low religious profile while privately adhering to the dictates of their faith—others responded as pseudo-Catholics, remaining Protestants at heart but publicly partaking in the sacraments and other ceremonies of the Roman

Catholic Church. The broader geographic and demographic context into which Protestants entered also affected their religious options as well as the responses of Church and state authorities.

Beginning in the 1810s, new immigration legislation permitted the arrival of thousands of non-Spanish immigrants and transients to the Spanish Caribbean each year, many of whom were Protestants. Transients could stay up to three months; those wishing to stay longer had to seek domiciliation and take an oath of Catholicity; those staying five years or longer were obligated to become naturalized Spanish subjects.[3] In the Spanish Caribbean, however, where most matters were subject to negotiation, these and other laws were corruptible and applied with utmost flexibility. French settlers and black laborers arriving in Vieques from the British West Indies were exempt from these regulations, the same way African slaves and Chinese contract laborers were exempt from most immigration requirements.[4]

Among the thousands of foreigners entering Cuba and Puerto Rico from predominantly Protestant countries, many stayed either permanently or for long periods of time. In Ponce, for example, a sizable immigration from the West Indies, Germany, the United States, and Great Britain settled in and established solid foothold in commerce and commercial agriculture. Foreign-born residents, a good proportion of them from Protestant countries, dominated Ponce's burgeoning commercial agriculture during the first half of the nineteenth century. In 1827, 80 percent of Ponce's planters were immigrants, and in 1845, 75 percent were. Foreign-born merchants, many of them associated with slave-trading activities, also came to dominate Ponce's sugar trade with St. Thomas and other regional trade entrepôts. Around 1870, several Protestants, among them José María Archevald, Thomas Davidson, William Lee, Thomas G. Salomons, James Gilbee, George Weichers, José Henna, Guillermo Oppenheimer, Robert Graham, and John van Rhyn figured among Ponce's wealthiest planters and businessmen.[5] This foreign-born elite was highly endogamic and intricately interconnected through marriage, co-godparenthood, and business links. Their members had multiple familial and business connections with Ponce's Spanish-speaking elite and were, therefore, subject to close social scrutiny.[6]

As Puerto Rico's premier sugar-producing region, Ponce also attracted a considerable permanent or semipermanent migration of black and mulatto skilled and semiskilled workers from the British, Dutch, Danish, and French West Indies. According to 1838 statistics, 39 percent of Ponce's immigrants, not counting imported slaves, were black or mulatto.[7] Sugarcane workers from these islands also settled in large numbers in Vieques, a smaller island under Puerto Rico's jurisdiction that experienced a sugar boom during the 1860s and 1870s. Beginning in the 1850s and 1860s, Vieques underwent dramatic demographic growth and economic transformations. The island's population quadrupled between 1846 and 1866, mostly as a result of a steady influx of sugarcane workers from the British West Indies. By 1871, Vieques had become an important agro-exporting center with a total of 3,700 inhabitants, 1,175 of whom were black Protestants from neighboring islands.[8]

In Cuba, Protestant immigrants arrived in even larger numbers, but it was a different migration playing a substantially different role and moving into a different position within the social ladder. Estimates produced in the mid-1870s point to around 2,000 foreign residents from the United States and about the same number of immigrants from Germany and Great Britain combined. Most of these foreigners settled in Havana, the island's mercantile and political center, and a smaller number in the sugar-exporting districts of Matanzas and Cárdenas.[9] Unlike the case in Ponce, where early-nineteenth-century immigrants were able to move into a virtual capital vacuum and take command of commercial agriculture, in Cuba very few foreigners from the Protestant North or elsewhere managed to make a dent in the sugar industry, in which Cubans remained dominant throughout the first three-quarters of the century. Havana and Matanzas's British, U.S., and German resident elite gravitated instead toward diplomatic, commercial, professional, and skilled-labor activities. Domiciliation request documentation for the 1850s show that the bulk of immigrants seeking permanent residence in Cuba were skilled or semiskilled artisans and technical workers: U.S. mechanics, Neapolitan cauldron makers, French carpenters, and the like. Records of non-domiciled foreigners in Matanzas (1844) reflect a majority of clerks, machinists, and carpenters, and very few property owners. The 1871 register of U.S. citizens in Cuba identifies 737 individuals by occupation. Among these, the dominant categories were merchants (38 percent), machinists (31 percent), skilled or semi-skilled artisans (13 percent), and professionals (9 percent). Out of the total 737, only 37 (5 percent) are identified as planters, agriculturalists, property owners, or "labradores." Another important category among Cuba's foreign-born residents was the seasonal and semipermanent mechanics and engineers who served the island's expanding sugar industry. By midcentury an estimated 1,000 to 1,500 mechanics, mostly from the United States and Great Britain lived in Cuba, many of them just for the grinding season.[10]

As a group, Havana's foreign-born residents from the Protestant North never achieved either the rank or visibility or the social and economic power of their counterparts in Ponce. Many of them actually were wretchedly poor; in the words of U.S. Consul Charles Helm: "destitute . . . broken down in health, scarcely able to walk, without money, and unable to speak the language of the country . . . crippled, sick, ragged, hungry, weeping."[11] Reflective of the social isolation of Havana's foreigners is the fact that many of them settled in the suburban districts of El Cerro and El Horcón, where they tended to reside in particular streets such as Tulipán and Buenos Aires.[12]

Transient foreigners added to the growing presence from predominantly Protestant countries in Cuba and to a lesser extent in Puerto Rico. The growing trade, particularly sugar, between the islands and the North Atlantic produced a large naval exchange with the United States and Great Britain. Each year thousands of sailors and officers from U.S., British, and other nations' vessels called in Havana, San Juan, and other Hispanic Caribbean ports. In the mid-1850s, a yearly average of 883 U.S. ships with 14,682 passengers visited the port of Havana alone; three decades later, the number of passengers more than doubled to approximately 32,000. Estimates for Puerto Rico suggest that as many as 8,000 North American sailors visited its ports each year. Some crews remained for weeks and even months while their vessels were being unloaded, prepared, and reloaded.[13]

Although similar laws and parallel historical processes opened the entire Hispanic Caribbean to foreign and Protestant penetration, geographic, economic, and social differences produced very different Protestant communities in Ponce, Havana, Matanzas, and Vieques. In Ponce, foreign Protestants were able to move into the upper echelons of society, establish firm and commanding economic positions, and interact intimately with the local elite. In contrast, the foreign elites settling in Havana and other Cuban jurisdictions were generally involved in much more mobile, temporary, and seasonal activities. They were also less cohesive as a community, less affluent, and virtually detached from society at large. The larger island also had a much larger transient, nonelite, white Protestant presence. Foreign black Protestants settling in Ponce and Vieques, for their part, established close bonds among themselves but had very little interaction with their white fellow Protestants and remained socially as well as economically marginal.

As attested by the considerable Protestant presence finding its way into the region, it is evident that the oath of Catholicity required of all long-term foreign visitors was more of an obnoxious inconvenience than a real obstacle keeping Protestants from settling in the Spanish islands. The oath, moreover, could not keep visiting Protestants from spending short periods of time on the islands. Contemporaries commented that few foreigners actually took the oath and that it was very mildly enforced. As reflected by domiciliation documents of scores of immigrants from predominantly Protestant countries, the process had many holes and lacked an adequate system of verification. The Briton George Booth, for example, arrived in Havana in 1818 with the intention of establishing himself as a carpenter. He claimed to be Catholic but said that he had no documentation to prove it. Booth received the domiciliation status a few days later as government officials took his word. He may have been Catholic, but the odds are that he was not. David Clark, also a Briton, declared upon his arrival in Cuba that he was Catholic. He failed to produce evidence but came up with three witnesses who had heard him say that he was a Catholic. Their testimonies sufficed. In 1841, a Philadelphia merchant surnamed Beylle was certified Catholic by a witness who claimed to have seen him in Catholic religious activities.[14]

Some foreigners who took the religious oath in the presence of Spanish officials quibbled by omitting the word "Roman," thus accepting allegiance to a less specific and inclusive Apostolic and Catholic Church. Others signed documents swearing adherence to the "C A R Church" which could have meant to stand for Catholic, Apostolic, and Reformed. George C. Backhouse, a British official stationed in Havana, reported that those kinds of omissions and substitutions were quite common and satisfactory to both Spanish officials and the "consciences of Protestant Foreigners who take the oath."[15] Some foreigners circumvented the requirement altogether by hiring agents to handle their domiciliation procedures. Yet others avoided presenting actual proof of Catholicity by paying a fee or by purchasing a certificate either on the islands or abroad. Still, the oath requirement remained a constant source of humiliation that hung over Protestants and could be, and at times was, used to harass and deport foreigners, forcing many to either lie or falsify documents.[16]

For the thousands of Protestants in the Spanish colonies of the Caribbean at any given time during the nineteenth century, the presence of a resident Protestant minister of their own faith would not become a reality until the early 1870s. Throughout most of the nineteenth century, foreign and native practicing Protestants had to settle for private home services, services aboard British or U.S. ships, and on occasion illegal private services held by a sojourning clergyman. The other options were to forgo Protestant practices and pass for Catholic or to truly convert to Catholicism.

As several travelogues and foreigners' diaries attest, many Protestants carried out private Sunday services either in the privacy of their own homes or quietly in hotel rooms. The English and American Episcopalian Prayer Books both provided the offices of mattins and evensong, which could be led by non-ordained individuals in private home services. The diaries of George C. Backhouse and his wife Grace attest that they held one or two home services most every Sunday during their stay in Havana during the mid-1850s, including the reading of the Scriptures, prayers, and sermons. After exploring other options, a contemporary Protestant visitor from the United States, Julia Woodruff, came to the conclusion that the best thing was "a quiet reading of our own helpful and satisfying Liturgy, in my own room."[17]

The calling of a British or U.S. man-of-war was a source of joy to many of the islands' practicing Protestants because public Protestant services were usually held aboard them on Sundays. British naval vessels provided Holy Communion for members of the Church of England, while their U.S. counterparts held services for Episcopalian, Methodist, Baptist, or other Protestant denominations. Non-ordained chaplains, usually ship captains, officiated most services, which generally included the reading of sermons and prayers and, on occasion, communion services.[18]

A few of the British and U.S. naval vessels calling in Spanish Caribbean ports had ordained chaplains who could perform Protestant sacramental ceremonies. These chaplains, however, were generally not the most inspiring sorts of ministers. Referring to the naval chaplain of the HMS *Alban*, Grace Backhouse said that the Reverend Mr. Hannan's visit had "resulted in no benefit to us with regard to the services of our Church." She described another British naval chaplain as "a sad subject!" Other Protestants left corroborating testimonies of their dissatisfaction with naval chaplains' sermons. Naval chaplains and other visiting clergymen at times ventured ashore and administered communion and other sacraments for the spiritually neglected Protestant communities of Cuba and Puerto Rico. These clandestine, amphibious services usually took place at the British, German, or U.S. consulates. Such visits were few and far between and only benefitted those belonging to the consular circle of relatives and friends.[19]

As far from ideal as sporadic visits by Protestant clergymen were, these remained about the only source of sacraments for the islands' crypto-Protestants. Pseudo-Catholics, or Protestants who passed for Catholics, participated in the Catholic rites. Protestants residing in the region and not willing to pass for Catholics had few options regarding these vital moments in their lives. Some parents waited months and years before having their children baptized by a passing clergyman of their own faith. Marriages were postponed indefinitely and Protestant couples lived in concubinage either because they rejected Catholic matrimony or because it was denied to them. Dying Protestants passed on, their minds tormented with images of gruesome burials in a godforsaken potter's field.

Holy Baptism

Foreign Protestants with greater social capital and whose actions were more closely monitored by other members of the elite tended to have their children baptized with Catholic rites. This was canonically acceptable to Anglicans and Episcopalians, who recognized as valid sacraments administered by Roman Catholic priests. In so doing, they also secured the legal inheritance rights of their children. This was the case among many foreign-born Protestants of the Ponce elite and among some of Havana's long-term resident foreign Protestants. The parish books of Ponce's Catholic Church show that the Davidsons, Salomons, Oppenheimers, van Rhyns, Penders, Lions, Dodds, Finlays, Ecklemans, Weichers, and other Protestant families that passed for Catholics had their newborn children baptized as Roman Catholics. Their high social status and visibility within Ponce's elite made not baptizing their children not an option. Baptizing them as Protestant would have been not only illegal but socially unacceptable, scandalous in the eyes of the Catholic members of society with whom they comingled.[20]

In contrast, Protestants with less social capital who were less vulnerable to social pressures could afford waiting for a visiting clergyman or not baptizing their children at all. This was particularly true within the somewhat socially aloof Protestants of Havana, who seemed to care little about what the Catholics thought, and among Ponce and Vieques's working-class black Protestants from the British West Indies. When Grace Backhouse asked Fanny Runge, the Lutheran sister of the wife of Havana's British consul-general, whether she intended to baptize her child, Runge responded by saying that she "had not thought about it." An Episcopalian priest reported that there were many unbaptized children among Havana's Protestants and that their parents remained "indifferent about the matter." The parish books of la Iglesia Salvador del Mundo of El Cerro, on the outskirts of Havana, include

virtually no entries with names from predominantly Protestant countries. There were also very few Catholic baptisms among West Indian
laborers who settled in Vieques. One finds just a few Anglo names in
the Catholic baptismal books of the Vieques parish during the 1850s
and 1860s.[21]

The other option for crypto-Protestants was to have their children
illegally baptized by a Protestant minister passing through the region.
They could not count on this, however, as these visits were infrequent
and brief. There is at least one recorded instance of a Ponce family traveling to St. Croix to have their child born outside Roman Catholic
Puerto Rico, where it would have been difficult to have the child baptized. This was the case of the Anglicans William Lee and Sarah Baggs,
whose three previous children, William, Charles Henry, and Ana Isabella, had died unbaptized in Ponce. When Grace Backhouse was
pregnant with her third child, she left Cuba; one of her reasons was "to
have my confinement in England where the child might receive Holy
Baptism."[22]

Some adult Protestants also partook of Catholic baptism after publicly renouncing their faith. This was the case, for example, of the Irish-
man John Nott, who in 1840 requested the sacrament of baptism from
the bishop of Puerto Rico. In a similar petition, Londoner Robert
McPherson declared that although he was a Calvinist since an early
age, he had realized that the Catholic Church "was the only one where
man can find eternal happiness." In 1870, Charles Basanta, the son of
Ponce's British vice-consul, abjured Protestantism and was baptized
Catholic at age twenty-eight.[23] Parish records of El Cerro's Nuestra
Señora del Pilar reflect at least two similar cases. On June 11, 1858,
María Luisa Iraste, a Protestant and a native of Venezuela, was bap-
tized Catholic as an adult, as was Emilia Bloisant of Alabama, who
first renounced her Protestant faith.[24]

Holy Matrimony

The sacrament of holy matrimony posed even greater difficulties and
challenges to Protestants residing in the Hispanic Caribbean, since un-

like baptisms, which Catholic priests did not deny even to the children of known heretics, church marriages were reserved exclusively for communicants of the Roman Catholic Church. In Puerto Rico, priests received strict guidelines that whenever either the bride or groom was from a Protestant country, no marriage be performed until the bishop could first verify the individual's claimed Catholicity. Foreigners were also required to obtain expensive and time-consuming Catholicity and *soltería* (bachelorhood or spinsterhood) certificates, from which natives were exempt.[25]

With regard to marriages, a similar pattern held true, whereby Ponce's foreign Protestants were more likely to go to greater lengths to comply with the social and religious mandate of Catholic matrimony. The sons and daughters of several of Ponce's pseudo-Catholic, Protestant families were married under the auspices of the Roman Catholic Church. Since confession was part of the prenuptial preparations, they went along with this requirement, which must have been very odious to some. Many had to make false declarations and even falsify documents to prove their Catholicity and secured witnesses—many of them also Protestant—to lie in their behalf. A small group of pseudo-Catholics regularly served as witnesses in most of these cases. In one instance, crypto-Protestant groom George Weichers, claimed that he was Catholic but was unable to prove this because he had no baptismal certificate and could not get one because his birthplace, Vienna, was too distant. Actually a native from Hamburg, Weichers got by with the testimony of Bernardo Eckelman, himself a pseudo-Catholic. In another case, twenty-eight-year-old Charles Basanta apparently could not pretend that he was born a Catholic, so he converted publicly to Catholicism before marrying Hortensia Miraihl, also a pseudo-Catholic. For these upper-class families, neither concubinage nor the public embracing of Protestantism were options.[26] The high propensity among them to marry Catholic reflected, in part, the critical importance of marriage as a means to secure upward social mobility, whether this was achieved through marriage with foreign-born women or with women of the local elite. In contrast, among Vieques's poor foreign laboring Protestants, there were virtually no Catholic marriages, since cohabitation and serial monogamy were acceptable options among the working poor of all races and religions. Even the island's highest authority, Governor Francisco Saínz, openly mocked the sacrament of matrimony by holding a long-term adulterous relation with a married woman named doña Pepa; even after the local priest intervened to put an end to the scandalous relation and had her banished from Vieques, the lovers continued their relation on a commuter basis.[27]

In Havana and Matanzas, the foreign Protestant population had lower social rank than in Ponce, was less immersed into greater society, and was far less concerned with social appearances and therefore less compelled to marry Catholic. Thus, pseudo-Catholic marriages were less prevalent in Cuba than in the more sparsely populated and less anonymous context of Ponce. Havana's crypto-Protestant couples were more likely to live in concubinage, which was reportedly quite widespread among Britons and North Americans. There were very few exceptions to this. In El Cerro's Salvador del Mundo parish, Carolina Smith of the state of New York renounced her Methodist faith and was baptized with Catholic rites in 1862 as a precondition to her Catholic marriage to Francisco Javier Molina y García, a member of a local wealthy family. They had already been married by a Methodist minister in New York but decided to ensure the legitimacy and inheritance rights of their two children.[28]

Those Protestants who rejected or were denied Catholic matrimony but still considered it a sin to cohabitate out of wedlock could either wait for a visiting clergyman or travel to the United States or some other destination in the Caribbean where marriage vows could be sanctified with fewer complications and expenses. At least four couples residing in Puerto Rico traveled to St. Thomas in 1855 to seek the marriage ceremony at All Saints Anglican Church: British Vice-Consul Charles Lindegren, an Anglican, and the Roman Catholic Rafaela Gautier; planter John Henry van Rhyn and Grace Louisa Basanta, both communicants of the Church of England; the Anglican planter Isaac Easton Bedlow and Lucy Dupont Penchoen; and the merchant Manuel Toro and Evelina Basanta of the Church of England. Toro and Basanta had married earlier with Catholic rites in Puerto Rico. A few years later, the marriage of Basanta's sister, Josephine, to Thomas Edward Lee was solemnized during a visit to Ponce by the Anglican bishop of Antigua.[29]

Traveling to St. Thomas or New Orleans to seek the sacrament of marriage was also an option for some Catholics who faced consanguinity or other obstacles. Dispensations were reportedly cheaper and more expediently granted in these destinations. Luis Bonafoux and Clemencia Quintero of Guayama and a Mr. Valton and Ms. Quilmin of the French West Indies and residing in Vieques, for example, traveled to St. Thomas to get married there; in the latter case, the Vieques priest had not been positively convinced of the fact that Valton was a widower. The register of marriages of the Dutch Reformed Church of Christiansted, St. Croix, includes entries for several weddings between residents of Puerto Rico, some of whom were Catholic. Church and state authorities could, and in some instances did, nullify matrimonial ties sought outside of the bride and groom's place of residence.[30]

"Don't Die Here"

The notoriously unhealthy climate of the region made the issue of funeral and burial rights particularly critical and pressing among unacclimated foreigners. Foreign visitors and travelers were especially vulnerable to the onslaught of tropical diseases. In Havana, mortality rates among recently arrived foreigners reached appalling levels of between 260 and 400 per thousand. One U.S. consul referred to mid-nineteenth-century Havana as of one the "foulest" ports in the world. Another observer dubbed it a "hot-bed of pestilence." Puerto Rico's principal ports were somewhat healthier but still a concern among foreigners, many of whom faced the prospect of a premature death there. On one occasion, U.S. Consul Charles De Ronceray said of San Juan: "[it is a place with] unhealthy climate, where a man's life is in danger."[31]

The death of ailing Protestant immigrants and visitors marked the end of their sufferings, but it also marked the beginning of a very sad, difficult, and frustrating period for their relatives, friends, concerned compatriots, and consular representatives. Survivors seeking decent funerals and adequate burials for their non-Catholic dead encountered numerous obstacles. One U.S. official stationed in Havana summarized the predicaments of deceased Protestants when he bluntly advised his compatriots: "Don't die in Cuba." In the words of another contemporary observer, "all that accompanies death . . . in Cuba is particularly repulsive. Difficulties are thrown in the way of the becoming burial of those who die out of the communion of the Holy Church of Ferdinand VII and Isabella II."[32]

Justifiably, many Protestant visitors and immigrants were highly anxious about the possibility of dying in the Catholic islands. This was a particularly pressing preoccupation among invalids and ill seamen. As U.S. Consul Andrew K. Blythe put it, "knowledge on the part of a sick person that his remains will be uncared for is calculated to produce a morbid effect upon the mind unfavorable to his recovery." Some foreigners wrote testaments, leaving specific instructions with friends and consuls in which they spelled out what was to be done in the event of their death. One visitor, after returning from a sobering tour of Havana's run-down Espada cemetery, instructed his hotel's attendant that if he were to die on the island, he must be buried at sea. "[A]nywhere," he added, "but in a Catholic country." Another visitor, a New Yorker suffering from consumption, was horrified by the mere thought of dying in Cuba. His only wish was that the steamer *Cahawba* arrive on time so he could die on board the vessel rather than on the island.[33]

Protestants wishing to get married or to have their children christened within their faith could continue with their lives while they waited for a visiting clergyman or until they traveled abroad to receive the desired sacrament. Dead Protestants and their survivors could do neither. The Catholic Church held firm control over funeral services, burials, and cemeteries. In the words of one critical contemporary, "the Mother Church is the mistress of ceremonies of all kinds. She owns the cemeteries practically, is interested in the sale of coffins and management of hearses, buries the dead, licenses the inhuming and exhuming of all bodies." Since licenses granted by parish priests were required before any corpse could be interred, the authority to determine who could and who could not be buried lay strictly within the Catholic Church. North

American and British foreigners were denied funeral ceremonies and burial in consecrated ground unless their surviving friends and relatives could produce evidence of their Catholicity. In Santiago de Cuba, the body of Consul Parsons was barred from the city's consecrated burial grounds for not being Catholic. The remains of James Gallagher, his U.S. counterpart in Ponce, came close to a similar fate, which in the end was avoided because during the course of the day a document was found—or fabricated—that attested to his Catholicity.[34]

Crypto-Protestants and nominal Catholics who either avoided Catholic rites or received Protestant sacraments were well aware of this situation and, not surprisingly, many of them were either converted to or returned to Catholicism during their last days. Abraham Nicolas Souquin, a Swiss agriculturalist residing in Puerto Rico, faced the disturbing prospect of dying outside the communion of the colony's official religion. He abjured his Protestant faith and converted to the Catholic faith before dying in San Juan's military hospital. In El Cerro's Salvador del Mundo parish, Enriqueta Winch y Shepherd, as she faced the possibility of death, renounced "the errors of the [U]nitarian sect," was baptized and received the last rites. A few years later, while awaiting execution, the Cuban Protestant revolutionary Luis Ayestarán reluctantly reembraced the religion into which he had been born. For her part, Tomasa Hernández of Ponce requested, on her deathbed, absolution for the sin of having received the sacrament of matrimony from a Protestant minister. She and her husband, Jaime Roura, attested that they were carrying a "great weight on their consciences and that they felt disturbed." They justified their actions on the grounds that the certificate of *soltería* required by the Catholic priest was too expensive for them to afford. As documented in the parish records of Ponce and El Cerro, dozens of Catholics living in concubinage sought to solemnize their vows shortly before their deaths. The prospect of being denied Catholic burial was at the crux of many of these decisions.[35]

There is also evidence that before the 1870s, many Protestants died as they had lived—as pseudo-Catholics—and were buried with the rites of the Catholic Church. Ponce's Salomons family, for example, who later hosted the island's first public Protestant service, owned a splendid mausoleum in Ponce's Catholic cemetery. The van Rhyns, Basantas, Miraihls, and most other Ponce Protestant families buried their dead as Catholics in the municipal burial ground. According to an 1849 police report, most Protestants were buried in the Havana's Catholic cemetery "under the false assurance of Catholicity." The same occurred in Matanzas.[36]

Most Protestants dying in the Spanish colonies that did not, or could not, pass for Catholics ended up in potters' fields or unfenced, unconsecrated, makeshift cemeteries in desolate and remote locations. One of these was built in the mid-1820s in the El Vedado section of Havana by a British hotel keeper named Francis Nichols. Upon Nichols's death, someone by the name of James Thompson took charge of the graveyard but following Thompson's death it fell into disrepair; the gate keys were lost, and sections of the walls collapsed. Scavenger animals roamed the ruined "American" graveyard and feasted on human remains. During the early 1840s, a yearly average of about forty corpses, including foreign Protestants, suicides, and the unbaptized, were buried in that location.[37]

Several foreign residents and travelers have left revolting descriptions of El Vedado's potter's field and other makeshift places for Protestant burial. The controversial British Consul-General David Turnbull raised cries of outrage in the early 1840s concerning the state of Protestant burial sites. He wrote an impassioned letter to Cuba's captain-general in which he underscored "the horrors which prevail at the place known at the Havana by the name of 'the American burial ground,' where dead bodies are left exposed in the face of day, and where the Vulture contends with the worm for his share of the human spoil." Other reports confirmed the deteriorating state of Havana's Protestant graveyard and the fact that vultures and other beasts profaned the bodies. At a later point, a traveler described what he saw there: "the ground [is] strewn with the bleaching relics of mortality, and in some corner is a heap, mostly of skulls, several yards high."[38]

There was another Protestants' burial ground in Matanzas. It measured half an acre and consisted of mass graves in which bodies were lined side by side; dirt was thrown over the first layer of cadavers and then the next layer was started above it. Scenes at the Matanzas Protestant burial ground moved a visiting Episcopalian bishop to write: "for the first time in my life I saw and realized what is implied in the phrase, 'the burial of a dog.'" Within the jurisdiction of Matanzas, there was a burial ground for non-Catholics in the area known as Playa de Judíos. An 1841 report described it as being in a state of abandonment, having a broken gate, and its dead "barely burried."[39]

Around the time in which El Vedado's graveyard fell into disrepair, Dr. Charles Belot, a hospital owner and physician serving the foreign community, created another option for Protestant burial. Dr. Belot, it so happened, not only could bury his mistakes, but he also managed to profit from them after he inaugurated a private cemetery near one of his clinics. In 1858, U.S. Consul Blythe denounced the practices of such lowland clinics, Dr. Belot's in particular, stating that their proprietors obtained "a large part of their profits" from burying the dead. He pointed out scathingly that patients were better clients dead than alive, for each death produced a net profit of seventeen dollars. Dr. Belot finally yielded to the mounting pressures and consented to surrender all profit in the futur [sic] from the private cemetery attached to the hospital."[40]

In neighboring Puerto Rico, with fewer foreign Protestants, and many of them passing for Catholics, there was no Protestant burial ground as such, but locations close to the coast or offshore, where the bodies of Protestants and other non-Catholics were cast into shallow graves without ceremony or mark. According to a description by the U.S. consul at San Juan, "the burying place [in Ponce] is often profaned by filthy animals roaming there in the night or in the second case left exposed to the open air and often washed away by the beating of the sea." Some foreign Protestants were not even allowed burial on the island. In January 1817, two foreign Protestants, James Coggeshall and his ship's mate died of yellow fever. According to Coggeshall's surviving brother, Charles, since ecclesiastical burial was out of question, he had to take care of the entire matter:

We accordingly had a coffin made on board, and on the following day in the afternoon, with our own crew took the body to a small uninhabited island [most probably, Cayo Cardona], about two miles from the main land of Porto Rico, and interred the remains of this worthy, brave and ingenious young man. To prevent them from being disturbed or desecrated, I left no trace of a grave, but levelled the ground so that the spot where his remains repose should not attract the idle curiosity of those who should hereafter visit this lonely island.

More than half a century later, Wilbert M. Clifford, a twenty-nine-year-old North Carolinian, died of yellow fever in Ponce during the summer of 1871, and local ecclesiastic and civil authorities refused to allow his remains buried anywhere on the island. Instead, they ordered his body interred on the neighboring Cayo Cardona, a location that had housed a lepers' colony since 1836.[41] In sharp contrast, as early as 1845, foreign Protestant laborers from the Lesser Antilles were granted funeral rights on the island of Vieques, where the Catholic Church had a much weaker presence. Foreign labor immigration was deemed essential to the peopling and development of this frontier island, and thus state authorities offered a greater extent of religious tolerance.[42]

Conclusion

Much to the chagrin of the region's state and church authorities, Protestants found their way into Cuba and Puerto Rico beginning in the first decades of the nineteenth century. Unable to worship freely according to their religious preference, the region's Protestants became either crypto-Protestants or pseudo-Catholics. In either case, the opportunities to live and die as practicing Protestants were few or nonexistent. Demography, geographic location, and the particularities of each setting's social structure had a strong influence on the religious choices of the foreign Protestant population and on the capacity of church and state authorities to enforce religious orthodoxy. In spite of—and perhaps precisely because of—their poverty and majority status, Vieques's working-class Protestants avoided pressure to comply with the dictates of the Catholic Church. Contrastingly, Ponce's foreign Protestants of high social standing felt compelled to pass for Catholics and to partake in the Catholic sacraments. The larger, more anonymous urban setting of Havana, especially its suburbs, allowed foreign Protestants more space to escape the demands of official Catholicism. Havana's Protestants, with less social capital at stake than their Ponce counterparts, felt less pressure to live and die as pseudo-Catholics.

The five and a half decades between the opening of the Spanish colonies to foreign, non-Spanish immigration and the declaration of religious tolerance in 1869 demonstrated the inherent tensions of a colonial system in transition, one seeking to hold on to old exclusivist restrictions while opening the Spanish sugar islands to trade with the Protestant North. Despite the fact that the mere residence of Protestants was illegal, the early Protestant populations that emerged in Ponce, Havana, Matanzas, and Vieques laid the foundations for the type of Protestant congregations that would eventually form in the 1870s and 1880s. Furthermore, one could very well argue that one of the keys to understanding the divergent trajectories of Cuban and Puerto Rican Protestantism during the twentieth century is to be found during the foundational stages of Protestantism in the region.

CHAPTER 5

Caudillos, Annexationism, and the Rivalry between Empires in the Dominican Republic, 1844–1874

Pedro Santana (1801–1864) was president of the Dominican Republic on three separate occasions between 1844 and 1861.

T raditionally, the annexationist tendencies of Dominican *caudillos* Pedro Santana and Buenaventura Báez have been simplistically dismissed as antinational maneuvers by self-serving strongmen.[1] That Santana and Báez were self-serving characters whose primary object was to stay in power is undeniable, but they were not the only Dominicans who wanted at one time or another to persuade other nations to annex their country. Similar sentiments and strategies were embraced by other national and regional leaders, among them Manuel Jimenes González, Matías Ramón Mella, José María Cabral, and prominent members of the Cibaeño bourgeoisie. Dominican annexationism also changed over time in terms of its intensity and the objects of its metropolitan choices: France, Spain, or the United States.

This chapter seeks to explain the motivations behind the Dominican *caudillos'* seemingly chronic annexationist desires from Dominican independence (1844) to the end of Báez's fourth presidential term (1874), as seen against the backdrop of imperial rivalries over the struggling Dominican Republic. It contends that Dominican annexationism peaked precisely during the periods of intensified international rivalry over the republic and that the nature of the *caudillos'* annexationist preferences was dictated by geopolitical circumstances beyond their control. This chapter, thus, establishes a connection between the evolution of North Atlantic imperial rivalries and political developments within the Dominican Republic that testifies to the importance of examining the effects of international politics on local affairs. It also focuses upon the activities of foreign envoys who intermittently sought to prod Haitian forces into invading Dominican territory and shows how the manipulation of racial issues was at the heart of conflicting

This chapter was originally published with the same title in *Diplomatic History* 17:4 (Fall 1993): 571–97. Reprinted with permission.

policies regarding the infant republic. In sum, this chapter seeks to shed new light on the historical phenomenon of nineteenth-century Dominican annexationism by looking at the broader Atlantic context, and in so doing, it suggests a paradigm applicable to other Caribbean experiences, most notably Cuban annexationism.

The First Republic (1844–1861)

The inhabitants of Spain's neglected Caribbean colony gained their independence almost by default during the general Latin American emancipation period in 1821. Although easily achieved, Dominican independence was short lived. Within a few weeks, Haitian forces invaded the infant republic and reunified the island under Haitian rule until 1844. After the fall of Jean-Pierre Boyer on March 24, 1843, various Dominican separatist movements coalesced to oust the Haitians.[2] In a conciliatory effort to promote Dominican unity against the Haitian foe, the Trinitario leadership of the new republic included a number of conservatives in the national junta and placed the army under a conservative *caudillo*, Pedro Santana.

Great Britain, France, Spain, and the United States paid close attention to developments in the new Caribbean republic. Following the Dominican declaration of independence in 1844, these nations immediately appointed envoys and secret agents to monitor the activities of their rival powers. Of all the North Atlantic powers, France was the most aggressive in its policy toward the Dominican Republic. Even before the republic's separation from Haiti, France had demonstrated interest in territorial concessions in the eastern part of the island. In December 1843, for example, the French envoy to Port-au-Prince maneuvered to acquire territorial cessions around the formidable Samaná Bay in exchange for clearing the Haitian debt to France. The infant republic resisted the idea that a portion of the Haitian debt should extend to the Dominican Republic, rightly arguing that Haiti had incurred the debt prior to the annexation of the Dominican Republic in 1822. Nevertheless, French agents continued to use the debt as a bargaining chip to exert pressure for territorial concessions, and they withheld diplomatic recognition from the struggling republic until it accepted responsibility for part of the Haitian debt.[3]

Spain also used the prospect of recognition as a means to extort concessions from the emerging nation. In May 1847, the governor of Puerto Rico advised the Spanish minister of state to use appropriate timing in granting recognition to the Dominican Republic. "It would be desirable," he wrote, "that the Spanish government proceed with great moderation before agreeing to any treaty with Dominican Envoys, in order to secure all possible advantages for Spain." In a later communication, he warned of growing British influence in the Dominican Republic and of the possible consequences of a British loan to the emerging republic. If the British made the loan, he concluded, Spain would no longer be able to swap recognition for territorial concessions.[4]

For its part, the U.S. Department of State maintained a very low-keyed policy toward the Dominican Republic, limiting itself to observing the activities of Europe's naval powers and gathering intelligence about the new republic. It was essentially a defensive position. Early in 1845, Secretary of State John Calhoun sent John Hogan as his agent to the Dominican Republic with instructions to gather information about the island's social and economic conditions. Hogan reported that French and British secret agents and other foreign envoys were active in the republic. Two years later, when President James K. Polk commissioned Francis Harrison as commercial agent in Santo Domingo, he ordered him to monitor the activities of European agents. In his reports, Harrison referred repeatedly to France's interest in Samaná and the presence of French agents there. Special agent Benjamin Green was later dispatched to the republic to keep close watch over British and French agents trying to gain concessions in Samaná.[5]

Despite the aggressive and expansionist designs of so many nations, Dominicans retained their political and economic autonomy and territorial integrity. The designs of one foreign nation were neutralized by those of others, producing a stalemate wherein France could not secure a portion of Samaná, British lenders could not force a loan, and neither Spain nor the United States could claim any significant concessions.

Tensions within the Dominican anti-Haitian coalition over the issue of national sovereignty mounted in the summer of 1844. Conservatives, church leaders, Santana and Báez and their troops, and the ruling junta under Tomás de Bobadilla all sought French aid in exchange for a protectorate and/or land concessions in Samaná. Meanwhile, the liberal Trinitarios remained firm in their nationalistic stance. Facing an impending arrangement with the French government, on June 9, 1844, Trinitario leaders Juan Pablo Duarte, Matías Ramón Mella, and Francisco del Rosario Sánchez staged a coup d'état in Santo Domingo and assumed control of the junta. They failed, however, in their next move; they could not wrest control of the army from Santana, as the rank and file refused to recognize the newly imposed Trinitario commander, Esteban Roca.[6] Reassuming leadership, Santana proceeded to march on Santo Domingo with two thousand loyal troops. By mid-July, he had gained control over the capital city and reinstated the conservative members of the junta, forcing Generals Duarte, Mella, and Sánchez to flee. Soon thereafter, the conservatives drew up a constitution. Although it provided for the separation of powers, Santana managed to assume dictatorial powers by imposing the infamous Article 210, which allowed him to govern by decrees for as long as the Haitian menace remained.[7]

Santana's first presidential term extended through August 1848, when he resigned and retired to his estate. During his tenure, his ministers had made numerous attempts to annex the Dominican Republic to a foreign nation or to establish a foreign protectorate over it. Annexationist overtures, in fact, anteceded the actual establishment of independence, as Dominican leaders had approached French representatives with offers of territorial concessions in Samaná in return for military aid against Haiti. Santana's envoys knocked on the door of practically every European monarch, making similar offers to Great Britain, Spain, and even the tiny kingdom of Sardinia. During the early years of Dominican independence, however, France continued to be the main target of Dominican annexationist aspirations.[8] All of these annexationist maneuvers proved fruitless, because the European powers checked one another's designs and because governmental transitions in France and Spain ended negotiations already in progress.

The course of international rivalry over the Dominican Republic was transformed by intensified U.S. expansionism during the peak of filibuster activity following the war with Mexico. European statesmen viewed the Caribbean as a monolithic unit and feared that either the U.S. government or the filibusterers would use the emerging republic as an expansionist beachhead. The activities of U.S. filibusterers were not, however, directed against the Dominican Republic, mainly because slavery had been abolished there and because it had an unacceptable majority of free blacks and mulattoes. During this period, white Southerners in the United States were trying to reduce the free black population, either by closing the roads to manumission or by reenslaving free blacks; most of these Southerners deemed a large population of free blacks unacceptable within a Southern, slave-based Caribbean empire. Thus, U.S. interests in the Dominican Republic during the 1850s were notably different from U.S. interests in Cuba. While most U.S. expansionists who coveted Cuba did so because of its potential in the expansion of agrarian, slave-based capitalism, a growing number of imperialists understood that the Dominican Republic had other things to offer, especially in terms of strategic naval possibilities and prospects for extractive, speculative ventures such as mining and real estate.[9]

During the 1850s, the European powers continued to check each other's moves but became increasingly concerned with the possibility of expansionist actions by the United States. European agents had begun to signal a growing U.S. presence in Dominican territory as early as 1850.[10] A polarized situation began to emerge over the next few years, with Europe and the United States on opposite sides. Great Britain remained firmly attached to the status quo. The British had no desire to establish new colonial possessions in the hemisphere, nor did they want any disturbances that might hamper British trade in the region. After all, since they already controlled between half and three-fourths of the Dominican Republic's foreign trade, why bother with costly imperial ventures there?[11] Meanwhile, French policy toward the Dominican Republic became less aggressive and increasingly defensive during this period. Fearing U.S. and British resistance, the French government repeatedly rejected Dominican offers for the establishment of a protectorate.[12]

Of all the European powers, Spain was the most preoccupied with U.S. designs in the Dominican Republic. In the summer of 1852, Spanish agents began to report details of expansionist schemes by U.S. citizens. One agent, José M. Pando, informed Cuba's captain-general about a plan to help a group of U.S. citizens emigrate to the republic, linked to a filibuster expedition to Cuba.[13] In another dispatch, the Spanish consular agent at Turks Islands reported that this migration project was part of a broader scheme whereby the United States would attempt to subjugate the Dominican people under a plantation system. By September 1852, the Spanish captain-general of Puerto Rico was recommending armed intervention to stop U.S. expansion. Later that year, the president of the Spanish Council of Ministers outlined a drastic strategy, suggesting that secret agents be dispatched and that ties with the Báez party be cultivated for use against the United States. He also recommended troop deployments. "All of this could be achieved," he noted, "without the entanglement of formally recognizing the independence of Santo Domingo, because this is not necessary, and besides, it is convenient to reserve the weapon of recognition for a more propitious and useful moment."[14] In all likelihood, Spanish agents purposely exaggerated the seriousness of the filibuster threat. Such reports, their aggressive rhetoric notwithstanding, reveal that the Spanish had assumed a defensive posture in response to the new, very palpable assertiveness in U.S. designs toward the infant republic of the Caribbean.

In 1849, a new factor further complicated foreign rivalries around the struggling Dominican Republic. Faustin Soulouque, the illiterate black emperor of Haiti who once swore "by the soul of his mother, that he [would] not leave a chicken alive on Dominican soil," invaded the Dominican Republic with ten thousand troops in an effort to reunite both parts of the island under his rule.[15] Each of the four concerned North Atlantic naval powers tried to use this situation to its own particular geopolitical advantage by underscoring either the republic's vulnerability or by pointing at how foreign influence would lead to more Haitian aggression. Under these pressing circumstances, official representatives from Great Britain, France, and the United States, along with delegates from Haiti and the Dominican Republic, negotiated and agreed on a ten-year truce. Within two years, however, multinational mediation fell apart, and the specter of Haitian invasion reemerged.

In sum, the decade leading to 1852 was one of profound transitions in terms of the balance of power in, and the extent of foreign influence over, the Hispanic Caribbean. During these years, the United States gradually assumed an offensive position in the region. The change in U.S. policy put the European naval powers on the defensive and forced them to coalesce in order to curb U.S. encroachment.

Manuel Jimenes González, who became president of the Dominican Republic in September 1848, inherited the problems of Santana's administration but also created new problems of his own. Following two years of reduced tensions with Haiti, Jimenes González proceeded to dismantle the national army. It was not a wise move. In 1849, Haitian troops attacked the republic again.[16] Renewed Haitian aggression had two salient effects. First, it prompted Dominican leaders to pursue annexation with greater vigor than before. On April 4, 1849, the Dominican Council of Ministers addressed a desperate letter to Puerto Rico's governor informing him of the invasion by "the usurping antisocial Haitian enemy" and requesting "all the aid that can be spared in favor of the Christian Dominican family." Two weeks later, the Dominican Congress passed a resolution offering the French government a protectorate over the country along with land concessions in Samaná.[17] Meanwhile, Jimenes González approached first British and later U.S. and French agents requesting protection and inquiring about the possibilities of annexation. When these overtures failed, a desperate Jimenes González offered his country to the Spanish crown. Congressional president Báez, for his part, continued to promote a French protectorate. Despite tepid responses from France, Báez ordered the French flag hoisted on April 4, 1849. In September, when the Haitian troops had been pushed back momentarily, a still-worried group of Santiagueños sent Santana a petition for their country's annexation to the United States. In the petition, they declared that they belonged to "the great family of American peoples," and underscored their desire "to enjoy the advantages of the 27 states of the Union."[18] All of these annexationist schemes failed—frustrated, like previous schemes, by the concerned powers, which actively checked one another's designs.

Haitian aggression also served to revive Pedro Santana politically. The National Congress called upon him to reassume command of the army and to mobilize the troops to face the Haitian invaders. On April 21, 1849, Soulouque's and Santana's forces clashed in the bloody battle of Las Carreras. The Haitian army came out badly beaten; Soulouque himself had to jump off a cliff in desperate retreat.[19] Following this victory Santana regained his status as a national hero.

After defeating the Haitians, Santana marched once again on Santo Domingo to reclaim leadership over the national government. This time, he chose not to participate directly in the national government, selecting instead Báez as his successor. Upon reaching the presidency, Báez initiated talks to pursue annexation to the United States. Meanwhile, Santana, believed to be the only one capable of defeating the Haitians, retained control of the military from his retirement at his El Prado estate. Conflict with Haiti did not abate until 1851, when the mediation of the North Atlantic powers fashioned a truce between the two nations. For the balance of his term, Báez, with the support of the Francophile and Hispanophile clergy, maneuvered to establish a European protectorate. The only thing that he achieved, however, was the further alienation of the Haitians, who initiated yet another military mobilization.[20]

The United States' influence over the Hispanic Caribbean continued to grow throughout the balance of the 1850s. The year 1854 was of particular importance, because anti-expansionists from the U.S. South and North temporarily canceled each other out as the Franklin Pierce administration embarked upon two different expansionist projects, one seeking to acquire Cuba, the other seeking territorial concessions in the Dominican Republic. In fact, 1854 was the high-water mark of U.S. interest in the Dominican Republic. Popular support in the United States for expansion into the Dominican Republic, however, was practically nonexistent. Interest in the Dominican Republic centered mainly around two considerations: first, the acquisition of a coaling station, preferably at Samaná, one of the hemisphere's finest bays; and second, the creation of extractive enclaves and potential markets that could be developed on an island free from the tariffs and other restrictions affecting Cuba and Puerto Rico.[21] Expansion into the Dominican Republic was arguably an exclusively Northern project.

In June 1854, U.S. Secretary of State William Marcy dispatched William Cazneau with instructions to negotiate the recognition of the Dominican Republic in exchange for the cession of a coaling station in Samaná. Cazneau's arrival in Santo Domingo sparked immediate concern among European consular agents. When his intentions became known, the Europeans tried to dissuade the Dominican government from signing any treaty that might surrender any portion of its national territory to the United States.[22] The British consul cautioned Juan N. Tejera, the Dominican minister of foreign affairs, that the proposed treaty should not be accepted, particularly because the United States had thus far refused even to recognize the country's independence. The French were even more forceful. According to Cazneau's reports, the French consul at Port-au-Prince instigated the persecution of those favorable to the treaty and achieved the closing of a pro-treaty newspaper, *El Porvenir*, whose editor barely escaped being sent to jail.[23] During the treaty negotiations, the European agents also called for an increased military presence. In light of what was believed to be an imminent invasion from the United States, the Spanish envoy to the Dominican Republic, Eduardo San Just, wrote to the captain-general of Cuba suggesting the deployment of a warship to join the British *Argus* and French *Mélange*. His desperate communication gave the impression that invading U.S. troops were on their way. Increased U.S. interest in the Dominican Republic further strengthened the European coalition. High-level British officials manifested their certainty that France would make common cause with Britain in defense of Dominican independence and territorial integrity.[24]

The issue of race was a key determinant in U.S. policy toward the Dominican Republic and, for that matter, toward the entire Caribbean region. During the 1840s and 1850s, successive U.S. administrations had to court white Southern support and were therefore very careful not to offend the white population's racial sensibilities. That white Southerners perceived the Dominican Republic as a struggling nation with a lawless, free, dark-skinned population made it very difficult for any administration to establish solid diplomatic relations with the republic, or even to grant recognition, which many deemed the first step toward annexation. Agents Hogan, Green, Cazneau, and Jonathan Elliot favored a stronger U.S. presence in the Dominican Republic to one degree or another. They also favored the acquisition of the whole island or at least of territories around Samaná Bay. Something of a correlation emerges from their reports between their perception of the racial characteristics of Dominicans and their desire to acquire the island: the more ardently expansionist the reporter, the lighter the racial portrayal of the Dominican people. Significantly, some of these envoys were Northern entrepreneurs who at one point or another established exploitative ventures on the island.[25]

The race issue also played a large part in the struggle against the cession of Samaná. Cazneau denounced the Europeans for working "incessantly to instill in the Dominicans the belief that native whites will be set aside and blacks enslaved, if Americans gain a foothold on the island." His wife and fellow diplomat, Jane Cazneau, called for an "armed colonization" to stop Soulouque.[26] Robert Schomburgk, the British consul, informed Lord Clarendon that he had spoken with the island's legislators about the U.S. treaty and drew "their attention to the humiliating clause of Article 3, by which nine-tenths of their population were rendered liable to arrest and imprisonment, should they, as per example, land in Charleston in South Carolina." Spanish secret agent Juan de Abril also highlighted the nonreciprocal nature of the treaty.[27]

In the end, the race issue killed the negotiations despite Cazneau's efforts to paint his country as seeking the elevation of people of color. On December 13, 1854, Juan N. Tejera notified Secretary of State Marcy that Dominicans would not agree to the treaty unless all their people, without racial distinctions, received the same rights and liberties in the United States as would be granted to U.S. citizens in the Dominican Republic. On this matter the United States proved unyielding. Marcy instructed agent Jonathan Elliot not even to consider any modifications, which would be contrary to the sentiment of many people in the United States. Finally, in December 1854, the Dominican Congress

rejected the treaty overwhelmingly. Even then the U.S. government refused to amend it, instead trying to circumvent the lower house of the
legislature and force it on the Dominican executive branch.[28]

The specter of a Haitian invasion of the Dominican Republic arose
once again during the treaty negotiations of 1854–1855. Evidence in-
dicates that the European naval powers prodded Haiti into action; in-
disputably, these nations stood to gain from Haiti's menacing presence.
According to diplomat-historian Sumner Welles, throughout this period, French and British envoys "lost no opportunity in impressing the
Emperor Faustin [Soulouque] with the danger which would threaten
his own domain should a slave-holding power such as the United States
obtain foothold on the Island." In November 1854, the Spanish minister of state instructed his envoy to Haiti not to antagonize Soulouque's
government and to associate with the French and British envoys, who
also opposed U.S. encroachments on the island. Eduardo San Just received orders to seek the aid of the British and French consuls and to
instill the fear of a racial war on Dominican authorities.[29] During this
period, Cazneau complained repeatedly about a French and British plot
to use Haitians to Africanize the Dominican Republic under Báez's
leadership. In a letter to expansionist John Quitman, he declared that
"under the specious title of 'the mediating powers,' France and England
always hold the negroes in readiness to be let slip like bloodhounds on
the whites at the east end of Hayti, if they prove, at any time, refractory
to European policy."[30] The renewal of Haitian expansionism in 1854–
1855 played neatly into the hands of the European powers trying to
check the designs of the United States. The British consul, for example,
based his anti-treaty campaign on the argument that the Dominican
Republic would never achieve peace with Haiti if it granted territorial
concessions to the United States.

In December 1854, the British and French consuls to the Dominican
Republic wrote to President Santana spelling out the conditions under
which they would mediate to appease Haiti. The first of six conditions
was that the republic should not "alienate, lease, mortgage or transfer
or donate, either permanently or temporarily, any portion of the
Dominican territory, particularly the Samaná Bay, to any government

whatsoever." Also included were prohibitions against the establishment of financial agreements with any foreign nation, the landing of foreign armies of adventurers, and the signing of any treaty that would not guarantee reciprocity of rights and privileges, regardless of race. These restrictions were obviously in reference to the United States.[31]

In part because of European opposition and interference, the treaty negotiations, which were led by Cazneau, were an uphill battle. At one point, a frustrated Cazneau scorned the Dominicans' position as "semi-colonial and irresponsible." He also protested against European meddling in direct communications with the British and French consuls.[32] In the end, the treaty did not materialize, not only because of foreign interference but also because of popular opposition from a society polarized under two *caudillos* who had aligned themselves with different international powers.

Of Great Britain, France, and Spain, the latter remained the most cautious in its policy toward the Dominican Republic. That caution did not signify a lack of interest, however. Spain stood to lose much if the United States gained a foothold in a territory located between its two remaining American colonies, Cuba and Puerto Rico. Spain's greatest fear was that the United States would take over Samaná and turn it into "an immense den of filibusterers." The Spanish captain-general of Puerto Rico kept a watchful eye on developments in the neighboring republic. He informed the Spanish minister of state of Cazneau's arrival in Santo Domingo and of his alleged intentions to promote a mass immigration to the Dominican Republic like the one preceding the annexation of Texas in the 1830s and 1840s. In later dispatches, he described the situation as "extremely complicated and dangerous" and said that he believed Cazneau's activities would lead to "incalculable evils."[33] Also active in checking U.S. encroachments were Spanish agents San Just and de Abril. The former had instructions "to use all available means to paralyze, if possible, the ambitious projects of the United States." Upon his arrival he reported that he thought "that the only way to put an end to so undesirable a situation is to oppose by force with the most rigorous resistance the pretentious designs that the United States have for this country."[34]

The tense international rivalry and the imminence of U.S. expansion into the Dominican Republic in 1854 led Spain to reevaluate its policy toward its former colony. Up to that point, Spain had avoided recognizing the Dominican Republic because, as the Spanish minister of state explained to Dominican envoy Matías Ramón Mella, recognition "could set a bad example before the eyes of the partisans of Cuban independence." Spaniards also shied from negotiating a protectorate for fear of provoking the United States.[35] But Cazneau's mission and the prospect of the United States receiving territorial grants in Samaná moved Spanish officials to reevaluate their position. Fearing the crystallization of a United States–Dominican treaty, Puerto Rico's governor recommended recognition. A few weeks later, San Just received instructions to initiate negotiations for recognition. As Sumner Welles aptly put it, "the revelation of the ambitions of the United States proved a stronger argument in persuading the Spanish Government to accord official recognition to the Republic than all of General Mella's eloquence."[36]

As noted above, around 1853, Dominican politics had become polarized between two *caudillos* representing different regions and different economic bases. Santana was a wealthy rancher from El Seibo; Báez was a landholder from Azua. Their struggle for power intensified as it became internationalized when both sought support from the North Atlantic powers. The resulting polarization in Dominican politics was a reflection of a growing polarization in northern Atlantic international relations. The United States absorbed the Santana party into its field and repudiated the Báez party, which it associated with the black segment of the Dominican population. This position was clearly reflected in a report from commercial agent Elliot. "The presidential term of Buenaventura Báez, *a mulatto*, expires on February 15," Elliot wrote. "He has been a great enemy of United States' nationals, his successor being General Pedro Santana, a much better person who I believe has warm feelings toward us, he is considered a *white man*, but I think has a slight mixture with the black race."[37]

Cazneau relayed information of a similar nature. He wrote Secretary of State Marcy that there was an Anglo-Franco-Haitian conspiracy in accord with Báez's so-called black party that sought to extinguish the Dominican Republic and turn it into an African dependency. In 1856, when the Santana-Báez polarization had become even sharper, Elliot spoke scornfully of Báez as "an ambitious black."[38] Cazneau also informed Lewis Cass that the black party planned a pro-Báez insurrection that, if successful, would mean the end of white predominance and white property, if not all white people. He added that France and Great Britain were behind this plot. Spanish envoys, for their part, aligned with the Báez faction. "Under the present circumstances," wrote the Spanish commercial agent, "[Báez's] victory would offer us complete protection against the projects of the *Yankees*." In an earlier report, he had characterized the Santana administration as being "of poor quality," "ignorant," and "perverse."[39]

At the termination of Báez's term in February 1853, Santana assumed the presidency for a third time. This term, however, he faced the opposition of Báez and his party, which, ironically, had been strengthened when Santana chose Báez as his successor in 1849.[40] The Dominican political scene for the next eight or nine years was to be dominated by the struggle for power between these two *caudillos* and their partisans, a rivalry reinforced and aggravated by the international tensions over the Dominican Republic. While Santana's party sought stronger links with, and the protection of, the United States, Báez and his pro-French or clerical party reaffirmed its Europhilia and its Catholicism. Before the polarization of international rivalry over the Dominican Republic between 1853 and 1855, annexationism had not been a divisive factor; many of the country's leaders, including Santana, Jimenes González, Báez, and Bobadilla had been willing to hand over their country to any power wishing to accept it. As Báez himself put it, he would favor "whatever Power[,] be it British, French or Anglo-American, whichever offered the best advantages."[41] Now, in the mid-1850s, geopolitical shifts forced the *caudillos* to choose sides: Santana looked westward to the United States; Báez looked east to France and Spain.

Tensions between these two groups became evident early on when Bishop Tomás de Portes refused to appear at Santana's inauguration. Santana then accused Báez and the clergy of conspiring to set Báez up as the country's dictator in perpetuity and of committing high treason. Tensions escalated over the issue of civil marriages versus church marriages and culminated in the banishment of several pro-Báez clergymen. Later, Santana issued a decree whereby prelates and church officials would henceforth be appointed by the state.[42] During the mid-1850s, it became clear that the Báez party enjoyed the full support of the Dominican Church, in part because of Báez's pro-Spanish and pro-European stance. Meanwhile, relations between the pro-U.S. Santana and the Church continued to deteriorate. This link between politics and religion ran parallel to the postures toward the Catholic Church embraced by annexationists and anti-annexationists in Cuba. In both cases, the party that gravitated toward the United States opposed Catholic exclusivism, while the party that gravitated toward Europe reaffirmed its ties with the Catholic Church.

When Santana returned to power, Báez and many of his partisans fled to St. Thomas, where they enjoyed numerous business contacts, particularly among the French. Only nine months into Santana's third term, the U.S. consul at Santo Domingo discovered a French scheme to overthrow Santana and replace him with Báez, who, according to Elliot, "most cordially hates Americans and all that is American and is purely a Frenchman in his heart." Spain also played a crucial role in this polarization. Consul Antonio María Segovia gave his full support to Báez and worked diligently to reinstate him in the presidency. He even began a naturalization campaign, granting Spanish citizenship and protection to hundreds of Baecistas, and set up an anti-Santana newspaper, *El Eco del Pueblo*. Segovia, who deemed Báez the only Dominican capable of restoring peace and progress, bore much of the responsibility for Báez's return to power in October 1856.[43]

The Santana administration was moving toward the U.S. pole at a time when the United States was again actively seeking to establish its presence in the republic. The Santana-Cazneau negotiations mobilized the opposition, which sought the support of the European envoys. The threat of U.S. penetration into the Dominican Republic also mobilized the Haitian government, which feared that the United States would try to reestablish slavery throughout the whole island. Thus, in November

1855, thirty thousand Haitian troops invaded the Dominican Republic once again, but by January of the following year they were repelled. Haitian aggression and French, British, and Spanish support of Báez further fueled Santana's pro–United States sentiments. He renewed his efforts to cede Samaná to the United States. In fact, the Santana administration offered the United States permission to conduct a naturalization drive like the one Segovia was carrying on for Spain, in exchange for the protection of four armed vessels. The official press also became ardently pro–United States, and the Santana administration adopted national emblems, such as spread eagles, strikingly similar to those of the United States.[44]

Spanish envoys continued to relay negative assessments of Santana's government. In a letter to the captain-general of Cuba, the Spanish commercial agent stated that Santana was a source of growing hostility toward Spanish subjects. The captain-general later requested the deployment of a vessel for the protection of Spanish subjects in the Dominican Republic.[45] Finally, in May 1856, Santana yielded to the mounting pressures; he retired once again and left the presidency to Manuel de Regla Mota, who in turn resigned in favor of Báez.

Once in power for a second time, Báez faced strong opposition from the bourgeoisie of El Cibao—the northern agricultural region that had its capital in the city of Santiago. In July 1857, after renewed efforts by Báez to siphon profits from the tobacco growers, Santiagueño professionals, merchants, and agriculturists rebelled and set up their own government. One of the first acts of the Santiago revolutionary government was to call upon the man who had twice defeated the Haitians and had twice marched triumphantly on Santo Domingo: Santana.[46]

Although in his inaugural proclamation, Báez had promised "the strictest impartiality" toward all foreign powers to avoid "the predominance of any of them," his short-lived second presidential term developed a strong anti–United States coloration. Just two days after his inauguration, an angry mob of his partisans gathered in front of the U.S. Commercial Agency in Santo Domingo and threatened to tear down its flag and other emblems. A few weeks later, the U.S. interim chargé d'affaires reported that since Báez had taken over, the general cry in the streets was "down with the Yankees, down with the eagle and the American flag." In the same communication, he requested protection for Santana, "who has proven to be a real republican and friend of the United States," and for the other "pro Americans." At one point the U.S. envoy desperately requested British protection for his quarters.[47]

Báez denounced the Santiago insurrection of 1857 as "pro–North American and filibusterer" and requested military aid from Puerto Rico's governor. The Baecista minister of foreign relations, Félix María del Monte, complained directly to U.S. Secretary of State Lewis Cass about the allegedly antigovernment activities of agent Elliot, accusing him of plotting against Báez, of being a partisan of Santana, and of insulting high government officials. He also informed Cass that according to a police report, Elliot had been seen in the streets apparently "crazed and cheering the enemies of the government."[48] Santana and the Santiagueño revolutionaries moved to put Santo Domingo under siege. Báez's troops held firmly inside the city walls for a little over a year, until the mediation of the French, British, and Spanish consuls allowed Báez to cede the capital in exchange for his life and those of his associates. Following the surrender, he fled, while most of the Baecista leaders and Baecista clergy sought exile in the neighboring Spanish colonies. Santana took power once again. Shortly afterward, a jubilant Elliot informed Cass that "the time has arrived when we can have a good station for our Navy and depots for our steamers in these waters."[49] The dramatic events of the next few months would prove that Elliot had celebrated too soon.

As the balance of power in the Hispanic Caribbean began shifting toward the United States in the 1850s, the European naval powers coalesced to check that nation's expansionist and hegemonic tendencies. Most European nations welcomed the U.S. Civil War because it moved the geopolitical clock back by ten to twelve years, enabling them once again to take the offensive in the Caribbean as well as in Mexico. The Civil War also further strengthened the informal European coalition vis-à-vis the United States.

Although the sympathies of Europe's policymakers were definitely with the Confederacy, the European powers at first pursued a cautious policy toward the crisis in the United States. The crisis leading to the separation of the North and South soon cleared the stage for European encroachments into regions of the hemisphere in which the Monroe Doctrine had been in force during the antebellum era. During the war, Spain annexed the Dominican Republic; France, Spain, and Great Britain launched a combined attack on Mexico that culminated in the establishment of a French emperor there; and negotiations went on to establish European protectorates over Texas and Ecuador. All of these developments would have been inconceivable before the war.

For some time before the Civil War broke out, France and Spain had considered reestablishing European control over Mexico and the Dominican Republic. Fear of the United States' reaction, however, deterred concrete action in that direction before the Civil War. The growing political crisis in the United States during the election year of 1860 spurred Spain into action, although formal annexation of the Dominican Republic would remain in limbo while the United States stood as a single unified nation. On December 8, 1860, the Spanish foreign minister, Leopoldo O'Donnell, instructed Cuba's captain-general to proceed with prudence, adding that it was better to wait for the final breakup of the Union. He warned that:

> the reunion of Santo Domingo brought about in such a manner as would give rise to suspicions not destitute of foundations, would not only turn the gaze of the terrified states of Latin America towards the United States, thus destroying the basis of our policy in America, the unity of our race, but also perhaps making the contending parties in America forget their internal discords, might lead them to group themselves under the Monroe Doctrine, a principle accepted without reserve by the slave states no less than by those where free labor prevails.[50]

Annexation and War of Restoration (1861–1865)

Spain annexed the Dominican Republic in the spring of 1861. It waited until the fighting between the North and South had actually begun.

Neither France nor Great Britain posed any serious opposition to Spain's move to retake the struggling Caribbean republic.[51] Spain carried out the annexation for a number of reasons. First and foremost was the fear that the Dominican Republic would fall victim to either U.S. or Haitian expansionism. The Spanish consul, Mariano Álvarez, warned in 1860 that "two different enemy races of the Dominicans covet this precious Antille," and in a similar report filed a few months later, Antonio Peláez Campomanes, a Spanish envoy entrusted with assessing conditions in the republic on the eve of its occupation, ominously predicted that "Santo Domingo will be Haitian or Yankee." There were good reasons for Spain's fear of U.S. encroachments in the Dominican Republic. A U.S. presence there could provide a foothold for filibusterers looking toward Cuba and Puerto Rico. As Consul Álvarez put it, control over Samaná would turn the United States into "the owners of the Gulf of Mexico, [a situation] that would hang like the sword of Damocles over our rich possessions."[52] Spanish policymakers also had reason to fear a Haitian victory over the Hispanic side of Hispaniola. Haitians would then represent a serious threat to both Cuba and Puerto Rico, where slavery still thrived. Thus, Spanish control over Samaná Bay was strategically vital for the preservation of both colonies.

Santana and his partisans had their own reasons for desiring annexation to Spain. Above all else, Santana wanted to strengthen his position and wipe out internal opposition to his regime with the support of Spanish troops. He had also come under attack from insurgent movements with strong Haitian ties. On the eve of his country's annexation by Spain, he cried "Haitians" and "Yankees" to accelerate the process under way and to deter coups like those in 1848 and 1856. Remarkably, up until the late 1850s, Santana had been an ardent promoter of annexation and concessions to the United States, but after 1859, when annexation to the United States was no longer plausible, he turned his attention to Spain.

On March 18, 1861, Santana, the *caudillo* who had previously been an ally of the United States and had promised to "look out for the conservation of independence," publicly declared his nation's annexation

to Spain. "Our anxieties and dangers are over!" he exclaimed. In Santana's words, the Dominican Republic went from being "a weak nation
whose independence was a vain title repeatedly blown around by powerful winds" to being "the robust child of a mighty power."[53] Within
two months, with an all-out war raging in the United States, Spain formally annexed the Dominican Republic.

The Dominican Republic that reentered the Spanish empire in 1861
differed markedly from its sister colonies to the east and west. For one,
it lacked a structured state apparatus and had few significant staple
crop plantations. Santana openly prided himself on delivering to Spain
a country without lawyers and newspapers. Under Spanish rule, however, the state grew in size and power. The national budget increased
almost twentyfold, from 241,000 pesos in 1860 to 4,476,000 pesos in
1863. Funds from Cuba and Puerto Rico and locally collected revenue
helped support the new bloated colonial bureaucracy. Spain now levied
taxes and duties similar to those collected in Cuba and Puerto Rico.
These taxes became a great source of irritation for the Dominicans,
particularly those engaged in international trade.[54]

The Catholic Church, which practically functioned as an arm of the
Spanish State, was also radically transformed. Like the Dominican
State, the Dominican Church during the First Republic had not
touched the lives of the majority of the people. Most Dominicans were
nominally Catholic, but few attended mass or partook of the basic
sacraments of baptism and marriage. According to General José de la
Gándara y Navarro, "illegitimate unions" were more common in the
Dominican Republic than anywhere else in Latin America. Another
contemporary observer noted that Dominicans "[d]o not attend mass,
do not go to confession, and some skip the sacrament of baptism to
avoid travelling a few miles."[55]

Annexation and the strengthening of Catholicism went hand in
hand. On September 5, 1861, Francisco Serrano stated that Catholic
sentiments were "inseparable from the pro-Spanish sentiment," and he
requested the appointment of a prelate "to fix" the Dominican Church,
a request fulfilled with the appointment of Bienvenido Monzón as archbishop of Santo Domingo in May 1861. A zealous prelate, Archbishop

Monzón was determined to purify the Dominican Church and to reestablish "religious unity" in the colony. His crusade had three principal targets: concubinage, Freemasonry, and Protestantism. Monzón first ordered parish priests to excommunicate all those living outside Catholic marriage. He then declared civil and Protestant marriages invalid.[56] Monzón also persecuted Freemasons, whose activities were widespread before annexation, barring them from communion until they recanted their vows and gave up their Masonic practices and documents. Monzón actively persecuted Protestants as well. Protestant churches in Samaná and Santo Domingo were taken over, burned, or confiscated for military purposes, forcing many Dominican Protestants to consider moving to Haiti in search of religious tolerance.[57]

Monzón's repressive religious policy alienated many Dominicans and ignited strong opposition to the Spanish colonial regime. Protestants, Freemasons, and poor peasants, who now had to pay for their marriages, burials, and children's births, became active opponents of colonial rule. Monzón soon lost the support of the native clergy. With the notable exception of Father Arturo Meriño, the Dominican clergy had welcomed annexation as a way to increase the economic and political power of the Church and to restore religious unity and orthodoxy. The Dominican clergy's pro-Spanish annexation attitude was short lived, however. Monzón and his clerics discriminated against the local clergy and cut some of its traditional sources of income. By 1863, most Dominican priests openly opposed the new Spanish colonial government.[58]

In summation, the annexation of the Dominican Republic alienated diverse sectors of society, even some that had originally advocated it. Intolerance, arbitrary government, and discrimination against Dominicans, coupled with a sustained agricultural and commercial crisis, fueled an all-out rebellion against Spanish rule. The Spanish had gotten themselves into a quagmire; the question now was how to get out of it gracefully.

Only six weeks into the new colonial era, rebellion began. On May 2, 1861, a Dominican general, José Contreras, and his followers, "most of whom were of color," rose up in arms.[59] Spanish troops quickly suffocated the uprising and executed its leaders. Opponents of Dominican annexation, some of whom had been in exile for many years in St. Thomas and Curaçao, also conspired against the Spanish government. In St. Thomas, Francisco del Rosario Sánchez, one of the patriots of the 1844 war of independence, organized the anti-annexationist exiles. Soon thereafter, his forces invaded Dominican territory, but he was captured and executed. Meanwhile, Baecista exiles in Curaçao came together under José María Cabral to form the Revolutionary Party of Dominican Regeneration.

Báez and his partisans, for obvious reasons, were anti-Santana and opposed annexation, not out of principle—for most had been and would again be annexationists themselves—but because of political rivalry. Báez, in fact, had been an accomplice of annexation; while his followers and relatives conspired against Spanish colonialism, he accepted a commission as a field marshal in the Spanish army. Another sector vehemently opposing annexation was the black and mulatto peasantry, which feared that Spain would try to reestablish slavery.[60] The abuses of the new government helped form a coalition of Freemasons, Protestants, merchants, Cibaeño agriculturalists, peasants, foreigners, and other dissatisfied Dominicans to join the war against Spain.

In order to be fully understood, the Dominican struggle for independence between 1861 and 1865 must be seen within its broader context. While the Dominican War of Restoration was not merely a reflection of the Civil War in the United States, the nature of that war, to a great extent, determined the configuration, alliances, and objectives of the Dominican struggle. Like the Civil War, the Dominican War of Restoration was an antislavery, anti-European struggle. Dominican patriots looked for support in Haiti, in the Union government, and among North American abolitionists. Meanwhile, Spain sought the support, or at least the sanction, of Great Britain and France.

The Haitian government of Fabre Geffrard supported Cabral's insurgency with supplies and allowed Dominican revolutionaries to cross the Haitian border at will. Geffrard had good reasons to aid the revolutionaries in their struggle against Spanish colonialism. First, Haitians feared that the Spanish presence would strengthen slavery in the region and be used against the free black societies of the Caribbean. Some even feared that the Spanish would reenslave dark-skinned Dominicans. Second, the Spanish occupation of Dominican territory not only blocked Haiti's historical aspirations to unify the island but also threatened the black republic's territorial integrity. This was proven true when the Spanish mobilized their forces in an attempt to impose on Haiti the old Dominican-Haitian border agreed upon in Aranjuez in 1777.[61]

Geffrard reacted to the Spanish annexation of Dominican territory with a fire-eating proclamation denouncing the hoisting of the flag that "authorizes and protects the enslaving of the children of Africa." He added that the "degraded banner" of Spain foretold the end of Haitian liberty and concluded by calling for armed struggle. "To the battle field!" he exclaimed. "It is necessary that Spanish domination come to an end in America. We shall force them out of St. Domingo."[62] Black solidarity with the revolt was also evident in other parts of the Caribbean. Shortly after Dominican annexation, 3,700 Jamaicans signed a petition demanding that Great Britain not recognize Spanish domination over Dominican territory. Free blacks in the Turks Islands later played an important role in supplying war matériel to Dominican insurgents. Aware of this, the Spanish government prohibited the entrance of free blacks into its new colony.[63]

A second wave of Dominican insurrectionary activity crested in mid-1863, this time in Santiago, in El Cibao. Increased taxes, arbitrary currency exchange policies, and an attempt to establish a state-run tobacco monopoly ignited a revolt among many of those who had risen against Báez in 1857 for similar reasons. Insurrection forces soon captured Santiago and set up a provisional government. Meanwhile, Cabral, a Baecista and therefore theoretically a rival of the Santiago bourgeoisie, joined the struggle against Spanish domination. This revolutionary coalition made considerable progress toward the overthrow of the colonial government.[64]

By the end of 1863, it was clear that the Dominicans were likely to succeed in their effort to force out the Spanish. In Spain, criticism of the annexation mounted. In January 1865, a bill was introduced in the Spanish Cortes for the abandonment of Santo Domingo.[65] It became law four months later, and all Spanish troops withdrew within three months afterward.

First Decade of the Second Republic (1865–1874)

Meanwhile, in the United States, President Andrew Johnson and Congress clashed in their policy toward the Caribbean. The president, the Department of State, and the Navy sought to expand into the Caribbean in order to establish coal depots and naval stations. The Civil War had made clear the importance of naval warfare, and such bases could, in the future, determine the outcome of a confrontation with any European power in the Caribbean. On December 9, 1868, Johnson declared that "comprehensive, national policy would seem to sanction the acquisition and incorporation into our Federal Union of the several adjacent, continental, and insular communities as speedily as it can be done. . . . The time has arrived when even so direct a proposition for an annexation of the two Republics of the island of St. Domingo would not only receive the consent of the people interested, but would give satisfaction to all other foreign nations."[66]

The newly expansionist Andrew Johnson administration also wanted naval stations in the Caribbean to service and protect commercial routes, particularly the projected isthmian route across Central America. In the winter of 1865–1866, Secretary of State William Seward personally toured the region in search of suitable locations for coaling and naval bases. A year later, Frederick Seward, the secretary's son and assistant, and Admiral David D. Porter visited the Dominican Republic to negotiate the purchase or lease of territory in the much-coveted Samaná Bay. They were instructed to seek sovereignty over Samaná or, as a second option, a thirty-year lease of the bay in exchange for $1 million in cash and another $1 million in weapons. Báez, then serving his third presidential term, proved eager to swap a strip of Samaná for guns and cash, which he needed to fight the insurgent opposition. Eventually negotiations collapsed because of U.S. congressional opposition.[67]

A new round of negotiations for the acquisition of territory in the Dominican Republic began during the early years of the Ulysses S.

Grant administration. Grant ordered General O. E. Babcock to support Báez's regime and to lay the groundwork for annexation of the Dominican Republic. Meanwhile, Commander E. K. Owen received orders to pursue and capture the *Telégrafo* and its commander, Gregorio Luperón, leader of the insurrection seeking to overthrow Báez.[68] Despite the active interference of the U.S. Navy in the region, the Dominican rebellion gained force and lent support to the overthrow in January 1870 of Haiti's pro-Báez and pro-U.S. president, Silvain Salnave. U.S. officials were quick to warn the new Haitian president, Nissage Saget, that the United States was "ready to make use of all of its might to prevent any intervention in the affairs of the Dominican government."[69]

During this period, the United States adhered to a policy, applied in Cuba as well as in the Dominican Republic, of obstructing popular rebellions that could lead to the establishment of independent, black-dominated regimes unless the economic interests of the United States were assured. Only when both the Civil War and the Dominican War of Restoration were over did the United States grant recognition to the Dominican Republic, where the strongman Báez seemed to provide the best guarantee for social order. Thereafter, the United States systematically intervened against the opposition to the Báez regime.

Grant's obsessive desire to acquire territory in the Dominican Republic did not abate following his failure to convince the U.S. Senate of its importance in 1871. His administration then proceeded to support the annexationist schemes of the Samaná Bay Company, a private speculative venture that successfully negotiated sovereignty over Samaná under a hundred-year lease, at $150,000 per year. Beginning on January 1, 1873, Samaná became an unofficial U.S. enclave, until later in the year, when the anti-Báez insurrection triumphed and rescinded the lease.[70]

The Civil War in the United States and the War of Dominican Restoration created new geopolitical realities. The Union's victory in the United States signaled the end of European political domination of the Dominican Republic. Dominican politics could no longer be based on the rivalry between those seeking annexation to the United States and those looking to Europe for protection. Moreover, Santana's death in 1864 left one of the parties of the First Republic without its leader. During the first years of the Second Republic, two barely distinguishable parties emerged: the Reds and the Blues. The Reds were essentially Baecistas, a more autocratic, more agriculture-based party, while the Blues were a more urban party that combined former Santanistas and liberals and had links with the northern commercial sector. Interestingly, the Red party not only attracted the traditional oligarchy but the nation's peasantry as well.[71] After the Spanish abandoned the republic, leaders of both parties looked to the United States for protection or annexation while they were in power and proved willing to accept a U.S. presence in Samaná in exchange for cash and arms in order to stay in control and curb Haitian hostility. When not in power, both became extremely nationalistic and opposed to annexation.[72] Some Blue leaders, like Gregorio Luperón and Arturo Meriño, however, remained firmly nationalistic.

The War of Restoration had provided the context for the temporary unification of different segments of Dominican society under a common anti-annexation banner. Baecistas and Cibaeños, tobacco growers and cattle ranchers, independent peasants and subordinate peons, blacks, mulattoes and whites, rose as one to free their country from Spanish domination. After their victory, however, this informal coalition collapsed just as it had after the declaration of Dominican independence in 1844. A similarly broad coalition of Santanistas and elements of the Cibaeño bourgeoisie had also collapsed after fulfilling its goal of overthrowing Báez in 1857. In all three instances—the independence movement (1844), the insurrection against Báez (1857), and the War of Restoration (1863–1865)—the northern liberal intelligentsia played a major leadership role. In all three cases, the men with the military power (Santana in 1844 and 1857 and Cabral in 1865) refused to hand over control to the Cibaeños. In all three cases, furthermore, the most economically dynamic region, El Cibao and its capital Santiago, failed to assume control over the central government. Southern and eastern *caudillos* were better able to mobilize the working masses, turning them into improvised soldiers at their whim. Patron-client relations between these *caudillos* and the republic's subordinate peonage continued to be at the crux of military, and therefore political, power.

The first years of the Second Republic was a period of great political instability. Nine different administrations governed the Dominican Republic between March 1865 and May 1868. Pedro Antonio Pimentel, the head of the Santiago provisional government, was unable to reach Santo Domingo because Cabral's troops blocked his path. Six months later, with opposition mounting, Cabral arranged Báez's return to power. As a conciliatory gesture, Báez included Pimentel and Cabral in his new cabinet.[73] At this point, the north became once again the focus of insurrection, this time around the Blue party under Luperón. By the spring of 1866, the Blue party succeeded in taking over the national government and proceeded to establish a triumvirate on August 10, which was also short lived. Blue leadership then yielded control to Cabral, then in the Blue party, because they believed he was the only one capable of keeping Báez out of power.[74]

True to his model, Santana, Cabral sought to consolidate his command by offering to sell Samaná and by seeking a U.S. protectorate. His weak grip on the national government, along with unfavorable political circumstances in the United States, however, frustrated his annexationist overtures. His antinational agenda, furthermore, alienated Luperón and other nationalists in his party, while the Baecistas exploited his annexationist plots to rally the opposition against him. This opposition included the Haitian government, now led by Salnave, who turned Haiti into a haven for Baecista rebels and supported them with funds and weapons. By January 1868, the Baecistas were in control again, and Báez became president for the fourth time in May.[75]

Even though the Baecista opposition to Cabral had rested on nationalist, anti-annexationist grounds, one of the first official acts of Báez's fourth administration was to approach the United States with offers to yield control over portions of the Samaná bay and peninsula. Only six days after his inauguration, Báez communicated to the United States his desire to come to an agreement whereby the United States would help him stay in power with "moral" and "material" support in exchange for sovereignty over Samaná. He set the price at $2 million for a fifty-year lease, with half the amount paid in cash and the other half in weapons. Báez used the traditional Dominican argument, claiming that the Haitians were behind Cabral and Luperón. Báez's secretary of state denounced Luperón as a man of "backward ideas" who believed that "the African race must predominate in the island and that it should band together to exterminate other races."[76]

As Báez's survival appeared more doubtful, he became increasingly desperate. By July 1868, he was talking of selling rather than leasing Samaná, and by October, he was advocating the establishment of a protectorate over the entire republic. He even signaled a willingness to annex the whole country to the United States.[77]

During his fourth presidential term (1868–1874) Báez became more repressive and authoritarian. He banished dozens of political opponents and treated guerrillas with a heavy hand. He also resorted to wholesale electoral fraud, rigging the February 1870 plebiscite to create the impression that Dominicans overwhelmingly supported annexation to the United States. The result of this farce was 15,169 votes in favor of annexation, 11 votes against. After the U.S. Senate rejected the annexation treaty, Báez sought desperately needed funds through the lease of portions of Samaná to a group of speculators from the United States.[78]

The Blue opposition to Báez and his pro-U.S. annexationism derived considerable support from foreign and domestic merchants and tobacco producers whose ties to the traditional tobacco markets were threatened by the prospect of annexation to the United States. The nationalist leader Luperón, himself a wealthy merchant from Puerto Plata, received monetary assistance from business associates in St. Thomas for the struggle against Báez and annexation.[79]

Báez's annexationist schemes won him the antipathy not only of the now nationalist Blue party of Luperón and Cabral but also of his former ally, the Dominican Church. In an amazing shift, Báez, who during the 1850s figured as the anti-U.S. *caudillo* of the black and clerical parties, now attempted to sell his country to the United States.[80] In the process, he was forced to assume anti-Haitian and anticlerical postures. The traditional interpretation of this annexationist flip-flopping has been that mid-nineteenth-century annexationists were merely self-serving politicians. A sounder explanation, however, can be found by looking at broader changes in the international climate. Dominican leaders paid close attention to political developments on both sides of the Atlantic, took note of shifts in the balance of power, and changes in international tensions, and acted accordingly. Their attentiveness and subordination to the broader Atlantic context explains why Santana, the "friend" of the United States, suddenly became an anti-U.S. Hispanophile in 1860, and why Báez, the man who "hated" the United States, became an ardent advocate of his country's annexation to the United States in 1865 1866 and again between 1868 and 1873. In 1860–1861, when Santana planned and achieved Spanish annexation, the United States endured a grave political crisis that created a vacuum in one of the poles of rivalry over the region. European nations took advantage of the situation and moved into the Caribbean region. Shortly after the Civil War, the United States once again assumed an offensive position in the region, this time without the antebellum restraints of sectional political compromises. In this context, Báez and the other annexationists of the Second Republic could no longer look to European powers for political support, and except for Spain, which maintained a precarious hold on Cuba and Puerto Rico, those nations retreated from the Hispanic Caribbean, never to return.

CHAPTER 6

Puerto Rico in the Whirlwind of 1898: Conflict, Continuity, and Change

U.S. cavalry troops occupying the town of San Germán
in western Puerto Rico, 1898.

In none of the theaters of the Spanish-American-Cuban-Filipino War, otherwise misnamed the Spanish-American War, was the war more splendidly little than in Puerto Rico. Actual hostilities broke in the morning of May 12, 1898, as Admiral William T. Sampson's formidable naval squadron spewed a storm of metal and fire over the fortified walls of the ancient city of San Juan. The bombardment, the first military assault on Puerto Rico in more than a century, lasted three hours and left a toll of only one dead Spanish soldier. A blockade of the island ensued, and a military invasion followed ten weeks later when U.S. troops under the command of General Nelson A. Miles disembarked in the southern port of Guánica on July 25. The fighting lasted only nineteen days, during which time only three U.S. soldiers lost their lives. Deaths on the Spanish side numbered only seventeen.[1]

In sharp contrast with the brevity and relative bloodlessness of the conflict in Puerto Rico stands the dramatic and far-reaching impact of the island's change of sovereignty as Spain was forced to cede its oldest remaining New World colony to the emerging "Colossus of the North." Arguably, no other country or region participating in the conflagration of 1898 was more lastingly or profoundly impacted by the war's aftermath than Puerto Rico. Even the island's name endured mutation with the hope that its new rulers could more easily spell and pronounce the name "Porto Rico." In 1898, the floodgates opened to a new system and worldview that clashed with those of Spanish colonialism. Their uneasy coexistence would shape the Puerto Rico of the new century.

The economic, social, and political transformations affecting Puerto Rico after 1898 involved a complex and shifting combination of impo-

A version of this chapter was published with the same title in *Magazine of History* 12:3 (Spring 1998): 24–29. Copyright © Organization of American Historians. All rights reserved. Reprinted with permission.

sition, resistance, and collaboration, and an interplay among the new colonial rulers, U.S. economic interests, old insular political and economic elites, and the dispossessed rural and urban masses. Manichaean good-versus-evil and us-against-them perspectives, which have dominated the Puerto Rican nationalistic understanding of the drama of 1898, have obscured the complexity of the transformations and have also concealed the many social and economic continuities between the nineteenth century under Spanish colonial rule and the twentieth century under the aegis of the United States.

The study of events in Puerto Rico during 1898, thus, demands careful attention to the construction of the historiographical edifice that emerged after the war. Much of what became the standard interpretation of the impact of 1898 is marked by mostly critical and anti-imperialist views produced during the most traumatic period in Puerto Rico's recent history: the Great Depression. Puerto Rico's first generations of professional historians and social scientists, who dominated the historiography of the 1940s, 1950s, 1960s, and much of the 1970s, failed to challenge this view. They held on to the crisis-ridden 1930s as a framework for comparison not only with the Spanish colonial past but also with the relative prosperity that followed and the ascent to power of the populist Partido Popular Democrático in 1941 and the post–World War II years. Not until the emergence of Puerto Rico's new historiography in the 1970s and 1980s, with its critical perspectives on life under Spanish rule, did a less idealized portrayal of the nineteenth century emerge. With its emphasis on social and economic aspects, Puerto Rico's new historiography recognized far more continuities between centuries than earlier generations of scholars were willing to concede.[2]

Puerto Rico on the Eve of the U.S. Invasion

On the eve of the U.S. invasion, Spain granted Puerto Rico a new charter establishing an autonomous government for the island. This concession resulted from a combination of geopolitical factors and developments in Spain's domestic political arena. The offer of autonomy to Cuba and Puerto Rico was, on the one hand, a last-minute effort by the Spanish government to respond to escalating pressures from the United States and a naive effort to appease Cuban insurgents who had been staging an all-out war of independence since 1895. On the other hand, it was a political payback from Práxedes Mateo Sagasta in return for the support of Puerto Rico's liberals, who helped the Spanish Liberal Party establish a majority in the Spanish Cortes.

While Cuba's patriots rejected the offer of autonomy, Puerto Rico's autonomists, even the Barbosista faction that had opposed the Sagasta pact, embraced it as the realization of longtime aspirations of self-rule within the framework of the Spanish monarchy. Although on paper the Autonomic Charter satisfied many of the goals of Puerto Rico's liberals, its true reach was never tested: U.S. troops invaded the island only six days after Puerto Rico's insular legislators took office.[3]

Writing from the vantage point of the crisis of the 1930s and beyond, nationalists and other Puerto Rican authors have viewed the Autonomic Charter of 1897 as the all-time high point of Puerto Rican self-rule and have exaggerated its scope and reach. Tomás Blanco, for example, praised the charter's provisions that limited the powers of colonial governors and erroneously claimed that similar legal provisions existed throughout the nineteenth century. Essayist Antonio S. Pedreira, for his part, viewed the concession of autonomy as the step that finally allowed Puerto Ricans to gain control over their "collective destiny." A few years earlier, Luis Muñoz Marín, son of autonomist leader Luis Muñoz Rivera, deemed Spanish colonial governors as purely ceremonial figures and painted an idealized picture in which "a native Cabinet with a native Premier [his father] ruled the green fields and polychromatic towns."[4] Much of the nationalistic historiography of later decades as well as the more politically moderate institutional historiography of the 1950s, 1960s, and 1970s embraced the interpretation of a far-reaching functional autonomy. Fernando Picó, one of the leading pens of Puerto Rico's new historiography, has recently challenged this view: "Under a state of war," Picó wrote, "the autonomous government was nominally functional in 1898, and precisely when it was necessary that it play a more active role, during the economic crisis brought about by the war, it did not function."[5]

The granting of the Autonomic Charter, nonetheless, did much to appease Puerto Rico's liberals and to guarantee their loyalty to the Spanish crown. Autonomists in general, but those of the Muñocista faction, in particular, exhibited unwavering loyalty to Spain.[6] Besides the autonomists, there was a separatist minority desiring the island's independence from Spanish rule, and a small annexationist group that aspired to turn Puerto Rico into a state of the United States. Despite their competing ultimate agendas, both groups found common ground in their anti-Spanish sentiments and collaborated within the Puerto Rico section of the New York–based Partido Revolucionario Cubano under the leadership of annexationists José Julio Henna and Roberto H. Todd. Some three hundred Puerto Rican separatists, meanwhile, fought Spanish troops on Cuban soil, but various attempts to extend the Cuban struggle to Puerto Rico failed because of lack of popular support.[7]

Political and constitutional developments in Puerto Rico during the 1890s, marked by closer, more cooperative bonds between the colony and its metropolis on the basis of the autonomic formula, were paralleled in the economic arena by closer trade ties between the island and Spanish and European markets in the coffee trade. Sugar, which had earlier dominated the island's exports, was now the second export staple and was on the wane; consequently the island's economic ties with the United States, the traditional market for the region's sugar, weakened as well. On the eve of the U.S. invasion, coffee accounted for 41 percent of the island's cultivated acreage while sugarcane comprised only 15 percent, and the total value of coffee exports was three times the value of sugar exports. In 1895, the United States absorbed slightly more than 10 percent of Puerto Rico's exports while Spanish, Cuban, and European markets received 84 percent of Puerto Rico's export output.[8]

The transition to agrarian capitalism and the shift toward coffee dominance later in the nineteenth century brought many social dislocations and produced a marked deterioration in the material conditions of the rural working classes. Contemporary observers like sociologist Eugenio María de Hostos, historian Salvador Brau, and novelist Manuel Zeno Gandía documented and dramatized the plight of Puerto

Rico's peasants during the era of the coffee boom.[9] However, a contrasting picture emerged in the 1930s. The Depression-era historiography painted a nineteenth-century Puerto Rico that had achieved prosperity and social harmony. In a muckraking essay, Muñoz Marín portrayed nineteenth-century Puerto Rico as a "penniless but content" society where the average peasant was well-fed and well-rested and had enough time for work, music, poetry, and life's other pleasures. The planter class, continued Muñoz Marín, owned mortgage-free land and unselfishly looked after the welfare of the working class. The romanticization of the past reached its highest level of hyperbole at the hands of nationalist leader Pedro Albizu Campos who viewed the nineteenth century as a time of "old collective happiness." "Puerto Rico was the healthiest country of the Americas," Albizu Campos claimed. "It was rich," he continued, and "figured at the vanguard of modern civilization."[10] Remarkably, while far from accurate, these Depression-era views shaped the historiography of the next four decades and persist in some contemporary portrayals of Puerto Rico under Spanish rule. The new historiography of the 1980s, including the works of social and economic historians such as Picó, Andrés A. Ramos Mattei, Francisco A. Scarano, Laird W. Bergad, and Guillermo A. Baralt, challenged these views by documenting the violent social and economic displacements and rapidly deteriorating conditions for the bulk of the island's laboring classes.[11]

The bombardment of San Juan and the naval blockade that followed strangled the island's economy and further aggravated existing social tensions. As a result of the blockade, foreign trade came to a virtual halt, leading to a serious scarcity of essential consumer goods, widespread commercial speculation, and even starvation among the population. The already profound monetary crisis deepened and placed agricultural loans beyond the reach of planters and farmers. Not surprisingly, wide segments of the rural peasantry resorted to theft and other forms of social protest.[12]

The War and the War Behind It

The question as to why the United States included Puerto Rico among its military and expansionist targets has long been debated in the historiography. Two leading interpretations have dominated this discussion. On the one hand, we find the "offshoot" or "sideshow" thesis sustained by Arturo Morales Carrión and Carmelo Rosario Natal, among others, which holds that the United States had little previous interest in acquiring the island of Puerto Rico, but at the insistence of Puerto Rican annexationists, namely Henna and Todd, and responding to the dynamics of war, U.S. officials decided to acquire the island. Other social scientists, for their part, have argued that rather than an improvised decision, the acquisition of Puerto Rico was a longtime goal that stemmed from economic and strategic interests.[13]

In any case, in the morning of July 25, the long-anticipated U.S. invasion of Puerto Rico began. The port of Guánica proved an excellent choice for landing site because it was near the heart of the island's southwestern region, where anti-Spanish sentiment had historically been strongest. Economically speaking, the southwest and its hinterland was the island's most dynamic region, with coffee production booming. It was precisely in the coffee-producing region where social dislocations and antagonisms had reached dangerously explosive levels.

The Spanish offered surprisingly little resistance to advancing U.S. troops. Throughout the island's southwest, the response of the resident Creole elite was welcoming and festive. Parades, fireworks, and the tolling of bells celebrated the arrival of General Miles's troops. Members of the Creole elite collaborated with the invading troops, providing information, supplies, and field hands.[14]

The recent historiography, particularly Picó's works, has paid detailed attention to the explosion of peasant violence during and shortly after the invasion. The *partidas sediciosas* or *tiznados* (as the armed bands of rural workers came to be known) raided, looted, and burned plantations and other sources and symbols of their oppression. Other acts of social vengeance included the burning of records of indebtedness and even the murder of some coffee planters. At first, U.S. officers welcomed the mobilization of armed bands of peasants who unleashed their rage against the remnants of Spanish colonial exploitation. One armed *partida*, for example, captured the town of Ciales and raised the U.S. flag. After the armistice of August 12, 1898, however, U.S. troops actively sought to demobilize the remaining *partidas sediciosas*.[15]

The Puerto Ricans' lack of resistance to the invading forces has long troubled the collective conscience of the Puerto Rican intelligentsia, particularly its most nationalistic exponents. Some have denied that this ever happened; others have recognized it as a chapter of national shame. Still others have attempted to neutralize it with a mythology of resistance that includes alleged anti-U.S. guerrilla activities under José Maldonado, known as Águila Blanca. Picó has recently documented that rather than a nationalist patriot, Águila Blanca was a common criminal who, while fleeing Spanish justice in New York, swore alliance to the United States.[16] A 1983 incident clearly illustrates the lingering desire for turn-of-the-century national heroism. Luis López Nieves published a story in the pro-independence weekly *Claridad* that told of a Puerto Rican victory in May 1898 against U.S. troops in the town of Seva. According to this fictionalized narrative, the United States concealed this military embarrassment by returning to Seva, destroying the town, and executing the surviving population. A massive cover-up followed that included the destruction of all documents alluding to Seva and the founding of a new town, Ceiba, in the ashes of heroic Seva. Unsuspecting readers produced a torrent of angry letters demanding inquiries into the Seva cover-up.[17]

The Aftermath of 1898

On October 18, 1898 the U.S. military formally assumed the administration of Puerto Rico. Two months later, on December 10, the Treaty of Paris formalized the cession of Puerto Rico to the United States in exchange for a $20 million compensation for Spain. Thus ended four centuries of Spanish colonialism in the New World. Between October 1898 and May 1900, three military governors ruled over Puerto Rico: General John R. Brooke (October 18 to December 9, 1898), General

Guy V. Henry (December 9, 1898 to May 9, 1899), and General George W. Davis (May 9, 1899 to May 1, 1900). On May 1, 1900, a civilian colonial government was finally established under the Foraker Act. Charles Allen became the island's first U.S. civilian governor.

The overwhelming majority of Puerto Rico's political actors responded to the new circumstances by seeking the island's annexation as a state of the United States. Muñoz Rivera, who had three years earlier denounced the annexationist option as "absurd, depressing and inconceivable," stated in 1898: "We must move rapidly toward our identity. The Liberal Party desires that Puerto Rico become a sort of California or Nebraska."[18] The virtual unanimity in favor of annexation responded to the confluence of divergent agendas: to the old autonomist leadership, it was a means to retain insular political power within the federation of the United States; to sugar planters, it represented the opening of the insatiable North American market for their crops; to labor leaders, it represented the right to organize and the hope of more progressive labor laws.

As a package, the decrees of the military governors successfully dismantled the institutional foundations the Puerto Rico inherited from Spain and facilitated the island's incorporation into the territorial orbit of the United States. General Brooke's decrees included measures to cease state support of the Catholic Church and the substitution of old forms of taxation for new ones. Some of the measures—and the temperament—of his successor, General Henry, proved odious and controversial in the eyes of local interests and produced a bitter distancing between the leaders of the party of Muñoz Rivera and the military authorities. Included among Henry's measures were a moratorium on foreclosures against mortgaged farmlands, which resulted in an unintended but catastrophic freeze in agricultural credit; the modification of marriage and divorce laws; and the declaration of the eight-hour workday. General Henry had the bad judgment to outlaw cockfights, the island's national pastime.[19] Among General Davis's decrees were the establishment of trial by jury and the extension of the right of habeas corpus. He also proved diligent and genuinely caring during the crisis brought by the San Ciriaco hurricane (August 8, 1899), which left more than 3,000 dead and $20 million in damages throughout the island, mostly in the coffee areas of the western central highlands.[20]

The imposition by the U.S. government of the Foraker Act in May 1900 further alienated broad sectors of the island's political and economic elites as it fell short of their aspirations. The initial hopes had by now turned to disillusionment. The Foraker Act offered fewer self-rule provisions than the Autonomic Charter under Spain. It organized Puerto Rico as an "unincorporated territory" of the United States and denied U.S. citizenship to the island's population, which overwhelmingly desired both statehood and U.S. citizenship. The Puerto Rican citizenship established by the Foraker Act was a legal fiction that lacked international recognition. Puerto Rican reactions to the Foraker Act were overwhelmingly critical. Even Henna, who had so ardently promoted the U.S. invasion of Puerto Rico, referred to life under the Foraker Act in dismal terms: "No liberty, no rights, absolutely no protection, not even the right to travel."[21] Later measures such as the imposition of English as the language of instruction in public schools further fanned nationalist opposition to U.S. colonial rule.

The period between the invasion and the passage of the Foraker Act allowed for the creation of the legal and constitutional bases for the far-reaching economic transformations of the next four decades. The economic provisions of the military governors and the Foraker Act formally incorporated Puerto Rico into the U.S. tariff and navigation systems, established the rate of monetary exchange at sixty U.S. cents per Spanish peso, and limited landownership by individuals and corporations to five hundred acres.

The sudden removal of Puerto Rico from the sphere of its traditional markets and its inclusion in the U.S. tariff and navigation systems resulted in the penalization of Puerto Rican coffee in the Cuban and European markets. The U.S. market did not absorb this loss because North American consumers preferred the cheaper, lower-quality coffee from Brazil. Puerto Rican sugar, on the other hand, received preferential access to the U.S. market: at first a 15 percent tariff, and tariff free after 1901.[22] These new tariffs had an immediate impact on the insular economy and commerce. By 1901, coffee's proportion among exports fell to 19.6 percent, while sugar's rose to 55 percent. This trend continued during the balance of the decade. In 1910, coffee represented only 10 percent of the export output and sugar reached 64 percent. In the process, the United States became the island's dominant trading partner, absorbing 84 percent of Puerto Rico's exports and supplying 85 percent of its imports.[23]

Profound social transformations accompanied the changes in the economy. The advent of a new form of capitalism based on the enclave model of absentee monopoly capitalism shook the island's social foundations and unleashed manifold social dislocations. Gradually but surely, the island's traditional agrarian elite endured displacement and subordination at the hands of absentee corporate capital that directly invested in sugar production. A study by Juan A. Giusti Cordero demonstrates, however, that this did not occur overnight. As late as 1920–1921, he maintains, "insular interests produced between 65 and 75 percent of the sugar output and controlled 75 percent of the sugar lands."[24] More immediate was the impact on the working classes. The new economic realities, particularly the shift away from coffee toward sugar, accelerated the proletarianization of the rural workforce and signaled losses in the autonomy and material conditions of the average worker. Prices of food and other essential items shot up, and unemployment and poverty became more widespread. Emigration became the only options for tens of thousands of Puerto Ricans in decades to come.

There is no question that many of the measures of the military governors and several provisions of the Foraker Act were misguided and were a detriment to the people of Puerto Rico, benefiting certain interests within the U.S. economy. It would be an oversimplification, however, to view the legal-constitutional package of 1898–1900 as a concerted effort to destroy the Puerto Rican elite, to impoverish the working classes, and to open the way for unbridled U.S. monopoly capital.[25] It would be equally distorting to view the Liberal, later Federal, elites as champions of the oppressed masses. The drama of 1898–1900 is far more complex. Some of the military government measures like the eight-hour workday, the adoption of trial by jury, and the reduction of the voting age from twenty-five years to twenty-one were bitterly opposed by Muñoz Rivera, Severo Quiñones, and other so-called liberals.[26] A recent work by Kelvin A. Santiago-Valles brings our attention to deep divisions in turn-of-the-century Puerto Rico and to the insular elite's classism and racism vis-à-vis the mulatto working classes of the coastal plains. These problems were neither new nor creatures of U.S. imperialism.[27]

In Puerto Rico, the war of 1898 was a short one with a long aftermath. The whirlwind of 1898 brought into conflict two distinct worlds: a Spanish world tied to the past and a North American world heralding the future. The feudal Spanish legacies of corporatist society, of inherited hierarchies, and of high regard for honor and prestige did not disappear with the arrival of a competing capitalist North American set of values with its alternative, market-driven forms of exclusion. In the aftermath of 1898, the feudal forms of exclusion and exploitation persisted—and arguably continue to persist—along with those of modern capitalism.

Political Culture in the Hispanic Caribbean and the Building of U.S. Hegemony, 1868–1945

Uncle Sam to Porto Rico:
"And to think that bad boy came near to being your brother!"
Chicago Inter Ocean, 1905; reprinted in John J. Johnson,
Latin America in Caricature (Austin: University of Texas Press, 1980).

D espite the seemingly endless possibilities for fruitful comparisons offered by the Hispanic Caribbean, there is a hardly justifiable dearth of comparative studies focusing on the region composed of Cuba, Puerto Rico, and the Dominican Republic.[1] This is particularly evident with regard to twentieth-century political history, where the sharply divergent trajectories of these three societies should have stimulated at least some comparatively focused scholarly attention. This interpretative essay, based on the extant secondary literature on the individual islands, seeks to begin to fill this void by tracing the development of Cuba, Puerto Rico, and the Dominican Republic's political cultures from a regional and comparative perspective.

While sharing many common circumstances and historical experiences, the resulting political cultures of Cuba, Puerto Rico, and the Dominican Republic are notably different and the traits that set them apart have roots buried deep into the nineteenth century, when the political ethos of the three nations began to unfold along markedly dissimilar paths that produced different political models and political struggles.

The term "political culture" is used throughout this chapter simply to mean the beliefs and behaviors of a particular group of people vis-à-vis the political processes of which they are part as either active or passive participants.[2] By political struggles and models, I mean the recurrent dominant manifestations of political action and organization that result from a particular political culture. Like other cultural manifestations, political culture is transmitted through various mechanisms of socialization: family influence, education, the media, and legislation. A given group inherits a political culture by learning from the previous generation (did their fathers fight in wars, join mass parties, or remain

This chapter was originally published with the same title in *Revista Mexicana del Caribe* 11 (2001): 7–55. Reprinted with permission.

politically apathetic?), by exposure to historical texts and educational materials (do textbooks glorify civilian and democratic institutions?), through music and popular culture (does the national anthem inspire the listener to bayonet the nearest Spaniard, as with Cuba's *La Bayamesa*, or to ask a beautiful woman out to dance, as with Puerto Rico's *La Borinqueña*?), and even by everyday iconographic messages (do statues in public parks depict sword-wielding men on horseback or politicians clad in three-piece suits?). Through these and other similar mechanisms, particular aspects of political culture are transmitted from one generation to the next, perpetuating values and behaviors such as the veneration of strong leaders, high or low voter participation, the propensity for military solutions, and the absence or prevalence of political suicide, to give but a few examples.

The structure of this chapter reflects the recognition of the overarching presence of the United States over a region often referred to as the "American Mediterranean," during a century widely recognized as the "American Century." It is precisely that dominant influence—economic, military, political, and even cultural—that provides the strongest argument for recourse to a regional chronology based on the evolution of U.S. presence in the Hispanic Caribbean. Still, U.S. desires and impositions over the region have had to contend with the particular circumstances and political cultures of each island. The building of U.S. hegemony over the region depended, in fact, on its success at confronting and manipulating the existing local political struggles and models in order to achieve at least partial consent for intervention and varying forms of domination; local political actors, while facing a formidable world power, struggled to assert their own interests, often limiting or redirecting the extent of the United States' imperial designs.

The periodization that stemmed from this perspective (1868–1898, 1898–1909, 1910–1929, and 1930–1945) reflects the evolving and negotiated results of the region's political cultures, in the light of impinging external forces. The dual titles used in this chapter for each period point to both a recognition of U.S. preponderant influence and the role played by insular political actors in determining their own fates, even if constrained by overwhelming foreign forces.

Overlapping Empires/Bullets or Ballots (1868–1898)

During the latter decades of the nineteenth century, the Hispanic Caribbean, when viewed as a region, endured a dual colonialism resulting from the oppressive reality of overlapping empires exerting different forms of domination over the region. Even though Spain retained formal colonial domination over Cuba and Puerto Rico until 1898 and several European powers vied for control over the precariously independent Dominican Republic, during the second half of the century the United States assumed the role of the region's dominant trading partner with the capacity to transform the islands' economies to suit its market demands. Growing economic power soon translated into political influence as well.[3]

During the last quarter of the nineteenth century, political struggles and political models in Cuba, Puerto Rico, and the Dominican Republic unfolded along clearly differentiated paths, responding to the particular political culture of each island. By that juncture, the three political cultures that would shape the following century's political developments had already assumed their respective pivotal positions within each of the individual components of the Hispanic Caribbean. In Cuba, the struggle for national sovereignty and social justice brought into conflict the revolutionary model of the island's insurgent masses versus the captain-general's model representing strong-armed Spanish colonial rule. In Puerto Rico, status definition along the lines of enhanced self-rule emerged as the dominant political struggle and was played out through the application of the lobbyist and parliamentary model. In the meantime, the central struggle in the Dominican Republic was the quest for the formation of a national state in opposition to the stubborn legacies of regionalist *caudilloism* and foreign intervention, its corresponding models being the authoritarian *caudillo* and controlled, *caudillo*-led mobilization of the masses.

The economic and historical backgrounds of the three societies of the Hispanic Caribbean begin to help explain the islands' divergent political trajectories. Despite sharing the same colonial status under Spanish rule until 1898, Cuba and Puerto Rico differed significantly in terms of the orientation of their economies and their links with the outside world. Cuba had become the world's leading sugar exporter on the basis of large-scale production, predominantly for the U.S. market, while Puerto Rico's economy gradually veered toward coffee production to satisfy European demands. Moreover, unlike the case with Cuba's economy, which by the middle decades of the nineteenth century had grown dependent on the U.S. market for its sugar, Puerto Rico's trade links were mostly within the Spanish commercial system that absorbed the bulk of the island's coffee and other exports. This helps explain why Puerto Rico's political actors sought to continue operating within Spain's imperial system. The Dominican Republic, for its part, had a peculiar history of earlier national independence followed by many decades of subordination to a variety of foreign powers that contested for trade and territorial concessions and even the annexation of the vulnerable republic. Its nominally independent status notwithstanding, the Dominican Republic endured the assault of many of the same external pressures afflicting the island colonies to its east and west.[4]

Cuba's older and more influential Creole elite—its plantocracy and associated intelligentsia—enjoyed a privileged economic and social standing that arguably would have allowed it to lead a challenge to Spanish rule at almost any time during the second half of the nineteenth century. Other considerations, however, such as the fear of sparking a racial war and concern over disrupting economic production and trade, forced Cuba's elites to waiver between loyalty to Spain and a variety of recurring radical options including separatism and annexation to the United States, whichever seemed to offer the best chances for maintaining social peace. The Ten Years' War (1868–1878) against Spanish colonialism exposed the persistent regional, class, and racial cleavages that thus far impeded a successful struggle for independence. By the mid-1890s, a wide multiclass and multiracial military coalition crystallized and was capable of mounting a politically and militarily feasible project of national liberation. During the Cuban War of Independence (1895–1898) the island's planters remained, for the most part, opposed to the armed struggle, however. Radicalized Cuban patriots saw them increasingly as an obstacle to the nationalist and progressive revolutionary agenda.[5]

Thus, in the Cuban context, the political struggle of the last three decades of the nineteenth century was played out as an all-out war of independence in which the revolutionary model of political action was used to demolish the increasingly despotic colonial captain-general's model. Conscriptions of able-bodied men by both armies and the reconcentration of hundreds of thousands of civilians by Spanish authorities, in effect, militarized most of the island's population. The unremitting quest for Cuban independence, which was intimately tied to growing aspirations of social justice, reflected a violent political culture in which differences were fought out in the battlefields and political might was measured on the basis of how many troops a given officer commanded. A concomitant development of this warrior culture was the possibility of social mobility through military service in a frontier-like context that helped blur otherwise rigid class and race distinctions. Extended warfare also produced a military class as potential breeding ground for the type of authoritarian *caudillo* that plagued Latin America after independence.

In marked contrast, neighboring Puerto Rico experienced a peaceful end of century as its political actors resorted to parliamentary, constitutional, and lobbying practices in their quest for concessions from Madrid's imperial authorities. Puerto Rican delegates were elected to Madrid's Cortes in 1869 and served there intermittently until the end of Spanish colonial rule. Neither independence from Spain nor annexation to the United States, the two alternating radical Cuban formulas, took much hold among Puerto Rico's political leaders. Quite significantly, Puerto Rico's counterpart to the Cuban Ten Years' War, El Grito de Lares (1868), lasted one day and left a toll of only four dead.[6] The island's Creole elite opted, instead, for the middle-of-the-road autonomist formula that promised a considerable extent of self-rule while remaining under the crown of Spain. In an 1873 speech on the floor of the Spanish Cortes, Puerto Rican delegate Joaquín M. Sanromá established a revealing comparison between his island and that of his rebellious neighbors: "Speak about Cuba, if you wish, I will speak to you about Puerto Rico; speak of war, I will speak to you of peace; speak about the country where passions simmer, where bullets whistle, where conspirators and their associates boil; I will speak to you about another country where reason prevails, where serenity reigns."[7] The Puerto Rican elite's inclination toward electoral and parliamentary solutions to its colonial dilemma became a defining characteristic of the island's political culture. Such strategies proved less disruptive to Puerto Rico's economy and society, thus helping preserve the existing rigid, hierarchical class structure.

The most obvious political difference separating the Dominican Republic from Cuba and Puerto Rico at the end of the nineteenth century was the fact that while the latter remained Spanish colonies, the former had achieved its independence. Actually, the Dominican Republic had gained its independence three times: in 1821 from Spain, in 1844 from Haiti, and once again from Spain in 1865. Political instability, *caudillo* warfare, foreign meddling and intervention, relative disconnection from the world trade system, and the absence of anything resembling a national state plagued the Dominican Republic throughout most of the nineteenth century. Between 1865 and 1879 alone, twenty-one different governments reached power.[8] As a by-product of chronic instability and warfare, several Dominicans of humble background, mostly black or mulatto, rose to positions of high authority, notably Gregorio Luperón and Ulises Heureaux. During the iron-fisted rule of *caudillo* Heureaux (1882–1899), the Dominican Republic finally entered a stage of sustained economic growth and incipient state building that made the republic more closely resemble its neighboring Spanish colonies.

Employing a combination of harsh repression and selective co-optation, Heureaux led his country through a process of state formation that included the creation of a national army and the expansion of the state bureaucracy. This process was financed by revenues stemming from rising sugar production and exportation. Foreign loans, which poured into the Dominican economy, also helped the consolidation of Heureaux's regime and the building of an agro-exporting infrastructure.[9] After nearly two decades of authoritarian rule, Heureaux left a mixed legacy. Paradoxically, while he laid the foundations for a modern national state, he also made his country more vulnerable to foreign meddling and control. As part of a loan agreement with a Dutch company in 1888, the Dominican Republic literally mortgaged its future tariff revenues, 30 percent of which subsequently had to be set aside to service the loan. In 1893, the Dominican debt was acquired by the San Domingo Improvement Company, which was controlled by U.S. bond-holders.[10] The company soon wrested from local authorities the privilege of managing the republic's customs houses. Thus, before century's end, U.S. financial interests dominated in the Dominican Republic. By that time, U.S. capital was also dominant among the republic's foreign investments. Control over Dominican foreign trade was yet another way in which U.S. economic interests outpaced their North Atlantic competitors, with the United States purchasing the bulk of the republic's sugar. A trade reciprocity treaty negotiated in 1891 would have sealed U.S. dominance over the Dominican Republic's commerce, but it did not materialize due to tenacious European opposition.[11]

In sum, political circumstances in the three components of the Hispanic Caribbean contrasted sharply from island to island. A revolutionary-military political culture gained ascendancy in Cuba, while a reformist-civilian one took hold in Puerto Rico. In the Dominican Republic, meanwhile, a *caudilloist*, authoritarian culture, brewing since the days of independence, culminated under the repressive regime of Heureaux. In all three countries, U.S. interests and influence, particularly commercial and financial, made headway as Spain and other European nations lost ground.

Laying the Foundations for U.S. Hegemony/Political Bifurcations (1898–1909)

The 1898–1899 juncture brought sweeping changes to all three components of the Hispanic Caribbean. The United States intervened militarily in Cuba and Puerto Rico, proceeding to pluck the islands like withering flowers from what was left of Spain's once impressive imperial bouquet. This intervention frustrated the ongoing struggles of the region: the revolutionary struggle in Cuba and the struggle for autonomic concessions in Puerto Rico. Regardless of how bleak the prospects of achieving those aspirations may have been had there been no U.S. intervention, the United States got the blame; and the frustrations of 1898 traumatized both islands' political elites to the extent that more than a century later, those wounds continue to ooze with no end in sight.

The end of the nineteenth century also brought profound transformations in Dominican politics. On July 26, 1899, an assassin's bullet brought Heureaux's rule to an end. The dictator's demise exposed the vulnerable nature of the Dominican state, which had thus far rested on personalistic and repressive means. Regional fragmentation had persisted, indeed, under the blood-laden coat of national unification. The other threat to the consolidation of the Dominican state, foreign intervention, lurked menacingly against the backdrop spectacle of *caudillo* warfare that followed Heureaux's rule. In all three societies, the first decade of the twentieth century witnessed political bifurcations that had been kept at bay by either despotic colonial rule or repressive dictatorship. Under the new sets of circumstances, Puerto Rico's political actors split along status options, while Cuba's split along Liberal-Conservative party lines and a host of Dominican *caudillos* surfaced seeking to control various regions and ultimately the national government.

Eighteen ninety-eight marked the beginning of a new era of U.S. presence and domination in the Caribbean. With a swift victory over Spain that year and the ensuing occupation of Cuba and Puerto Rico, the United States entered a phase of direct administration of conquered territories. Although a long record of U.S. expansionism predated the 1898 interventions, this was the United States' first experience administrating heavily populated territories with distinct cultures and without the intention of welcoming them as states of the federal union. While the Dominican Republic did not figure among the United States' end-of-century acquisitions, Heureaux's assassination led to a convulsive period of *caudillo* warfare that made the republic increasingly vulnerable to foreign interference, particularly at the hands of the United States, which aggressively asserted its regional preeminence. The republic, then, became the object of U.S. desires, much like neighboring Cuba and Puerto Rico. In geopolitical terms, all three societies came to constitute a geographical unit of vital importance for the defense of navigation routes and the projected Isthmian Canal.

A first phase of U.S. imperial presence in the western Caribbean began in 1898 and lasted until about 1909. During that decade, the United States managed to install the bases of colonial and neocolonial domination over Cuba, Puerto Rico, and the Dominican Republic. In all three instances, this required some measure of military intervention, the restructuring of legal-constitutional foundations inherited from Spain, the establishment of alliances with particular political groups in the insular contexts to achieve hegemonic control, and the securing of preferential trade and economic concessions. In each of the components of the Hispanic Caribbean, these efforts required different mechanisms, depending on the specific U.S. designs and on how far the United States could go in each case. The United States, thus, had to contend and negotiate with the circumstances and political culture of each society. In Cuba, where three decades of war made clear the impossibility of long-term, direct colonial rule, it required three years of military occupation (1899–1902), the imposition of the Platt Amendment (1901) and the Reciprocity Treaty (1903), and a second military intervention (1906–1909). In Puerto Rico, it involved two years of military rule (1898–1900), the imposition of the Foraker Act (1900), and continued colonial rule thereafter. In the Dominican Republic, U.S. intervention took the form of small-scale military actions in 1903 and 1904 and the assumption of control over Dominican customs houses in 1905, an arrangement that was formalized in 1907. All of these mechanisms of domination, seen together as a group, reflect a level of coherence that has not been fully recognized due to the persistent fragmented view of the Hispanic Caribbean's history. Though varied in their implementation and reach, these mechanisms yielded astonishingly similar results for the United States.

The timing of U.S. intervention in the ongoing Cuban War of Independence in 1898—three years into the struggle—secured two principal goals of the United States, namely, a quick victory over Spain and control over the Spanish colonies in the conflict's aftermath. By 1897,

Spain's grip over Cuba had been weakened to a point at which victory for Cuban patriots seemed to be at hand. By that juncture, the war had ruined the island's economy and had decimated its population. Early on, the war had turned into one of destruction and extermination. An estimated half a million people died as a direct result of the conflagration; another 100,000 sought exile to escape the horrors of one of the bloodiest and most brutal war the Americas had ever witnessed. The island's economy was utterly devastated, the vast majority of its sugar mills destroyed. Those were the conditions in the Pearl of the Antilles when the United States occupied it in 1898.[12]

The U.S. military also intervened in Puerto Rico, but the situation there was different on many counts. First, Puerto Ricans had not fought for independence from Spain. Although there was widespread dissatisfaction with Spanish rule and many Puerto Ricans fought and died on Cuban soil, it did not translate into armed revolt on the smaller island.[13] Puerto Rico's reformist politicians, in fact, realized their aspirations of an autonomous government not as a result of fighting Spain but rather as a result of remaining loyal while war ravaged through Cuba. The majority faction of Puerto Rico's autonomists, headed by Luis Muñoz Rivera, bartered its loyalty and support for the Liberal Party in the Spanish Cortes in exchange for concessions of enhanced self-rule. Significantly, when Cuban patriot Antonio Maceo fell in battle, Puerto Rico's autonomists publicly celebrated his death as Muñoz Rivera assured Spain: "We are Spaniards and wrapped in the Spanish flag we shall die." Naively hoping to appease the Cuban insurgents, Spain, in a last-ditch effort, offered autonomy and reforms to both islands. These reforms were welcomed in Puerto Rico but rejected outright in Cuba, where advocating autonomy was treated as a treasonous act by the Cuban Republic-in-Arms.[14]

The brevity and relative bloodlessness of the U.S. military campaign in Puerto Rico spared that island from the extreme social dislocation and economic ruin that befell Cuba. Wartime disruptions, however, were serious enough to further weaken the island's planter class and to make it more vulnerable to the onslaught of U.S. capital in the war's immediate aftermath. Comparatively speaking, however, Puerto Rico's white social and economic elite remained more intact than its counterparts in Cuba and the Dominican Republic, where destruction, exile, confiscations and other ravages of war severely eroded their standing. The wars also allowed a degree of social mobility to blacks and mulattos in the Dominican Republic and Cuba which produced leaders like Heureaux, the Maceos, Quintín Banderas, Juan Gualberto Gómez, among others. Significantly, Puerto Rico's most visible end-of-century mulatto political leader, Dr. José Celso Barbosa, moved up socially not in the battlefields but by earning a medical degree at the University of Michigan.

Following the United States' victory over Spain, both Cuba and Puerto Rico endured military rule under the U.S. flag. In Puerto Rico, it lasted until May 1900, when a civilian colonial government was established under the provisions of the Foraker Act. The act recognized Puerto Rico as an unincorporated territory of the United States while denying U.S. citizenship to the island's one million inhabitants. The U.S. military government in Cuba lasted until 1902. The Cuban independence that followed, however, was mediated by the Platt Amendment to the Cuban Constitution. One of its most insidious articles established that the United States retained the right to intervene militarily to guarantee peace, protect property, and maintain stability. Most Cubans rejected and many protested the humiliating clauses of the Platt Amendment, but notwithstanding their opposition, it was imposed as a precondition to the U.S. recognition of independence. As Governor Leonard Wood warned, "There will be no Republic if the amendment is not approved."[15]

The U.S. military governments in Cuba and Puerto Rico shared many similarities but also varied according to the particular circumstances of and the different long-term policy goals for each island. The resulting realities reflected the negotiation between new imperial designs and old political cultures. On both islands, the military intervention reduced the powers of municipal governments, the traditional power base of the Creole elites. Also, the powers and privileges of the Catholic Church endured erosion as a result of various secularizing military decrees. Not only had the Church served as an arm of the

Spanish colonial state, it also remained an obstacle to the desired Americanization of the newly acquired territories. In the Cuban case, one of the most urgent matters was the demobilization and disarmament of the Cuban army of liberation, moves deemed critical for the erection of a stable neocolonial edifice and the future consolidation of hegemony that would make the use of forceful intervention no longer necessary.[16] Although disarmament was achieved with relatively small investment on the part of the United States, it did not eradicate the warrior culture that had developed over the previous half century. War veterans continued to have enormous political influence particularly in the countryside, where they acquired sugar mills or *colonias* (cane farms).[17] This was made patent four years later, when a massive insurrectionary army challenged the established insular government. In Puerto Rico, the island that the United States wanted to and could manage to retain indefinitely, the constitutional and juridical foundations of North American hegemony were laid during the military occupation. These were more far-reaching than those applied in Cuba.[18]

In the war's aftermath, the United States fostered and manipulated fragmentations within insular politics that thus far had remained hidden by the unifying forces of war, dictatorship, and the promise of enhanced self-rule. During and after the military interventions, the United States meddled in local politics to keep the region's political actors divided and to secure the collaboration of particular groups. In Puerto Rico, following a very brief honeymoon during which both factions of the old autonomists welcomed the invading troops, tensions arose between the military authorities and the Federalist Party of Muñoz Rivera. By 1899, hostility had grown to the point that Governor Guy V. Henry's administration included very few Federalists: the dispensation of political patronage and the absence of a clear agenda regarding the island's status became key weapons for the manipulation of insular politics. Puerto Rican historiography has tended to present the escalating tensions between Muñocistas and U.S. governors as a clash between liberal-minded nationalists and reactionary imperialists; in reality, though, many of the issues over which Muñoz Rivera's partisans and the colonial rulers clashed had to do with the beleaguered Creole elites' desire to defend their threatened privileges vis-à-vis the rights of the subordinate working-class masses. Although not altogether satisfied with the military government and the Foraker Act, the island's Republicans, heirs of the old Barbosista autonomist faction, were able to establish collaborative relations with U.S. rulers. For their collaboration, the insular Republicans were rewarded with patronage. During 1900–1904, when the Federalists were a parliamentary minority, U.S. colonial administrators, with the help of Barbosa's Republicans, put in place new civil and penal codes. In 1904, the Federal Party disbanded and the bulk of its supporters regrouped in the new Unionista Party. Although the Unionistas constituted a multi-status party—they were willing to go with either independence, statehood, or an intermediate option—their orientation was increasingly autonomist, even leaning toward independence. Shortly after the Unionistas secured a majority in the insular legislature in 1904, colonial administrators maneuvered to reduce the powers of the legislature through an amendment to the Foraker Act. When the Unionistas tried to use the Foraker Act to their advantage by blocking the island's budget in 1909, the U.S. Congress responded by, once again, amending the existing legislation, thus further frustrating the Unionista leadership.[19]

In the Cuban case, U.S. colonial authorities also played politics, choosing favorites and fueling antagonism among the island's political actors. The Cuban revolutionary leadership, particularly its more socially radical faction, found itself in a situation of a leadership vacuum. Three of its four most respected and capable leaders (José Martí, Antonio Maceo, and Calixto García) died during or shortly after the war. A fourth one, Máximo Gómez who died in 1905, was not Cuban and therefore could not realistically aspire to be Cuba's first president. Early on, Governor Leonard Wood applied pressure so that Cuba's constitutional convention would include more moderate and conservative delegates. It was clear that U.S. policymakers had a preference for the pro-U.S. and socially conservative Tomás Estrada Palma, who represented the civilian wing of the anti-Spanish struggle.[20] Estrada Palma, who was sixty-seven years old at the time, briefly counted on the support of the Nationalist and Republican parties that made possible his election to the presidency in 1902. His major opponent, General Bartolomé Masó, withdrew his candidacy shortly before the elections. Estrada Palma's administration was not openly critical of the Platt Amendment and proved welcoming to U.S. economic interests.

By 1905, the virtually unanimous support for Estrada Palma had crumbled and a more populist and more anti-Plattist Liberal Party had formed under José Miguel Gómez, a veteran general of the war against Spain and *caudillo* from the province of Las Villas; intellectual, anti-annexationist Alfredo Zayas Alfonso; and mulatto patriot and journalist Juan Gualberto Gómez. Veterans, urban dwellers, and popular sectors tended to support the Liberal Party to a greater proportion than the Conservative Party of Estrada Palma. Also, by that juncture, politics had become a means of social mobility and capital accumulation for Cubans who had been displaced from the economic arena by U.S. capital and Spanish merchants. Access to political power, thus, became of paramount importance to political *caudillos* and their partisans. Despite the expansion of suffrage for the 1905 elections, the party of Estrada Palma held on to power through widespread fraud. The Liberals responded with a massive insurrection, consisting of about 25,000 men. Despite the Liberals' opposition to the Platt Amendment, by rebelling, they were forcing U.S. intervention as a means to reach control of the insular state. Interestingly, the Estradistas also wanted to provoke U.S. intervention, demonstrating that like the Liberals they had accepted the reality of the Platt Amendment. Indeed, as time went on, it became increasingly evident that no major ideological differences separated Liberals from Conservatives.[21]

Political chaos led to a second U.S. intervention in Cuba in September 1906. It was motivated by U.S. fears of the mobilization of the Liberal Party, the one party that could recombine the two revolutionary agendas of national sovereignty and social justice. If the Liberals were in fact to become the island's ruling party, it was necessary for the intervention government of Charles Magoon to establish legal and judicial mechanisms to limit the power of insular politicians and guarantee the unchallenged dominance of the United States. During Magoon's tenure as provisional governor (1906–1909), Cuba's laws endured a profound overhaul affecting municipal, electoral, public service, judiciary, and military legislation. Moreover, manipulation of patronage and outright corruption under Magoon co-opted, demilitarized, and deradicalized the Liberal leadership, which by then had been tamed enough to be an acceptable option to win the elections of 1908.[22]

U.S. officials did not have the same opportunities to manipulate internal Dominican politics during the first decades of the twentieth century, as they did in Cuba and Puerto Rico, where a military presence was established. Politics in the Dominican Republic, furthermore, was more a matter of *caudillo*-led mobilizations than electoral politics. Still, the United States exerted a great deal of political pressure during the convulsed aftermath of Heureaux's dictatorship. On the other hand, Dominican *caudillos* often courted U.S. support to gain or retain power. In October 1899, Juan Isidro Jimenes was elected to the presidency and was overthrown in 1902 by fellow *caudillo* Horacio Vásquez, who in turn was toppled in 1903 by Carlos F. Morales, who incredibly led a revolt against his own government. There were no major ideological differences separating the various *caudillos* contesting for power, as made evident by the personalistic nature of their movements and the ever-shifting political alliances. A momentary semblance of political stability was reestablished in the Dominican Republic following the ascent to power of the Vásquez partisan Ramón Cáceres in 1906. He came to represent a somewhat less repressive version of Heureaux. During his tenure, regional warfare was reduced, the economy expanded, and better relations with U.S. capital were established.[23]

Along with the imposition of new legal-juridical packages and the direct meddling in internal politics came new forms of economic domination. Cuba and Puerto Rico, as well as the Dominican Republic, came under the control of U.S. economic interests. Long before 1898, the needs and designs of the U.S. economy had exerted considerable, arguably dominant, influence over the Cuban economy. The new century brought a new set of circumstances allowing U.S. monopolistic capital to gain virtual control over sugar production, mining, railroads, the utilities, and banking in the Hispanic Caribbean.

In spite of, and perhaps because of, the chronic instability in the Do-

minican Republic, U.S. interests gained control over Dominican finances. The San Domingo Improvement Company continued to hold
the bulk of the Dominican foreign debt. U.S. control over the Dominican debt proved to be irritating to European bondholders, who pressured Dominican authorities to deal directly with them. European
warships were actually deployed to the republic's territorial waters in
1900 and 1903, seeking to collect part of the debt owed to European
bondholders. President Jimenes yielded to the growing pressures and
momentarily reduced the privileges of the San Domingo Improvement
Company. These developments pushed the U.S. government to apply
the Roosevelt Corollary to the Monroe Doctrine, by virtue of which
U.S. troops landed in the Dominican Republic in 1903 and 1904 to avert
the risk of European intervention.[24] What followed was the U.S. government's takeover of Dominican customs houses and the confiscation
of 55 percent of all yearly customs receipts to service foreign debts. The
remaining 45 percent was allotted to the Dominican government for its
operational costs. Although this arrangement was not immediately approved by the U.S. Senate, it was nonetheless imposed on the Dominican Republic in the form of a protocol beginning in February 1905.
The following year, the Dominican foreign debt was renegotiated and
acquired by a single lender: Kuhn, Lock, and Company of New York.
The customs receivership was finally formalized in 1907. The U.S.
takeover of Dominican customs houses represented the establishment
of a virtual protectorate because it included many restrictions similar
to those imposed on Cuba by virtue of the Platt Amendment: tariff
rates could not be altered nor could the foreign or domestic debts be
increased without U.S. authorization.[25]

Economic measures imposed by the U.S. military governments on
Cuba and Puerto Rico had far-reaching economic and social repercus-
sions. Instead of taking steps to alleviate the crisis endured by the islands' planter classes, military governors imposed measures that froze
agricultural credits and further debased the value of land. Such measures made the region's planters even more vulnerable to the unfair competition posed by the torrent of U.S. capital that poured into Cuba and
Puerto Rico after the war. Moreover, military authorities made scan-

dalously generous concessions to U.S. corporations and entrepreneurs who soon gained control over the islands' mining resources, utilities, banking systems, and transportation infrastructures. In Cuba alone, an estimated $30 million were invested by U.S. corporations and capitalists during the military occupation of the island.[26] A presidential decree of 1901 targeting Puerto Rico and a reciprocity treaty negotiated in 1903 between Cuba and the United States further reduced the islands' economic autonomy, pushing them deeper into the commercial orbit of the United States. In 1901, Puerto Rico was fully integrated into the U.S. tariff system, its exports gaining free access to the U.S. market and U.S. exports entering the island duty free. The reciprocity treaty of 1903 reduced the tariff on Cuban sugar by 20 percent and allowed U.S. exports to enter the island at tariff reductions ranging from 25 to 40 percent. During his provisional governorship, Magoon dug Cuba deeper into debt by arranging for several million dollars in loans.[27]

The various economic decrees and other impositions by the U.S. government on Cuba and Puerto Rico had immediate results on the islands' economic orientation, trade relations, and landholding patterns. Cuba's decades-long trend toward a sugar monocrop economy and dependence on the U.S. market continued to gain strength. The new economic measures had an even greater impact on Puerto Rico, where at century's end, the economy had been based on the exportation of coffee for the Cuban and European markets. While in 1897, coffee represented 66 percent of Puerto Rico's exports and sugar 22 percent, and the United States absorbed only 20 percent of all Puerto Rican exports; as early as 1901, sugar constituted 55 percent of all exports, the ratio of coffee exports had fallen to only 20 percent, and the United States received a whopping 85 percent of Puerto Rico's export output.[28]

The postwar years signaled the arrival of yet another form of U.S. economic penetration into the Hispanic Caribbean. Before 1898, direct U.S. investment in Cuba had been small and even more negligible in Puerto Rico. Beginning in 1898, U.S. capital flowed to both islands, where it faced minimal competition from the crippled insular planter classes. By 1902, the American Tobacco Company, a seemingly invincible trust, had gained control of over 80 percent of Cuba and Puerto

Rico's tobacco exports. Fully three-fourths of Cuba's cattle industry came under U.S. control shortly after 1898, and by 1905, only a quarter of Cuba's land belonged to Cubans. By the end of the first decade of U.S. domination, only 7 percent of the total capital in Puerto Rico was in Puerto Rican hands, and by 1911, U.S. holdings in the Cuban economy were valued at $220 million.[29]

By 1909, the United States had successfully established the legal and institutional bases of colonial and neocolonial domination over Cuba, Puerto Rico, and the Dominican Republic. The extent of direct control over the local state apparatuses and insular economies was a negotiated result that varied in each case according to local circumstances. In the Cuban case, the United States sought to halt revolutionary mobilization and to impose stability by reviving the captain-general's model, whether be it applied by a Wood, an Estrada Palma, or a Magoon. Liberal *caudillos* became acceptable once legal and constitutional guarantees were firmly in place, and more so once they demonstrated the ability to control the unruly masses. In Puerto Rico, the goal was to retain the island as a territorial conquest of ambiguous political status and to play favorites with the most pro-U.S. political actors. In the Dominican case, the most viable option to achieve stability was to support and befriend promising centralizing *caudillos* the likes of Cáceres. In the Hispanic Caribbean, the politics of bifurcation and fragmentation served either to consolidate colonial rule, as in Puerto Rico, or to justify stability-seeking interventions, as in Cuba and the Dominican Republic.

Adjusting the Hegemonic Apparatus/Persistent Bifurcations (1910–1929)

The period between 1910 and 1929 marked yet another stage in the process of extending and securing U.S. domination in the Hispanic Caribbean. Whereas the first decade of U.S. dominance over the region witnessed the installation of the legal and institutional bases of colonial or neocolonial domination (Foraker Act, Platt Amendment, Reciprocity Treaty, customs receivership), the second and third decades of the twentieth century saw radical readjustments in U.S. policy that responded to both challenges stemming from the region and challenges involving the broader Atlantic context, including the outbreak of World War I. Greater adjustments to the neocolonial apparatus, including extended military intervention, were required in the Dominican Republic and Cuba, where the bases for the achievement of hegemony had been only partially installed. Although the existing direct colonial rule over Puerto Rico required less adjusting and no further military intervention, there too domestic needs made necessary the restructuring of relations between the U.S. government and its Puerto Rican subjects and continuing manipulation of insular political divisions. Special attention was also given to the region in response to the geopolitical challenge posed by Germany during World War I, as military-strategic considerations became of paramount importance.[30]

Political developments within the three components of the Hispanic Caribbean continued to unfold along the lines marked by the respective political culture of each island. The three frustrated political struggles continued to play central roles in each society and the U.S. government continued to use or confront them according to its hegemonic aspirations. In the Cuban case, U.S. strategy was to continue dividing the heirs of the revolutionary struggle in order to separate the military leadership and the *caudillos* from the masses and their aspirations for social justice. In the Dominican case, with its chronic anarchy and less developed state, the primary desire of U.S. interests was the island's pacification and the hope that a strong unifying leader would emerge and maintain order throughout the national territory. In Puerto Rico, the apparent goal was to maintain the division among political groups and to keep the island in a limbo state as far as political status went. In all three societies, reaching political power whether via ballots or via bullets became a matter of increasing importance, given the insular elites' persistent lack of economic power.

Political struggle in Puerto Rico during the 1910s continued to center around the perennial status issue. That issue became increasingly pressing for two major reasons. First, there was widespread dissatisfaction with the Foraker Act's limitations on native political power, and this pushed growing numbers of Unionistas to the ranks of *independentistas* (partisans of independence). In 1912, a splinter of the Unionista Party created the Partido de la Independencia; the next year, Unionistas made independence their platform's sole status option. Second, the colonial political system, as it stood, took on farcical characteristics because the Unionistas, who received electoral majorities in every election since 1904, had less actual power and influence than the minority Republicans, who enjoyed better relations with U.S. colonial authorities. Through the dispensation of patronage, U.S. authorities were able to gain and retain the support of the pro-statehood insular Republican Party. Another development in Puerto Rico's party politics during the 1910s was the emergence of organized labor as an important political force. In 1915, Santiago Iglesias Pantín's Federación Libre de Trabajadores formed the Partido Socialista, which would continue to play major roles in electoral politics in many years to come.[31]

In Cuba, political struggles during the 1910s also took on greater importance in light of the lingering legacies of the war and the establishment of a neocolonial system that left Cubans virtually out of other avenues for economic power. Access to positions of political authority turned out to be one of the few remaining means for social mobility and capital accumulation, as an increasing number of Cubans came to see the state as the preferred source of income. As a reflection of this, political parties turned into power-seeking machines built around *caudillos*, who could mobilize ballots and, if necessary, bullets. Ideology was a matter of secondary importance, and party alliances shifted continuously.[32] Also during this period, due to the limitations imposed by the Platt Amendment and other neocolonial restrictions, the political struggle in Cuba retained the warrior side of the revolutionary struggle while its radical social manifestations were temporarily submerged due to the impossibility of their implementation. Cuba's chief political-military *caudillos*, whether Liberal or Conservative, had learned that U.S. support was critical for their survival and that the best way to guarantee that support was demonstrating that they could keep the masses under control.

José Miguel Gómez, the Liberal *caudillo* who governed Cuba between 1908 and 1912, became a master at controlling the masses having learned from the results of Estrada Palma's failure to achieve that objective. Instability under Estrada Palma had led to a protracted U.S. intervention that, among other things, reduced the ability of political chiefs to have direct access to the state's coffers. In 1912, he suppressed the mobilization of thousands of blacks, who out of frustration had left the Liberal Party and created their own: Partido Independiente de Color. A total of between 3,000 and 7,000 blacks were killed during the brutal repression of the 1912 "race war."[33]

In the 1912 elections, Conservatives under veteran General Mario García Menocal confronted a divided Liberal Party and defeated Zayas. Menocal's administration proved to be even more corrupt than previous ones and even more distant from the social revolutionary desires of labor and the general population. He also strove to demonstrate that he could maintain the masses under firm control. The Conservative Party tried to hold on to political power through electoral fraud in 1916, and this led to yet another insurrection in 1917, when 10,000 Liberals mobilized to topple the Conservative government. This revolt, popularly known as La Chambelona, was the fourth large-scale insurrection since Cuban independence.[34]

Dominican politics were even more unstable, even though the state there was far more underdeveloped and therefore offered less of a bounty for those seeking political power and economic gain. The period following Cáceres's assassination in 1911 was marked by anarchy and intensified *caudillo* warfare to the detriment of the Dominican economy. A total of six different administrations ruled the republic between the fall of Cáceres in 1911 and U.S. military intervention in 1916, averaging terms of ten months in office. In 1912, the U.S. government took steps to restore stability by deploying 750 troops and intensifying its meddling in Dominican politics, including pressuring the Dominican government to organize a national army under the direction of U.S. officers. Jimenes was elected president one more time in 1914 but remained in power only until May 1916, when he resigned in protest to the impending U.S. occupation. By then, U.S. policy makers had recognized the chronic nature of political instability on the island and the weakness of the Dominican state and had reached the decision that

major surgery was needed and that it would require an extended intervention. The intervention was also motivated by the fact that some
Dominican *caudillos* could prove vulnerable to German pressures, most
notably *caudillo* Desiderio Arias, whose pro-German stance was no
secret.[35]

The mid-to-late 1910s were years of escalating political turmoil
throughout the Hispanic Caribbean. *Caudillo* warfare continued to
plague Cuba and the Dominican Republic, and both Cuba and Puerto
Rico experienced greater mobilization of their popular classes, which
increasingly operated independently of the traditional oligarchies and
entrenched political bosses. World War I gave more urgency to U.S. desires for political stability in the region and for loyalty to the United
States in light of the growing German menace. Concern over German
expansionism in the Caribbean was the main reason driving the United
States to purchase the Danish Virgin Islands in 1917. Defensive and
strategic considerations, including the defense of the Panama Canal,
also played a determining role behind the U.S. interventions in the Dominican Republic (1916–1924), Haiti (1915–1934), and Cuba (1917–
1921). Political instability had proved to be endemic in these societies,
and the looming German threat made it all the more dangerous. The
war context also highlighted Puerto Rico's strategic relevance and the
importance of the Puerto Ricans' loyalty to the United States, including
the possibility of conscripting Puerto Rican soldiers for the war efforts.
These considerations made the Woodrow Wilson administration somewhat more attentive to the Puerto Ricans' demands for political reform.
While in Cuba and the Dominican Republic the United States responded with military intervention, in Puerto Rico the response was a
new constitutional package that came to be known as the Jones Act.

The Jones Act had the seemingly contradictory effects of, on the one
hand, bringing Puerto Rico closer to the United States and, on the
other, granting it a greater degree of self rule. It made the island's upper
legislative body elective and granted U.S. citizenship to the people of
Puerto Rico. The insular governor, however, remained an appointee of
the U.S. president, as did the members of the insular cabinet. The extension of citizenship, no longer openly advocated by most insular po-

litical leaders, had the backing of the U.S. War Department and Bureau of Insular Affairs, and President Wilson deemed the entire legislative package as vital during the context of war.[36] In part because Puerto Ricans played a minimal role in the process leading to the passing of the Jones Act and in part because it delivered too little, too late, it did not satisfy the aspirations of the island's political elites. Rather than solving the status question, the Jones Act intensified the status struggle. The Unionistas, who continued to enjoy comfortable electoral majorities, began to push for enhanced self-rule immediately after the act's passage.[37] Highly emblematic of the centrality of the status issue was the fact that Puerto Rico's most important elective post was that of the Resident Commissioner to Washington, D.C. The old electoral and lobbyist culture persisted but Washington had replaced Madrid as its sphere of action.

Another factor complicating Puerto Rico's political equation during the 1910s and into the 1920s was the fact that political struggles were played out triangularly, as sociologist Ángel G. Quintero Rivera has pointed out. On one side of the triangle stood the Unionistas, who represented the interests of the beleaguered insular *hacendado* class; on the next side, stood the colonial state with its local allies in the insular Republican Party; and the third side represented the island's working classes, which had often been at odds with the Unionistas for their anti-labor stances.[38] This triangle became fertile breeding ground for the coalition electoral agreements that characterized Puerto Rican party politics between 1924 and 1944. In 1924, as the Socialists' influence continued to grow, the U.S. government pressured the insular political elites into coalescing to block the ascendancy of the party and its affiliated mass labor union. The pro-independence Unionistas, now under the leadership of Antonio R. Barceló, obliged and joined in an electoral pact with the most conservative segment of the pro-statehood Republican Party to form the Alianza Puertorriqueña.[39] This forced the remaining Republicans and the Socialists to form their own electoral alliance: La Coalición. Much to the disadvantage of labor's aspirations, both the Alianza and the Coalición became power-seeking machines operating in a context of weakness vis-à-vis U.S. colonial rule. The formation and longevity of the cross-class Coalición was indicative of the centrality of the status issue which often brought together militants from socially opposed parties.

The extent of U.S. intervention in Cuba and the Dominican Republic during the 1916–1917 juncture went far beyond the constitutional tailoring that occurred in Puerto Rico. Whereas Puerto Rico remained relatively peaceful and its political elites continued to operate within established electoral and constitutional frameworks, Cuba continued to endure recurrent armed uprisings against the established government and the Dominican Republic continued to be submerged in *caudillo* warfare. Earlier attempts at state building along the patterns of Western representative democracy had only partially succeeded, and the previous legal impositions proved to lack the scaffolding of the necessary social and economic conditions.

As mentioned earlier, in Cuba, another civil war (La Chambelona) erupted in 1917 when José Miguel Gómez's supporters rose up in protest of Menocal's attempt to retain power via fraudulent elections. This latest revolt, with war in Europe as its backdrop, led to yet another U.S. intervention between 1917 and 1921, despite Menocal's insistence that he had the situation under control. During and following this intervention, the United States began a more active and direct role in the administration of Cuban affairs. During the presidency of Zayas, who succeeded Menocal in 1921, U.S. officials pressured insular politicians to produce favorable legislation, taxation rates, economic concessions, and even specific budgetary allotments. While U.S. officials achieved a greater degree of influence in Cuban politics, U.S. financial and corporate interests exerted other forms of control that curbed Cuban autonomy. It was dollar diplomacy at its best.[40]

For the 1924 elections, the newly formed Popular Party of Zayas presented Menocal as its presidential candidate to confront Gerardo Machado y Morales of the Liberal Party. Of humble background—a butcher by trade—Machado had risen within the ranks of his party as a result of his exploits during the War of Independence and later in La Chambelona. Machado won by a wide margin and managed to amass multi-party support for his administration which came to be known as

"Cooperativismo." By 1927, Machado had decided to seek reelection, and he maneuvered to extend his term by forcing a new constitution on the Cuban people.[41]

Meanwhile, the Dominican Republic presented even greater challenges to U.S. desires for stability because of the extent of *caudillo* warfare that plagued it and the persistent absence of a functional national state. The achievement of political and economic hegemony necessitated an extended military intervention producing sweeping legal and constitutional measures that could build a sound neocolonial edifice from the ground up. Still, however, the problem remained that a modern centralized state required a parallel social development that could not be legislated into existence within a single generation. Wilsonian democracy could not flourish in a social context characterized by a weak and subordinate elite and a population with an illiteracy rate of around 90 percent.[42]

U.S. troops landed in the Dominican Republic in May 1916, and the military occupation of the country was officially declared on November 29. The various decrees of the military occupation, which lasted until 1924, point to a highly coherent package of state-building measures. The most immediate goal was the disarming of the *caudillo*-led armies with the object of putting an end to regionalist warfare that had plagued the country for seven decades. The next step included the formation of a professional, and hopefully apolitical, national military force that would secure the monopoly over the use of force.

National territorial integration through road building and other infrastructural developments was aimed at reducing regional antagonisms and facilitating the economy's development along the lines of the enclave plantation model. Several military measures were clearly directed toward the elimination of barriers against U.S. monopoly capital. A new land-tenure law of 1920 put an end to the ancient practice of holding communal lands and made it easier for U.S. corporations to acquire extensive tracts of land, especially in El Seibo and San Pedro de Macorís. New tariffs put in place in 1919 and 1920 made it possible for Dominican sugar to be exported to the United States virtually duty free, while eliminating tariff protection of Dominican manufactures.[43]

Viewed as a package, occupation legislation aimed at creating a neo-colonial state that was strong enough to guarantee internal stability but vulnerable and dependent enough not to pose a challenge to U.S. economic interests.

Dominican opposition to the U.S. occupation came from two major sources: the *gavilleros* (peasant and sugar worker guerrillas) and the urban-based, nationalist intelligentsia. *Gavillero* resistance surfaced in the eastern provinces of El Seibo and San Pedro de Macorís, where U.S. capital and new land-tenure legislation threatened the subsistence of large segments of the traditional peasantry. Meanwhile, the urban intelligentsia unleashed an unremitting national and international campaign denouncing U.S. occupation. Nationalist agitation peaked during the crisis of 1920, when sugar prices hit rock bottom; before the end of the year, U.S. military governor Thomas Snowden announced his government's plans to withdraw the occupation forces. The last troops left in 1924.

The postintervention political panorama in the Dominican Republic included many of the old political actors, men like Horacio Vásquez, Federico Velázquez, and Luis Felipe Vidal, who had cooperated with the occupation forces and had accepted the terms of the troops' withdrawal as imposed by the United States. In 1924, an aging Vásquez was elected president and Velázquez, his opponent, was elected vice president. The major new political actor was the national military force that had been created and trained by the U.S. military during the occupation. Since 1925, the Dominican armed forces were led by Rafael Leónidas Trujillo, a thirty-four-year-old Vásquez protégé of mixed racial ancestry and humble background. U.S. occupation had also dealt a near-mortal blow to the regional *caudillos* and had further debilitated the standing of the Dominican economic elites. What remained after the intervention was a handful of old-time politicians, some with reduced personal armies, and a well-armed military under the leadership of Trujillo, an ambitious and cruel young man who resented the Dominican elites.

The application of the various hegemonic mechanisms during the 1910s and 1920s produced the desired results of U.S. control over the economies of the Hispanic Caribbean. By the late 1920s, the dominance of U.S. capital over the region was well established. Preponderant control had been achieved not only in terms of virtual exclusivity in foreign trade but also in direct ownership of extensive sugar lands. Although U.S. corporate ownership of sugar lands had expanded consistently during the first two decades of the twentieth century, the crash of 1921 accelerated the passing of agricultural land to U.S. corporate interests in all three societies. The four largest U.S. sugar corporations in Puerto Rico came to own 24 percent of the sugar land and controlled half of the sugar production. While total U.S. investments in Puerto Rico reached an estimated $120 million by 1930, U.S. investments in Cuba surpassed $1.2 billion in 1924, and four years later, U.S. corporations produced 75 percent of the island's sugar output. U.S. control of Dominican sugar production was even higher, with nearly all sugar lands and a quarter of all agricultural land in U.S. hands. A parallel pattern of U.S. dominance was evident throughout the region in banking, finances, mining, ranching, the utilities, and transportation.[44]

Depression and Noninterventionist Hegemony/ The Era of the National *Caudillos* (1930–1945)

The 1930s stand out as a clear watershed in the history of the Hispanic Caribbean. The most obvious reason for this was the Great Depression, whose worldwide reverberations afflicted the economies of Cuba, Puerto Rico, and the Dominican Republic in ways similar to its effects on other agro-exporting societies during that critical decade. The 1930s also represented profound shifts in the region politically and geopolitically. The region's relations with the United States changed notably with the application of a new U.S. policy package that came to be known as the Good Neighbor Policy. We also find the ascendancy of new political actors in the region, who represented new generations and different social and economic backgrounds. Significantly, however, the political cultures and their respective struggles and models with deep roots in the nineteenth century continued to shape the course of politics in the three societies of the Hispanic Caribbean.

The Great Depression had a deleterious impact on the Hispanic Caribbean, given the region's long-standing dependence on the exportation of sugar to the United States. Cuba's sugar export quota to the United States was cut in half in 1930, and the Hawley-Smoot Tariff Act further reduced Cuba's sugar exports. This had a drastic impact on salary and employment levels: rural wages dropped 75 percent as a quarter of the island's workers lost their jobs. Puerto Rico's economy also went into a tailspin, unemployment there reaching 60 percent in 1930. The Depression also afflicted the Dominican economy, where collapsing sugar prices translated into a 50 percent reduction in wages and mass layoffs among government employees. The deterioration of living conditions for the working classes in the region spurred a flurry of labor strikes, particularly in Puerto Rico and Cuba. Radical, and often violent, political movements, like the Nationalist Party in Puerto Rico, and the ABC secret organization and the Directorio Estudiantil Universitario in Cuba became increasingly active during the 1930s.[45]

The profound social and economic crisis also shook the incumbent governments of the Hispanic Caribbean, not unlike in other parts of Latin America between 1929 and 1933. Throughout Latin America, the effects of the Great Depression debilitated the power base of the traditional agrarian oligarchies, creating a power vacuum that was soon filled by other social sectors, including the urban bourgeoisies, the middle classes, and organized labor. Populist, multiclass coalitions emerged among the republics of Latin America and, in some instances, achieved political power through controlled mobilization of the masses and through electoral means. There were no comparable agrarian oligarchies in Cuba, Puerto Rico, and the Dominican Republic, and the political power of the region's political actors remained limited by a variety of neocolonial mechanisms imposed by the United States. Still, political transition in the Hispanic Caribbean during the 1930s came to represent a rift with the past. Cuba, Puerto Rico, and the Dominican Republic endured similar political crises during the early 1930s, but responses in each case varied in reflection of the particular political culture of each society. In Cuba, political struggles continued to follow the two inherited models: revolutionary mobilization and the captain-general; in the Dominican Republic, they were played out along the authoritarian model of limited, selective mobilization of the masses; in Puerto Rico, despite increased and radicalized nationalist mobilization, political struggles remained focused on the electoral model with special attention to the perennial status issue.

A variety of circumstances, both global and regional, allowed the development of a new U.S. policy toward the Hispanic Caribbean characterized by the end of direct U.S. military intervention and the application of other forms of hegemonic domination. For one, the 1930s witnessed the virtual elimination of European competition for influence over the region both politically and economically. Of equally great significance is the fact that the 1930s saw the rise to power of pro-U.S. authoritarian *caudillos* in Cuba and the Dominican Republic who provided political and social stability that made U.S. direct intervention no longer necessary. Political scientist Jorge Domínguez has referred to this transition as the end of the imperialist stage of the United States and the beginning of the hegemonic phase. Other students of U.S. foreign policy have concurred that the advent of the Good Neighbor era was more the result of new geopolitical and political circumstances than of any profound philosophical shift or major change in U.S. objectives.[46] Indeed, decades of raising, adjusting, and readjusting the hegemonic edifice, in addition to the culmination of favorable geopolitical circumstances, allowed the Franklin D. Roosevelt administration to dismantle the scaffolding of empire through intervention now that domination had been established with a degree of local consent. Stability-producing insular leaders were also able to submerge political fragmentations through varying degrees of combinations of repression and co-optation.

The 1930s marked the beginning of a clearly defined new era in Dominican politics under the fist of Trujillo, perhaps the most brutal dictator in Latin America's history. In the late 1920s, his predecessor, Horacio Vásquez, maneuvered to extend his term in office in a fashion similar to Machado's constitutional tinkering in Cuba. This move weakened the already feeble legal foundations of the Dominican Republic. Trujillo had already become a powerful player in Dominican politics from his position as head of the national armed forces. While trying to appear loyal to Vásquez, Trujillo plotted to topple him with the support of Santiago politician Rafael Estrella Ureña and *caudillo* Desiderio Arias. Following the collapse of Vásquez's regime, Trujillo ran for president and won in May 1930 through fraud and intimidation, amassing 99 percent of the votes. Soon thereafter, he went after Estrella Ureña, Arias, northern *caudillo* Cipriano Bencosme, and any other possible challenger to his regime. In 1930, Trujillo was able to move into a virtual power vacuum in which the military, under his command, gained a virtual monopoly over the use of force. The U.S. government, which was highly responsible for the conditions leading to Trujillo's rise to power, immediately recognized the regime, its unconstitutionality notwithstanding.[47]

Trujillo's rule was the culmination of a long tradition of authoritarian state-building dating to the ill-starred birth of the republic. He followed in Heureaux's bloody footsteps, taking his predecessor's goals and methods to new levels of violence and sophistication; he also incorporated some of the aesthetics of the old *caudillo*, such as the use of ostentatious nineteenth-century military uniforms with plumed field marshal hats, flashy epaulets, and a chest full of self-awarded medals.[48] This latest in a succession of tyrants inherited a state in the process of centralization, and he further strengthened the central government and its executive branch. Significantly, Trujillo's nation-building program also included nationalistic and protectionist measures. As early as 1931, he attempted to regain control over the nation's customs houses. During the Depression, Trujillo also implemented various protectionist tariffs that allowed for some import substitution.[49]

Besides economic power as the nation's wealthiest man, Trujillo enjoyed enormous military power. He expanded the nation's armed forces and, in the process, created a new economic elite that was both dependent on and loyal to his leadership. Significantly, mixed-race Trujillo loyalists moved up socially and militarily as a result of their services to the regime. Through fraud and intimidation, Trujillo was reelected in 1934, and the puppet candidate of his choice, Jacinto B. Peynado, won the elections in 1938; almost comically, both candidates received 100 percent of the vote. By that point, Trujillo's regime had assumed clearly totalitarian features. Though falling far short from the Wilsonian dreams of a successful tropical democracy, Trujillo fulfilled other U.S. desires, namely the achievement of stability and the creation of a climate friendly to U.S. investments and commerce. The United States supported Trujillo's regime and turned a blind eye to his domestic excesses of brutality. Even the atrocious 1938 massacre of around 18,000 Haitians under his direct orders received only mild official protests from the United States. Trujillo's ironfisted regime had clearly fulfilled the new U.S. goal of stability without intervention. Simply put, hegemony was secured through a local tyrant.[50]

The 1930s also saw a transition in Cuban politics with generational and class overtones and the eventual ascent to power in Cuba of a military *caudillo*, Fulgencio Batista y Zaldivar, who achieved political stability by cunningly combining repression and co-optation. The devastating effects of the Great Depression made Machado increasingly vulnerable to the opposition posed by his old political rivals and new political actors representing a new political generation and different sectors of Cuban society; the severe economic crisis made his administration unable to finance his support through government contracts and *botellas* (no-show state jobs). Machado responded by repressing the island's increasingly agitated and radicalalized labor and student movements: adversaries like student leader Julio Antonio Mella were targets of assassination plots and violent mobs called *porras* were let loose against opponents. If Gómez had not already done so, Machado demonstrated that Liberals could serve as good heirs of the captain-general's model as their Conservative Party counterparts did.[51]

Machado faced both old-model *caudillo*-led insurrections, like the failed one staged in August 1931 by Carlos Mendieta and Menocal, and the growing opposition from organized labor, armed student organizations, and middle-class armed groups. In one instance, the ABC went to the extreme of executing Senate President Clemente Vázquez Bello—a Machado partisan—with the ultimate intention of luring Machado and his staff to the Colón Cemetery, where ABC operatives had buried a large number of explosives. Although this plot failed because Vázquez Bello was interred elsewhere, hundreds of acts of political violence left a bloody toll. The dictator's response to an increasingly militant opposition was to tighten the screws of repression.[52]

By early 1933, the U.S. government withdrew its support from Machado as it became clear that he was losing control of the situation and that the post-Machado transition could require the kind of intervention that the new Roosevelt administration wanted to avoid. Machado fled the island on August 12 in the face of pressures from the meddling U.S. Ambassador Sumner Welles, the Cuban armed forces, and most other sectors of Cuban society; his partisans, meanwhile, endured the violent wrath of anti-Machado mobs that ransacked houses and dragged corpses down Havana's streets. Carlos Manuel de Céspedes y Quesada, son of Cuba's founding father, momentarily assumed the presidency with support of the U.S. government.[53]

Three weeks later, on September 3, a revolutionary coalition reached power, representing a new generation of civilian and military leaders who revived many of the revolutionary goals of the generation of '95. Ramón Grau San Martín, Batista, and Antonio Guiteras soon emerged as the leading figures of the post-Machado era. Reflective of the Grau San Martín–led revolutionary government's progressive social agenda were several measures of land reform, utility-rate control, expansion of suffrage, and establishment of the eight-hour workday. During the early months of the revolutionary government, the state nationalized U.S.-owned estates and factories while radical workers established soviets in seized plantations. Nationalism also manifested itself with the unilateral abrogation of the Platt Amendment by the Grau San Martín government as well as moves to wrest control of the Isle of Pines from U.S. control.[54] For a while, it seemed as if the dual revolutionary goals of national liberation and social justice, which first merged during the War of Independence, would be achieved by the generation of '33.

Neither the post-Machado political chaos nor the radicalization of the revolutionary government that followed were welcomed by U.S. interests and their representatives in Cuba. The U.S. government withheld recognition from the Grau San Martín government as Welles maneuvered to propel Batista to the center of political power. Batista soon transferred his support to Carlos Mendieta, and Grau San Martín's government collapsed on January 15, 1934. In a revealing move, the U.S. recognized Mendieta's government only five days after it assumed power. The power behind the throne, however, was Batista, who ruled through puppet presidents until 1936, when he staged a coup against Miguel Mariano Gómez and assumed direct power until 1940. Significantly, he was elected president in clean elections in June 1940 and willingly stepped down in 1944 when a now acceptable Grau San Martín replaced him as chief executive. Like Trujillo, Batista enjoyed good relations with the United States. His regime was propped with favorable sugar quotas and sugar tariffs of the 1934 Jones-Costigan Act, and he was rewarded with the abrogation of the Platt Amendment also in 1934.[55]

Batista's first regime (1933–1944), while serving many of the same U.S. needs and sharing some characteristics with Trujillo's, differed from it in many regards. This was true because Cuban society more closely resembled Argentina and Brazil than its neighboring Dominican Republic. Batista's brand of authoritarian populism was closer to the regimes of Juan Domingo Perón and Getulio Vargas than to those of Anastasio Somoza, Sr., and Trujillo. The existence of a large urbanized middle class and national industrial bourgeoisie and the higher extent of labor organization and mobilization in Cuba necessitated a negotiated and corporatist type of government that at the time was neither necessary nor possible in the Dominican Republic. Batista was also heir to a different political culture, one that intermittently combined aspirations for social justice and national sovereignty. He did share with Trujillo a mixed racial ancestry, the accomplishment of social mobility through military exploits, and a deep-seated contempt for old oligarchs and their heirs.

Like other contemporary populists, Batista relied on a shifting combination of co-optation and repression. Batista successfully suppressed his opposition and proceeded to cultivate harmonious and collaborative relations with a now tamed organized labor and co-opted leaders of the Cuban Communist Party, the ABC, and other former foes. Batista's government also exhibited a reformist strain that has often been overlooked. In fact, he allowed the implementation of many of the goals of the Revolution of 1933, acceptable to the United States if implemented by a strong-handed *caudillo*. Among his regime's noteworthy reforms were a mild agrarian reform, measures of rent and utilities control, and the establishment of numerous rural schools run by the military. Batista succeeded at imposing the captain-general's political model while diffusing the revolutionary goals through populist reformism.[56] The successful achievement of political stability during Batista's dictatorship, especially during the crisis years of the Great Depression, earned the dictator the support of the United States.

In Puerto Rico, meanwhile, the years of the Great Depression brought about major social dislocations with multiple political ramifications. Political transitions there during the 1930s were marked by ideological, generational, and geographical differences. In 1932, the Republican and Socialist coalition achieved its first electoral victory, bringing to a close almost three decades of control of the insular legislature by the Unionista, later Liberal, parties. This coalition, however, was different from the one formed in 1924, for it now included the Republican bourgeoisie, which faithfully represented the interests of sugar producers. Patronage and the aspiration of turning Puerto Rico into a state of the United States solidified an otherwise seemingly unholy alliance of political forces.[57] As a result, the Socialist wing of the coalition lost credibility among labor and other political groups such as the Nationalists, and years later, the Partido Popular Democrático managed to attract the support of the masses and organized labor.

The pro-statehood Republican-Socialist coalition led by Rafael Martínez Nadal and Bolívar Pagán, though victorious at the polls in 1932 and 1936, failed to achieve cooperative relations with U.S. colonial administrators appointed by the progressive Roosevelt administration. Just as in the 1910s and 1920s, one party triumphed at the polls while another enjoyed better working relations with the continental colonial administrators. United States authorities were quick to recognize that the Socialist Party had lost its influence and control over labor, that the Republicans represented dangerous reactionary interests, and that the most viable way to ride the Depression was through the application of

top-down palliative reforms of the New Deal administered in association with local reformers. They also recognized that the application of
reforms could weaken the increasingly violent Nationalist Party of
Pedro Albizu Campos. In this process, members of the younger reformist wing of the Liberal Party, like Luis Muñoz Marín, Carlos
Chardón, Guillermo Esteves, and Rafael Fernández García, played increasingly important roles, and many were incorporated into the bureaucracy of the newly formed New Deal agency called the Puerto Rico
Emergency Relief Administration (PRERA) and later the Puerto Rico
Reconstruction Administration (PRRA). The Liberal Party's reformists, though mostly pro-independence, were pragmatic politicians;
they recognized the urgency of the current crisis and subordinated the
status issue to other more pressing matters. They also converged ideo-
logically with the New Deal reformists in Washington.[58]

In 1938, Muñoz Marín and other reformists abandoned the Liberal
Party and founded the Partido Popular Democrático, which emerged
victorious in the elections of 1940 and achieved landslide victories over
the next fifteen years. Though a civilian and democratically inclined,
Muñoz Marín, once elected as senator (1941–1949) and later as governor (1949–1965), came to play the role of stability-producing, state-
building, strong leader parallel to the roles played by Trujillo and
Batista in the neighboring islands. Conditions in Puerto Rico, such as
the existence of a firm U.S. colonial apparatus and a long tradition of
electoral democracy, did not make necessary the application of extensive martial and repressive means that were in place in Cuba and the
Dominican Republic. The quasi-military Nationalists, however, had
abandoned electoral politics after the elections of 1932 and faced un-
relenting persecution at the hands of the colonial state's police forces,
culminating in the arrest and conviction of Albizu Campos and several
of his associates in 1936 and the Ponce massacre in 1937.[59]

In summation, the 1930–1945 period marked the definite achievement of U.S. hegemony in the Hispanic Caribbean. The foundational
bases for hegemony had been successfully installed during the first
decade of the twentieth century and were readjusted according to local
conditions during the second and third decades. In each case, the

United States used the local political culture to achieve its goals. In the Dominican Republic, the means was Trujillo, a figure like Heureaux but far more sinister. In Cuba, it was Batista who reconciled the stability of the captain-general's model with toned down aspirations of the revolutionary tradition. Both *caudillos* produced the conditions that guaranteed U.S. interests without recourse to direct meddling in local politics or intervention. In Puerto Rico, hegemony culminated with the gradual transference of local power to reformist-oriented politicians led by Muñoz Marín.

By 1940–1941, there were clear indications of the success of U.S. hegemony in the Hispanic Caribbean. Trujillo's regime entered its second decade and boasted brutality-imposed stability and economic growth. Quite significantly, the United States returned the nation's customs houses to Dominican hands in 1941, and in 1947, Trujillo paid off the national debt that had burdened the Republic for over a century. Trujillo also managed to nationalize the U.S.-owned electric company and buy the also U.S.-owned National City Bank and most of the island's sugar plantations.[60] President Batista, meanwhile, allowed and even promoted the creation of a new and very progressive constitution in 1940, which fulfilled many of the revolutionary goals of 1895 and 1933. According to historian Robert Whitney, this transition to democracy was possible only after "state violence [was] unleashed against the *clases populares* and the various opposition groups."[61] Muñoz Marín, for his part, enjoyed excellent collaborative relations with the colonial administration of Rexford G. Tugwell (1941–1946) and other like-minded New Dealers.[62] It would be a matter of a few years before the U.S. president would appoint the first Puerto Rican governor (1946) and later allow the people of Puerto Rico to elect their own governor (1949).

The three Caribbean *caudillos*, despite many differences, played similar roles as stabilizing figures that helped consolidate local consensus for U.S. hegemony through the application of various combinations of coercion and co-optation. Looking at their respective societies in comparative perspective, a significant paradox becomes apparent: the two most unstable, war-torn, and undemocratic countries (the Dominican

Republic and Cuba) allowed the emergence of two dictators of humble background and mixed racial ancestry who helped end the era of the white oligarchs; while in the most stable and democratic of the three (Puerto Rico), the son of a nineteenth-century white patrician inherited his father's social standing and leadership role. In the process, the forces that allowed his rise to power battled and defeated the Nationalist movement led by Albizu Campos, a mulatto of working-class background.[63]

Crisis of Hegemony/Persistent Political Cultures

Developments in the 1950s, 1960s, and 1970s, against the backdrop of the Cold War, demonstrated the vulnerability of the hegemony that the United States had finally achieved. The recent past has also made evident the persistence of the region's centuries-old struggles along the lines of deeply ingrained political cultures as well as the threat of resurfacing political bifurcations.

In 1956, a large-scale revolutionary struggle erupted against Batista's second dictatorship, which had become increasingly brutal and rested more and more on the authoritarian captain-general's model. The Cuban Revolution's triumph in 1959 made evident very soon that Fidel Castro's government, in its own way, reconciled the revolutionary and the captain-general's models. While certainly not a friend of the United States, Castro managed to impose the stability that neither Valeriano Weyler nor Estrada Palma nor Machado nor Batista could ever produce; redistribution of wealth, political imprisonment, executions, reconcentrations, repression, and massive exile served to submerge political fragmentations, producing a lasting mirage of unanimity.

Trujillo's regime, meanwhile, while useful as an anti-communist ally of the United States, became increasingly brutal during the 1950s and early 1960s, to the point that it lost the support of two of its staunchest backers: the U.S. government and the Dominican Catholic Church. Like Heureaux's sixty years earlier, it came to an end by an assassin's bullet on May 30, 1961, and was followed by a period of civil war that culminated with yet another U.S. intervention in April 1965. *Trujillismo* lingered, however, during the twelve-year U.S.-backed rule of Joaquín Balaguer, formerly a lackey of Trujillo's.

In Puerto Rico, meanwhile, Muñoz Marín and his Populares led the country through a process of unprecedented economic prosperity and social development between the 1940s and 1960s, turning what had been the Caribbean's poorhouse into the "Showcase of Democracy" and the hemisphere's model for economic development. Economic boom, the orchestration of the massive exodus of hundreds of thousands of Puerto Ricans to the United States, and the successful suppression of the Nationalist resurgence of the 1950s and other dissonant voices produced a semblance of political unanimity parallel to those imposed by the one-party regimes of Trujillo and Castro. Significantly, Puerto Rico's politicians—like their predecessors a century before—contrasted the island's stability and loyalty to the situation in nearby Cuba. As the Partido Popular Democrático's grip over power eroded and the status issue reemerged with a vengeance in the 1960s, the island's politicians once again resorted to delegations to Washington, referendums, and plebiscites hoping for a final status solution. Significantly, the Puerto Rican great-grandchildren of the nineteenth-century patrician and *hacendado* class still hold on to social, political, and economic power while their Cuban and Dominican counterparts have faded into oblivion in exile or God knows where.

Notes

Introduction

1. See, for example, Manuel Moreno Fraginals, Frank Moya Pons, and Stanley L. Engerman, eds., *Between Slavery and Free Labor: The Spanish-Speaking Caribbean in the Nineteenth Century* (Baltimore: Johns Hopkins University Press, 1985); Andrés A. Ramos Mattei, *Betances en el ciclo revolucionario antillano, 1867–1875* (San Juan: Instituto de Cultura Puertorriqueña, 1987); Laird W. Bergad, "Dos alas del mismo pájaro? Notas sobre la historia socioeconómica comparativa de Cuba y Puerto Rico," *Historia y Sociedad* 1 (1988): 143–54; and Roberto Marte, *Cuba y la República Dominicana: Transición económica en el Caribe del siglo XIX* (Santo Domingo, DR: Universidad APEC, [1988]). See Gert J. Oostindie, "España y el resurgimiento desigual del Caribe Hispánico, 1760–1860," in María Justina Saravia Viejo, coord., *Europa e Iberoamérica, cinco siglos de intercambios*, proceedings of the 9th International Congress of the History of the Americas (Seville: AHILA, 1992), 2: 705–24; Luis Martínez-Fernández, *Torn between Empires: Economy, Society, and Patterns of Political Thought in the Hispanic Caribbean, 1840–1878* (Athens: University of Georgia Press, 1994); and Christopher Schmidt-Nowara, *Empire and Antislavery: Spain, Cuba, and Puerto Rico, 1833–1874* (Pittsburgh: University of Pittsburgh Press, 1999).

Chapter 1

1. Juan Pérez de la Riva, "Desaparición de la población indígena cubana," *Universidad de La Habana* 196–197 (1972): 61–84.
2. Philip D. Curtin, *The Atlantic Slave Trade: A Census* (Madison: University of Wisconsin Press, 1969), 46; and David Eltis, Stephen Behrendt, David Richardson, and Herbert S. Klein, eds., *The Trans-Atlantic Slave Trade: A Database on CD-ROM* (New York: Cambridge University Press, 2000).
3. Joan Casanovas, *Bread, or Bullets! Urban Labor and Spanish Colonialism in Cuba, 1850–1898* (Pittsburgh: University of Pittsburgh Press, 1998), 48–56.

4. Juan Pérez de la Riva, "Demografía de los culíes. Chinos en Cuba (1853–1874)," in Juan Pérez de la Riva, ed., *El Barracón: Esclavitud y capitalismo en Cuba* (Barcelona: Editorial Crítica, 1978), 55–87.
5. John L. Offner, *An Unwanted War: The Diplomacy of the United States and Spain over Cuba, 1895–1898* (Chapel Hill: University of North Carolina Press, 1992), 80, 111–13; Louis A. Pérez, Jr., "North American Protestant Missionaries in Cuba and the Culture of Hegemony, 1898–1920," in Louis A. Pérez, Jr., ed., *Essays on Cuban History: Historiography and Research* (Gainesville: University Press of Florida, 1995), 55; and Casanovas, *Bread*, 103.
6. Consuelo Naranjo Orovio, "La emigración española a Iberoámerica desde 1880 a 1930: Análisis cuantitativo," in Instituto Cubano del Libro and Instituto de Cooperación Iberoamericana, eds., *Nuestra común historia: poblamiento y nacionalidad* (Havana: Editorial de Ciencias Sociales, 1993): 116–55; and Louis A. Pérez, Jr., *Cuba: Between Reform and Revolution*, 3rd ed. (New York: Oxford University Press, 2006), 154–57.
7. Sidney W. Mintz, "The Caribbean as a Socio-cultural Area," *Journal of World History* 9:4 (1966), 931.
8. V. S. Naipaul, *The Overcrowded Baracoon* (New York: Knopf, 1973), 259, quoted by Sidney W. Mintz, "The Caribbean Region," in Roberta Marx Delson, ed., *Readings in Caribbean History and Economics: An Introduction to the Region* (New York: Gordon and Breach, 1981), 6.
9. Antonio Benítez Rojo, *The Repeating Island: The Caribbean and the Postmodern Perspective* (Durham, NC: Duke University Press, 1992), 66–68; Gumersindo Rico, "Prólogo," in *Nuestra común historia*, vii–x; Manuel Moreno Fraginals, *Cuba/España España/Cuba: Historia común* (Barcelona: Editorial Crítica, 1995); José Sánchez-Boudy, *Filosofía del cubano . . . y de lo cubano* (Miami: Ediciones Universal, 1996); Louis A. Pérez, jr., *On Becoming Cuban: Identity, Nationality, and Culture* (Chapel Hill: University of North Carolina Press, 1999); Eduardo Torres-Cuevas, "Patria, pueblo y revolución," in *Nuestra común historia*, 1–22; Nicolás Guillén "Balada de los dos abuelos," in *Nueva Antología*, 4th ed. (Mexico City: Editores Mexicanos Unidos, 1986), 43–45; and Carlos Franqui, *Diary of the Cuban Revolution* (New York: Seaver Books, 1980), vii.
10. Pedro Francisco Bonó, "Apuntes sobre las clases trabajadoras dominicanas," in Emilio Rodríguez Demorizi, ed., *Papeles de Pedro F. Bonó, para la historia de las ideas políticas en Santo Domingo* (Santo Domingo, DR: Editorial Caribe, 1964), 190–245; and Fernando Ortiz, *Contrapunteo cubano del tabaco y el azúcar* (Havana:

Jesús Montero, 1940).

11. Fernando Ortiz, *Los factores humanos de la cubanidad* (Havana: Molina y Compañía, n.d.), 16, reprint of article published in *Revista Bimestre Cubana* 45:2 (1940).

12. Curtin, *Atlantic Slave Trade.*

13. Franklin W. Knight, *The Caribbean: The Genesis of a Fragmented Nationalism*, 2d ed. (New York: Oxford University Press, 1990), chap. 2; H. Hoetink, "'Race' and Color in the Caribbean," in Sidney W. Mintz and Sally Price, eds., *Caribbean Contours* (Baltimore: Johns Hopkins University Press, 1995), 55–84; Benítez Rojo, *Repeating Island*, 70; and Antonio Benítez Rojo, "La cultura caribeña en Cuba: Continuidad *versus* ruptura," *Cuban Studies/Estudios Cubanos* 14:1 (Winter 1984), 11.

14. Knight, *Caribbean*, 366–67.

15. Ortiz, "Los factores," 24.

16. Benítez Rojo, *Repeating Island*, 68; and Benítez Rojo, "Cultura caribeña," 2.

17. José Luis González, *El país de los cuatro pisos y otros ensayos* (Río Piedras, PR: Ediciones Huracán, 1980), 19–20; and Sidney W. Mintz, *Caribbean Transformations* (New York: Columbia University Press, 1989), 35–37.

18. Guillén "Balada," 43–45.

19. Hoetink, "'Race,'" 57.

20. See Sidney W. Mintz and Richard Price, *The Birth of African-American Culture: An Anthropological Perspective* (Boston: Beacon Press, 1992), 10–14, 45.

21. Ortiz, *Contrapunteo*; 11; Knight, *Caribbean*, 14; Mintz, *Caribbean Transformations*, 146–48; Benítez Rojo, *Repeating Island*, 53; and Arcadio Díaz Quiñones, "De cómo y cuándo bregar," in Arcadio Díaz Quiñones, *El arte de bregar* (San Juan: Ediciones Callejón, 2000): 19–87.

22. Ortiz, *Contrapunteo, passim*; and Bonó, "Apuntes," 199.

23. Benítez Rojo, "Cultura," 7, 10; and Benítez Rojo, *Repeating Island*, 45.

24. González, *País*, 19–20.

25. Ángel G. Quintero Rivera, *¡Salsa, sabor y control! Sociología de la música "tropical"* (Mexico City: Siglo XXI Editores, 1998); and Díaz Quiñones, "De cómo y cuándo bregar," 26–28.

26. Ortiz, *Contrapunteo, passim*; González, *País*, 19–20; and Benítez Rojo, "Cultura," 7.

27. Hoetink, "'Race,'" 58.

28. Ramiro Guerra y Sánchez, *Azúcar y población en las Antillas* (Ha-

vana: Cultural, S.A., 1927). Also see O. Nigel Bolland, "Creolization and Creole Societies," in O Nigel Bolland, ed., *Struggles for Freedom: Essays on Slavery, Colonialism and Culture in the Caribbean and Central America* (Belize City: Angelus Press, 1997), 7–10.

29. Ortiz, *Contrapunteo, passim.*

30. Eric Williams, *From Columbus to Castro: The History of the Caribbean* (New York: Vintage Books, 1984), 28–29; W. R. Aykroyd, *The Sweet Malefactor* (London: Heinemann, 1967); V. S. Naipaul, *The Middle Passage* (New York: Vintage Books, 1990), 57; George Beckford, *Persistent Poverty: Underdevelopment in Plantation Economies of the Third World* (New York: Oxford University Press, 1972), 10; Maurice Lemoine, *Sucre amer* (Paris: Eucre, 1981); Sidney W. Mintz, "Enduring Substances, Trying Theories: The Caribbean Region As OIKOUMENÊ," *Journal of the Royal Anthropological Institute* 2:2 (June 1996): 297; and León Ichazo, director, *Azúcar amarga* (First Look Films/Overseas Film Group, 1996).

31. Benítez Rojo, "Cultura," 6, 1; González, *País*, 12, 18–19; and Miguel Barnet, "The Culture That Sugar Created," *Latin American Literary Review* 8:16 (Spring–Summer 1980), 46.

32. Barnet, "Culture," 46.

33. Benítez Rojo, *Repeating Island*, 73.

Chapter 2

1. Sidney W. Mintz, *Sweetness and Power: The Place of Sugar in Modern History* (New York: Viking Press, 1985), 148.

2. Williams, *From Columbus*, 383; Manuel Moreno Fraginals, *El ingenio: Complejo económico social del azúcar*, 3 vols. (Havana: Editorial de Ciencias Sociales, 1978), 3: 36; Mintz, *Sweetness*, 144; and Laird W. Bergad, *Cuban Rural Society in the Nineteenth Century: The Social and Economic History of Monoculture in Matanzas* (Princeton, NJ: Princeton University Press, 1990), 162.

3. José García de Arboleya, *Manual de la isla de Cuba*, 2d ed. (Havana: Imprenta del Tiempo, 1859), 238; and Leví Marrero, *Cuba: Economía y sociedad*, 15 vols. (Madrid: Editorial Playor, 1971–1992), 10: 101.

4. A series of ravishing hurricanes hit the Cuban coffee regions in the mid-1840s, causing enormous destruction. See Louis A. Pérez, Jr., *Winds of Change: Hurricanes and the Transformation of Nineteenth-Century Cuba* (Chapel Hill: University of North Carolina Press,

2001). A variety of sources provide data on the number of estates, among them: Thomas William Wilson, *The Island of Cuba in 1850; Being a Description of the Island, Its Resources, Productions, Commerce & Co.* (New Orleans: La Patria, 1850), 7; Arthur F. Corwin, *Spain and the Abolition of Slavery in Cuba, 1817–1886* (Austin: University of Texas Press, 1967), 295; Franklin W. Knight, *Slave Society in Cuba during the Nineteenth Century* (Madison: University of Wisconsin Press, 1970), 39; and Marrero, *Cuba*, 10: 176.

5. Knight, *Slave Society*, 40–41.
6. Richard Henry Dana, Jr., *To Cuba and Back: A Vacation Voyage* (Carbondale: Southern Illinois University Press, 1966), 129; and Ramón de la Sagra, *Cuba, 1860: Selección de artículos sobre agricultura cubana* (Havana: Comisión Nacional Cubana de la UNESCO, 1963).
7. Wilson, *Island*, 7; Marrero, *Cuba*, 10: 176; and Knight, *Slave Society*, 39.
8. Marrero, *Cuba*, 10: 250; and Roland T. Ely, *Cuando reinaba su majestad el azúcar: Estudio histórico-sociológico de una tragedia latinoamericana* (Buenos Aires: Editorial Sudamericana, 1963), 539. See also testimony of José Julián Acosta at the Junta de Información, February 6, 1867, in España, Ministerio de Ultramar, *Cuba desde 1850 a 1873* (Madrid: Imprenta Nacional, 1873), 72.
9. Marrero, *Cuba*, 10: 194–95; and Marte, *Cuba*, 296.
10. Moreno Fraginals, *Ingenio*, 1: 272; Knight, *Slave Society*, 38; Bergad, *Cuban Rural Society*, 109–14; and García de Arboleya, *Manual*, 200–201. For an assessment of the origins, development, and impact of Cuban railroads, see Gert J. Oostindie, "Cuban Railroads, 1803–1868: Origins and Effects of Progressive Entrepreneurialism," *Caribbean Studies* 20:3–4 (1988): 24–45; and Oscar Zanetti Lecuona and Alejandro García Álvarez, *Sugar and Railroads: A Cuban History, 1837–1959* (Chapel Hill: University of North Carolina Press, 1998).
11. Ely, *Cuando reinaba*, 446–47; and Knight, *Slave Society*, 69.
12. García de Arboleya, *Manual*, 137–38; Knight, *Slave Society*, 39; Wilson, *Island*, 7, Corwin, *Spain*, 295, Marrero, *Cuba*, 10: 176; and Moreno Fraginals, *Ingenio*, 1: 222.
13. Cristóbal Madan [Un Hacendado, pseud.], *Llamamiento de la isla de Cuba a la nación española* (New York: E. Hallet, 1854), 32.
14. For data on Chinese and Yucatecan labor imports, see Crawford to Lord Clarendon, August 7 and 16, 1855, in Great Britain, Parliament, House of Commons, *British Parliamentary Papers* [Slave Trade], 95 vols. (Shannon, Ireland: Irish University Press), 1968–

1971 (hereinafter cited as *BPP*), vol. 42, Class B, 397–401. Also see Bergad, *Cuban Rural Society*, 250–51; Ely, *Cuando reinaba*, 616; "Report of Coolie Importations to Cuba, June 14, 1858," National Archives, Washington, DC (hereinafter cited as NA), Records of the Department of State, Record Group 59 (hereinafter cited as RG 59), Despatches from U.S. Consuls in Havana, roll 39; and *La Gaceta de La Habana*, January 30, 1856.

15. Raúl Cepero Bonilla, *Azúcar y abolición* (Havana: Cenit, 1948); Moreno Fraginals, *Ingenio*, 1: 27, 49; and Fe Iglesias García, "The Development of Capitalism in Cuban Sugar Production Based on Slave Labor in Cuba, 1860–1900," in Manuel Moreno Fraginals, Frank Moya Pons, Stanley L. Engerman, eds., *Between Slavery and Free Labor: The Spanish-Speaking Caribbean in the Nineteenth Century* (Baltimore: The Johns Hopkins University Press, 1985), 59.

16. Rebecca J. Scott, *Slave Emancipation in Cuba: The Transition to Free Labor, 1860–1899* (Princeton, NJ: Princeton University Press, 1985), 89; Laird W. Bergad, "The Economic Viability of Sugar Production Based on Slave Labor in Cuba, 1859–1878," *Latin American Research Review* 24:1 (1989): 95–113; and Bergad, *Cuban Rural Society*.

17. David Eltis, "The Nineteenth-Century Transatlantic Slave Trade: An Annual Time Series of Imports into the Americas Broken Down by Region," *HAHR* 67:1 (February 1987): 109–38; and David Murray, *Odious Commerce: Britain, Spain, and the Abolition of the Cuban Slave Trade* (New York: Cambridge University Press, 1980), 244, 259.

18. Susan Schroeder, *Cuba: A Handbook of Historical Statistics* (Boston: G. K. Hall, 1982), 107; Knight, *Slave Society*, 181; and Dana, *To Cuba*, 45.

19. According to an 1850 report by the British judge of the Havana Mixed Commission, three or four cargoes of Brazilian slaves arrived yearly to the island. *BPP*, 7: 173–77. See Arturo Morales Carrión, *Auge y decadencia de la trata negrera en Puerto Rico (1820–1860)* (San Juan: Instituto de Cultura Puertorriqueña, 1978), 200–203.

20. Luis Manuel Díaz Soler, *Historia de la esclavitud negra en Puerto Rico* (Río Piedras, PR: Editorial Universitaria, 1967), 407–8.

21. *La Verdad*, editors, *Cuestión negrera de la isla de Cuba* (New York: La Verdad, 1851), 4; and Ely, *Cuando reinaba*, 585.

22. Crawford to Lord Clarendon, August 29, 1853, quoted in Murray, *Odious Commerce*, 247–48; U.S. Congress, "Stephen R. Mallory of Florida on the Acquisition of Cuba," 35th Congress, 2d session,

Congressional Globe (February 25, 1859), vol. 28, pt. 2, 1328; and Robert W. Gibbes, *Cuba for Invalids* (New York: W. A. Townsend, 1860), 39.

23. Murray, *Odious Commerce*, 266; Robert W. Schufeldt, "Secret History of the Slave Trade in Cuba," *Journal of Negro History* 55:3 (1970): 218–35; Fuller quoted in Marrero, *Cuba*, 10: 269; also see Corwin, *Spain*, 118; and Crawford to Lord Russell, February 5, 1861, *BPP*, vol. 5, Class B, 16–19.

24. Franklin W. Knight, "Origins of Wealth and the Sugar Revolution in Cuba, 1750–1850," *HAHR* 57:2 (May 1977): 249.

25. Knight, *Slave Society*, 231–53; Robert Louis Paquette, *Sugar Is Made with Blood: The Conspiracy of La Escalera and the Conflict between Empires over Slavery in Cuba* (Middletown, CT: Wesleyan University Press, 1988), 45; Bergad, *Cuban Rural Society*, 14–15, 22–23; and Moreno Fraginals, *Ingenio*, 1: 63.

26. Justo Zaragoza, *Isla de Cuba, suspensión de conventos y contribución extraordinaria de guerra* (Madrid: n.p., 1837), 24.

27. Ely, *Cuando reinaba*, 324–25; and Bergad, *Cuban Rural Society*, 174.

28. Marrero, *Cuba*, 10: 210; and V. De Roches, *Cuba under Spanish Rule* (New York: Great American Engraving and Printing, [1869?]), 15–17.

29. *La Gaceta de Puerto Rico*, vol. 17, no. 137, quoted in Lidio Cruz Monclova, *Historia de Puerto Rico (siglo XIX)*, 3 vols. (Río Piedras, PR: Editorial Universitaria, 1952), 1: 292.

30. Pérez, *Cuba*, 85; Francisco López Segrera, *Cuba: capitalismo dependiente y subdesarrollo (1510–1959)* (Mexico City: Editorial Diógenes, 1979), 114; and Manuel Moreno Fraginals, "Plantations in the Caribbean: Cuba, Puerto Rico and the Dominican Republic in the Late Nineteenth Century," in Moreno Fraginals, Moya Pons, and Engerman, eds., *Between Slavery and Free Labor*, 16.

31. See Demoticus Philalethes, *Yankee Travels through the Island of Cuba* (New York: D. A. Appleton, 1856), 64–65; Dana, *To Cuba*, 111–12; John S. Thrasher, *A Preliminary Essay on the Purchase of Cuba* (New York: Derby and Jackson, 1859), 77; and James Rawson, *Cuba* (New York: Lane & Tippet, 1847), 12.

32. Ely, *Cuando reinaba*, 306–7.

33. Ely, *Cuando reinaba*, 330–31; Paquette, *Sugar*, 46–47; Corwin, *Spain*, 136–37; Marrero, *Cuba*, 10: 269–71; and Marte, *Cuba*, 178–79.

34. Data from "Balanzas mercantiles," housed in Centro de Investigaciones Históricas de la Universidad de Puerto Rico, Río Piedras

(hereinafter cited as CIH).

35. Francisco A. Scarano, "Inmigración y estructura de clases: Los hacendados de Ponce, 1815–1845," in Francico A. Scarano, ed., *Inmigración y clases sociales en el Puerto Rico del siglo XIX* (Río Piedras, PR: Ediciones Huracán, 1981), 23.

36. Cuban *ingenios* produced a mean of 391 tons (1860), while Puerto Rico's averaged around eighty-seven tons (1845). Francisco A. Scarano, *Sugar and Slavery in Puerto Rico: The Plantation Economy of Ponce, 1800–1850* (Madison: University of Wisconsin Press, 1984), 66–67.

37. Andrés A. Ramos Mattei, "La importación de trabajadores contratados para la industria azucarera puertorriqueña: 1860–1880," in Scarano, ed., *Inmigración y clases sociales*, 126; Laird W. Bergad, *Coffee and the Growth of Agrarian Capitalism in Nineteenth-Century Puerto Rico* (Princeton, NJ: Princeton University Press, 1983), 68. Andrés A. Ramos Mattei, *La hacienda azucarera: Su crecimiento y crisis en Puerto Rico (siglo XIX)* (San Juan: CEREP, 1981), 22–23; and Laird W. Bergad, "Agrarian History of Puerto Rico, 1870–1930," *Latin American Research Review* 13:3 (1978), 65–66.

38. Scarano, *Sugar and Slavery*, 5.

39. Quoted in Morales Carrión, *Auge y decadencia*, 134–35.

40. Scarano, *Sugar and Slavery*, 5.

41. H. Augustus Cowper to Lord Clarendon, February 11, 1866, in Centro de Investigaciones Históricas, *El proceso abolicionista en Puerto Rico: Documentos para su estudio*, 2 vols. (San Juan: Instituto de Cultura Puertorriqueña, 1974), 1: 53.

42. Fernando Picó, *Libertad y servidumbre en el Puerto Rico del siglo XIX* (Río Piedras, PR: Ediciones Huracán, 1979).

43. Curtin, *Atlantic Slave Trade*, 31–44, 88.

44. José A. Curet, "De la esclavitud a la abolición: Transiciones económicas en las haciendas azucareras de Ponce, 1845–1873," in Andrés A. Ramos Mattei, ed., *Azúcar y esclavitud* (San Juan: privately printed, 1982), 84–85.

45. De Ronceray to Cass, August 22, 1860, NA, Record Group 84, Records of Foreign Service Posts (hereinafter RG 84), San Juan, vol. 7228.

46. Morales Carrión, *Auge y decadencia*, 11–14.

47. Jay Kinsbruner, *Not of Pure Blood: The Free People of Color and Racial Prejudice in Nineteenth-Century Puerto Rico* (Durham, NC: Duke University Press, 1996), 445; Rafael María de Labra y Cadrana, *La cuestón de ultramar* (Madrid: Nogueras, 1871), 25; and Bergad, *Cuban Rural Society*, 99.

Chapter 3

1. There is an ample and rich body of nineteenth-century travel accounts by U.S. and European visitors to Cuba. For a partial listing, see Luis A. Pérez, Jr., *Cuba: An Annotated Bibliography* (New York: Greenwood Press, 1988), 19–28.
2. Antonio C. N. Gallenga, *The Pearl of the Antilles* (London: Chapman and Hall, 1873; reprint, New York: Negro Universities Press, 1970), 36, 29; Nicolás Tanco Armero, "La Isla de Cuba," in *La Isla de Cuba en el siglo XIX vista por los extranjeros*, ed. Juan Pérez de la Riva (Havana: Editorial de Ciencias Sociales, 1981), 112; and [John George F. Wurdemann], *Notes on Cuba* (Boston: J. Munro and Co., 1844), 40.
3. Census of 1861, reproduced in Cuba, Instituto de Investigaciones Estadísticas, *Los censos de población y viviendas en Cuba* (Havana: Instituto de Investigaciones Estadísticas, 1988), 1: 111–13. The gender imbalance among rural slaves aged 12–60 was, at midcentury, 136,000 males to 69,256 females. Among urban slaves of the same age group, however, the imbalance was inverted and much lighter: 22,891 men to 25,232 women. John S. Thrasher, "Preliminary Essay," in Alexander Humboldt, *The Island of Cuba* (New York: Derby & Jackson, 1856), 75; Richard Robert Madden, *The Island of Cuba: Its Resources, Progress, and Prospects* (London: Partridge & Oakey, 1853), 4; García de Arboleya, *Manual*, 116; and Verena Martínez-Alier, *Marriage, Class and Colour in Nineteenth-Century Cuba* (Ann Arbor: University of Michigan Press, 1989), 57.
4. Census of 1861 in Cuba, *Censos*, 1: 111–13.
5. See Johanna S. R. Mendelson, "The Feminine Press: The View of Women in Colonial Journals of Spanish America, 1790–1810," and June E. Hahner, "The Nineteenth-Century Feminist Press and Women's Rights in Brazil," both in Asunción Lavrin, ed., *Latin American Women: Historical Perspectives* (Westport, CT: Greenwood Press, 1978). Also see Antonio de las Barras y Prado, *Memorias, La Habana a mediados del siglo XIX* (Madrid: Ciudad Lineal, 1925), 178.
6. Martínez-Alier, *Marriage*, 109, xiii.
7. *La Verdad*, editors, *Cuestión negrera*, 8.
8. Philalethes, *Yankee Travels*, 11 (italics in original).
9. Thrasher, "Preliminary Essay," 69–71. Political governor of Havana to the captain-general of Cuba, March 3, 1855, Archivo Nacional de Cuba (hereinafter ANC), Gobierno Superior Civil, *legajo* 1373, file 53615.

10. Philalethes, *Yankee Travels*, 11. Quote from Condesa de Merlín [Mercedes de Santa Cruz y Montalvo], *Viaje a La Habana* (Havana: Editorial de Arte y Literatura, 1974), 107. For other sources on female seclusion, see Gallenga, *Pearl*, 29; de las Barras y Prado, *Memorias*, 178; Benjamin Moore Norman, *Rambles by Land and Water; or, Notes to Travel in Cuba and Mexico* (New York: Paine & Burgess, 1845), 28–29; Gibbes, *Cuba for Invalids*, 11; and W.M.L. Jay [Julia Louisa M. Woodruff], *My Winter in Cuba* (New York: E. P. Dutton, 1871), 123.

11. [William Henry Hurlbert], *Gan-Eden; or, Pictures of Cuba* (Boston: J. P. Jewett, 1854), 12; and Dana, *To Cuba*, 10.

12. Condesa de Merlín, *Viaje*, 107.

13. Quote from Gallenga, *Pearl*, 28; see John Mark, *Diary of My Trip to America and Havana* (Manchester, UK: J. E. Cornish, 1885), 66; Henry Tudor, *Narrative of a Tour in North America, Comprising Mexico, the Mines of Real del Monte, the United States, and the British Colonies with an Excursion to the Island of Cuba*, 2 vols. (London: James Duncan, 1834), 2: 120; de las Barras y Prado, *Memorias*, 116–17; Fredrika Bremer, *The Homes of the New World; Impressions of America*, 2 vols. (New York: Harper and Brothers, 1854), 2: 376; and José María Gómez Colón, *Memoria sobre la utilidad del trabajo de la muger pobre en la isla de Cuba y medios para conseguirlo* (Havana: Imprenta de Manuel Soler, 1857), 49–50.

14. Gallenga, *Pearl*, 29.

15. Norman, *Rambles*, 29; George Augustus Henry Sala, *Under the Sun: Essays Mainly Written in Hot Countries* (London: Tinsley Brothers, 1872), 142; Julia Ward Howe, *A Trip to Cuba* (Boston: Ticknor and Fields, 1860; reprint, New York: Negro Universities Press, 1969), 43.

16. Maturin Murray Ballou, *Due South; or Cuba Past and Present* (Boston: Houghton, Mifflin, 1885; reprint, New York: Young People's Missionary Movement, 1910), 175; and Dana, *To Cuba*, 17.

17. Tanco Armero, "Isla de Cuba," 135; Philalethes, *Yankee Travels*, 16–19; [Hurlbert], *Gan-Eden*, 42; Samuel Hazard, *Cuba with Pen and Pencil* (Hartford, CT: Hartford Publishing, 1871), 161.

18. James J. O'Kelly, *The Mambí Land; or, Adventures of a Herald Correspondent in Cuba* (Philadelphia: J. B. Lippincott, 1874), 26; also see: [Wurdemann], *Notes on Cuba*, 42; and Gallenga, *Pearl*, 36.

19. Jay, *My Winter*, 204, 294.

20. Bremer, *Homes*, 2: 281.

21. James William Steele, *Cuban Sketches* (New York: Putnam's Sons, 1881), 214; and Howe, *Trip*, 43–44, 85.

22. Rachel Wilson Moore, *Journal of Rachel Moore, Kept during a Tour to the West Indies and South America, in 1863–64* (Philadelphia: T. E. Zell, 1867), 37; and Jay, *My Winter*, 70–71.

23. Howe, *Trip*, 44–45; other sources on *volantas*: Richard J. Levis, *Diary of a Spring Holiday in Cuba* (Philadelphia: Porter and Coates, 1872), 25; Ballou, *Due South*, 219–21; Anthony Trollope, *The West Indies and the Spanish Main* (reprint, London: Frank Cass, 1968), 144; Condesa de Merlín, *Viaje*, 210; Hazard, *Cuba*, 176–77; and Jay, *My Winter*, 48.

24. Hazard, *Cuba*, 158; and Jay, *My Winter*, 204, 294.

25. Henry Anthony Murray, *Lands of the Slave and the Free; or, Cuba, the United States, and Canada*, 2 vols. (London: J. W. Parker and Son, 1855), 1: 281–83; Jay, *My Winter*, 28–29; and Hazard, *Cuba*, 176–77.

26. Ballou, *Due South*, 219–29; Frances Erskine Calderón de la Barca, *Life in Mexico* (London: J. M. Dent and Sons, n.d.), 10; Murray, *Lands*, 1: 283; Bremer, *Homes*, 2: 266; and [Hurlbert], *Gan-Eden*, 10–11.

27. Sala, *Under the Sun*, 147; John Stevens Cabot Abbott, *South and North; or, Impressions Received during a Trip to Cuba and the South* (New York: Abbey & Abbot, 1860), 44; Jay, *My Winter*, 20–28; and James Mursell Phillippo, *The United States and Cuba* (London: Pewtress, 1857), 433, 31.

28. Condesa de Merlín, *Viaje*, 101–7; [Carlton H. Rogers], *Incidents of Travel in the Southern States and Cuba* (New York: R. Craighead, 1862), 81; and Sala, *Under the Sun*, 141.

29. Reau Campbell, *Around the Corner to Cuba* (New York: C. G. Crawford, 1889), 9.

30. Hazard, *Cuba*, 160–77; Levis, *Diary*, 25; Condesa de Merlín, *Viaje*, 210; Trollope, *West Indies*, 144–50; Tanco Armero, "Isla de Cuba," 131; and Gibbes, *Cuba for Invalids*, 11.

31. Ballou, *Due South*, 159; and Phillippo, *United States*, 432.

32. Jay, *My Winter*, 26–27; and Tudor, *Narrative*, 2: 116–17.

33. Philalethes, *Yankee Travels*, 189–90; William Cullen Bryant, *Letters of William Cullen Bryant*, 4 vols. (New York: Fordham University Press, 1975–1984), 3: 27–28; [Wurdemann], *Notes on Cuba*, 42; Campbell, *Around the Corner*, 28; and Jay, *My Winter*, 70.

34. Amelia Matilda Murray, *Letters from the United States, Cuba and Canada* (New York: Putnam, 1857), 244.

35. Hazard, *Cuba*, 157; Jay, *My Winter*, 30, 70; and Howe, *Trip*, 45.

36. Hazard, *Cuba*, 431; and [Wurdemann], *Notes on Cuba*, 22.

37. Silvia Arróm, *The Women of Mexico City* (Stanford, CA: Stanford

University Press, 1985), 65–66.

38. Captain-General Valentín Cañedo to the president of the Council of Ministers, July 5, 1853, Archivo Histórico Nacional, Madrid (hereinafter AHN), Ultramar, *legajo* 1683, file 28.

39. Condesa de Merlín, *Viaje*, 145.

40. Bryant, *Letters*, 3: 31; [Wurdemann], *Notes on Cuba*, 22; George W. Williams, *Sketches of Travel in the Old and New World* (Charleston: Walker, Evans & Cogswell, 1871), 13. Jay, *My Winter*, 167; and Ballou, *Due South*, 139.

41. Richard Burleigh Kimball, *Cuba and the Cubans; Comprising a History of the Island of Cuba, Its Present Social, Political and Domestic Conditions, etc.* (New York: Samuel Hueston, 1850), 153; Rogers, *Incidents*, 88; Jay, *My Winter*, 58. Also see priest of the Church of Monserrate to the captain-general of Cuba, September 1, 1868; and superior civilian governor of Cuba to the chief of police of Havana, September 3, 1868, both in ANC, Gobierno Superior Civil, *legajo* 743, file 25436.

42. Hazard, *Cuba*, 127; [Rogers], *Incidents*, 89. [Wurdemann], *Notes on Cuba*, 22; Jay, *My Winter*, 58; and Calderón de la Barca, *Life in Mexico*, 13.

43. Norman, *Rambles*, 101; and Jay, *My Winter*, 191.

44. Quotes from: Norman, *Rambles*, 38; Hazard, *Cuba*, 130; and Rogers, *Incidents*, 89.

45. Steele, *Cuban Sketches*, 175.

46. [Kimball], *Cuba*, 153.

47. Dana, *To Cuba*, 28–29; Hazard, *Cuba*, 184; and Steele, *Cuban Sketches*, 147.

48. Condesa de Merlín, *Viaje*, 208; Ballou, *Due South*, 136; Rogers, *Incidents*, 147; Ballou, *Due South*, 135–36; [Wurdemann], *Notes on Cuba*, 82–83; Rogers, *Incidents*, 85; Philalethes, *Yankee Travels*, 201; Gibbes, *Cuba for Invalids*, 39; Bryant, *Letters*, 3: 28; Mark, *Diary*, 66; and Phillippo, *United States*, 430.

49. Hazard, *Cuba*, 404.

50. J. T. O'Neil, "Porto Rico," in Richard S. Fisher, ed., *The Spanish West Indies: Cuba and Porto Rico* (New York: J. H. Colton, 1861), 153; Philalethes, *Yankee Travels*, 18; Murray, *Lands*, 1: 289; Steele, *Cuban Sketches*, 58–59; Kimball, *Cuba and the Cubans*, 147: de las Barras y Prado, *Memorias*, 91; and Ballou, *Due South*, 128.

51. O'Neil, "Porto Rico," 153; Philalethes, *Yankee Travels*, 18; Murray, *Lands*, 1: 289; Steele, *Cuban Sketches*, 58–59; Kimball, *Cuba and the Cubans*, 147; de las Barras y Prado, *Memorias*, 91; Ballou, *Due South*, 128; and Hazard, *Cuba*, 420–21.

52. Hazard, *Cuba*, 300; Ballou, *Due South*, 136; and Jay, *My Winter*, 82.

53. Hazard, *Cuba*, 300.

54. Beth K. Miller, "Avellaneda, Nineteenth-Century Feminist," *Revista/Review Interamericana* 4 (Summer 1974), 177–83.

55. [Rogers], *Incidents*, 85; and Henry Ashworth, *A Tour in the United States, Cuba, and Canada* (London: A. W. Bennett, 1861), 50.

56. García de Arboleya, *Manual*, 176; and Howe, *Trip*, 146.

57. Jay, *My Winter*, 208; and Tudor, *Narrative*, 2: 121.

58. Martínez-Alier, *Marriage*, 71–99; Gómez Colón, *Memoria*, 49–50; and de las Barras y Prado, *Memorias*, 115.

59. Jorge Domínguez, *Insurrection or Loyalty: The Breakdown of the Spanish American Empire* (Cambridge, MA: Harvard University Press, 1980), 19; García de Arboleya, *Manual*, 304; Howe, *Trip*, 202; Steele, *Cuban Sketches*, 141; and Ballou, *Due South*, 128.

60. Steele, *Cuban Sketches*, 139.

61. Howe, *Trip*, 83.

62. Steele, *Cuban Sketches*, 63.

Chapter 4

1. There exists a modest body of published sources on Protestantism in the nineteenth-century Hispanic Caribbean. Most of it examines the post-1869 period. The best general source on Cuba is Marcos Antonio Ramos, *Panorama del protestantismo en Cuba* (San José, Costa Rica: Editorial Caribe, 1986). See Justo L. González, *The Development of Christianity in the Latin Caribbean* (Grand Rapids, MI: Wm. B. Eerdmans, 1969); Harold Greer, "Baptists in Western Cuba," *Cuban Studies* 19 (1989): 61–77; and Luis Martínez-Fernández, "'Don't Die Here': The Death and Burial of Protestants in the Hispanic Caribbean, 1840–1885," *The Americas* 49:1 (July 1992): 23–47.

2. See, for example, Archivo Histórico Diocesano de la Archidiócesis de San Juan (hereinafter cited as AHDASJ), Justicia, Procesos Legales, Certificaciones de Soltería, Ponce, *legajo* J-182; and various documents in Archivo del Arzobispado de La Habana (hereinafter cited as AALH).

3. See Puerto Rico's 1815 Cédula de Gracias in *Boletín Histórico de Puerto Rico*, ed. Cayetano Coll y Toste, 14 vols. (San Juan: Tipografía Cantero Fernández, 1914–1927), 1: 297–304; and Cuba's "Real Cédula de 21 de octubre de 1817, sobre aumentar la población blanca de la isla de Cuba," ANC, Gobierno Superior Civil, *le-*

gajo 1657, file 82745. Also see Francisco Ramos, *Prontuario de dis-pociciones oficiales. Disposiciones más notables del Gobierno Superior desde 1824 a 1865* (San Juan: Imprenta de González, 1866), 212–16.

4. French settlers in Vieques reportedly lived many years on the island without seeking domiciliation. Governor of Puerto Rico to the Spanish Minister of Government, November 18, 1851, CIH, Transcripts of papers relating to Vieques, 209–10.

5. In 1876, there were 811 foreigners among the 33,514 residents of Ponce. See Eduardo Gandía Neumann, *Verdadera y auténtica historia de la ciudad de Ponce desde sus primitivos tiempos hasta la época contemporánea* (San Juan: n.p., 1913), 85; Scarano, *Sugar and Slavery,* 81–82; Ivette Pérez Vega, "Las oleadas de inmigración sobre el sur de Puerto Rico: El caso de las sociedades mercantiles creadas en Ponce (1816–1830)," *Revista del Centro de Estudios Avanzados de Puerto Rico y el Caribe* 9 (January–June 1987): 114–23; Padrón de productos y capitales, Ponce, 1869–1870, and Riqueza territorial, 1871–1872, both in Archivo Histórico de Ponce (hereinafter cited as AHP) *legajo* 31, boxes 30A and 30C; Secretaría del Gobierno Superior Civil de la Isla de Puerto Rico, *Registro central de esclavos* (*6to. Depto.*) (San Juan, 1872) (microfilm at CIH); and Andrés A. Ramos Mattei, *Hacienda azucarera*, 22.

6. Albert E. Lee, *An Island Grows: Memoirs of Albert E. Lee, Puerto Rico, 1872–1942* (San Juan: Lee and Son, 1963), 3.

7. Of a total of 227 foreigners (1838), race was determined for 208, of whom 127 were white and 81 were *pardos*. Statistics for 1838 in Archivo General de Puerto Rico, San Juan (hereinafter cited as AGPR), Gobernadores Españoles, Ponce, box 14.

8. *La Gaceta de Puerto Rico*, December 28, 1872, 3. On Vieques, see Juan Amédée Bonnet Benítez, *Vieques en la historia de Puerto Rico*, 2d ed. (San Juan: F. Ortiz Nieves, 1977); Antonio Rivera Martínez, *Así empezó Vieques* (Río Piedras: La Universidad de Puerto Rico, 1963); Robert Rabin Siegal, "Los tortoleños: Obreros de Barlovento en Vieques: 1864–1874, " in Archivo Histórico de Vieques (hereinafter cited as AHV); and Ramos Mattei, "Importación de trabajadores," 125–42.

9. Edward Kenney to Bishop Whittingham, April 1, 1876, Maryland Diocesan Archives, Baltimore (hereinafter cited as MDA), Cuba, folder V; Gobierno de Cuba, *Cuadro estadístico de la siempre fiel Isla de Cuba, correspondiente al año 1846* (Havana: Imprenta del Gobierno y Capitanía General, 1847), 69, 77; Register of Americans [in Cuba] from January 1, 1871, to December 31, 1871, NA,

RG 84, Havana, c.14.1.

10. Domiciliation files for 1855 in ANC, Gobierno Superior Civil, *legajo* 796, file 27003; Registry of non-domiciled foreigners, Archivo Histórico Provincial de Matanzas (hereinafter cited as AHPM), Negociado de Órden Público y Policía, *legajo* 58, file 6001; Register of Americans [in Cuba] from January 1, 1871, to December 1, 1871, NA, RG 84, Havana, c.14.1; Paquette, *Sugar*, 187; Edward Kenney to Bishop Whittingham, April 1, 1876, MDA, Cuba folder V.

11. Consul Helm cited in Pérez, *On Becoming Cuban*, 23.

12. For information on the life of foreigners in Havana and El Cerro, see Luis Martínez-Fernández, *Fighting Slavery in the Caribbean: The Life and Times of a British Family in Nineteenth-Century Havana* (Armonk, NY: M. E. Sharpe, 1998). See Roberto Gómez Reyero, "Informe histórico sobre la casa # 256 de la Calle Tulipán entre Santa Catalina y Falgueras. Cerro," Archivo del Museo del Cerro, Havana (hereinafter cited as AMC), file 4,1,10.

13. Andrew Blythe to William Cass, July 20, 1857, NA, RG 59, Despatches from U.S. Consuls in Havana, microfilm roll T20, vol. 36; Pérez, *On Becoming Cuban*, 23. Estimate for Puerto Rico based on sixteen men per ship and data from Charles De Ronceray to Cass, July 29, 1859, United States, Department of State, San Juan Consulate, *Despachos de los cónsules norteamericanos en Puerto Rico (1818–1868)*, ed. CIH, (Río Piedras: Editorial de la Universidad de Puerto Rico, 1982), 390.

14. Consul-General Joseph T. Crawford to Lord Palmerston, 22 January 1852, Public Record Office, Kew, UK (hereinafter cited as PRO), Foreign Office (hereinafter cited as FO), 72, 866; Domiciliation documents of George Booth and Guillaume Perrone, ANC, Gobierno Superior Civil, *legajo* 1656, file 82742; Domiciliation documents of David Clark, idem, *legajo* 787, file 26754; testimony of Luis Mariátegui on behalf of Juan Emilio Beylle, AALH, Matrimonios Ultramarinos, file 25 (January 1841).

15. Grace Backhouse to Catherine Backhouse, January 6, 1854, and George Backhouse to his aunt, August 3, 1853, in John Backhouse Papers, Special Collections Department, Perkins Library, Duke University, Durham, NC (hereinafter cited as Backhouse Papers). Also see domiciliation papers of Mary Callaghan, ANC, Gobierno Superior Civil, *legajo* 791, file 26855, and of Jorge Y. Finlay, AHDASJ, Justicia, Procesos Legales, Certificaciones de Soltería, Ponce, *legajo* J-182.

16. David Turnbull, *Travels in the West; Cuba with Notices of Porto*

Rico and the Slave Trade (London: n.p., 1840; reprint, New York: Negro Universities Press, 1968), 67; Declaration of Jorge Y. Finlay, AHDASJ, Justicia, Procesos Legales, Certificados de Soltería, Ponce, *legajo* J-182; James Kennedy to Lord Palmerston, June 21, 1850, and Crawford to Lord Palmerston, January 22, 1852, both in PRO, FO 72, 886; and Spanish minister of Gracia y Justicia to the president of the Spanish Council of Ministers, Transcripts of papers pertaining to Vieques, CIH, 267–72.

17. Joseph John Gurney, *A Winter in the West Indies* (London: J. Murray, 1840), 211; Moore, *Journal*, 32; George Backhouse to his Aunt, August 3, 1853, Diary of Grace M. Backhouse, March 25–27, April 10, June 9, 1853, and April 9, 1854, Backhouse Papers; and Jay, *My Winter*, 157.

18. Ramos, *Panorama*, 78; Diary of Grace Backhouse, February 4, 11, and 18, March 4, 1855, Backhouse Papers; [Rogers], *Incidents*, 173–75; Murray, *Letters*, 257; and Diary of William Norwood, March 24, 1844, Virginia Historical Society, Richmond.

19. Grace Backhouse to Mary Backhouse, 30 June 1853, Backhouse Papers; Hiram H. Hulse, "The History of the Church in Cuba," *Historical Magazine of the Protestant Episcopal Church* 6:2 (June 1937): 249; (1971); and George A. Leakin to Dear Madam, March 16, 1906, Archives of the Episcopal Church, Austin, TX, Cuba Scrapbook.

20. Books of Baptisms of Ponce's Roman Catholic Church, microfilms at CIH.

21. Grace Backhouse to her mother-in-law, March 3, 1854, Backhouse Papers; baptismal entry of Gustavo Runge, July 14, 1858, Book of Baptisms no. 3, Iglesia Salvador del Mundo, El Cerro, Havana; Rev. Kenney's Report of 1874 in Edward Kenney, *Report of Our Mission in Cuba: October 1874–October 1877* (Detroit: Diocesan Printing Office, 1878), 15; and Books of Baptisms of Vieques's Roman Catholic Church, microfilms at CIH.

22. Lee, *An Island Grows*, 5; and Grace Backhouse to Catherine Backhouse, March 25, 1855, Backhouse Papers.

23. AHDASJ, Justicia, Procesos Legales, Papeles de Extranjeros, *legajo* J-229; and idem, Justicia, Procesos Legales, Certificados de Soltería, Ponce, *legajo* J-182.

24. Lourdes Sampera González, "Breve reseña: La Parroquia el Salvador del Mundo del Cerro," file 6,1,1, AMC.

25. See Circular by Bishop Gil Esteve, December 23, 1852, AHDASJ, Gobierno, Circulares; also see files in AHDASJ, Justicia, Procesos Legales, Certificaciones de Soltería, *legajos* J-181 and J-182; and

AALH, Matrimonios Ultramarinos.

26. Books of Marriages of Ponce's Roman Catholic Church, microfilms at CIH; AHDASJ, Justicia, Procesos Legales, Certificaciones de Soltería, *legajos* J-181 and J-182.

27. Books of Marriages of the Roman Catholic Church of Vieques, microfilms at CIH; Declaration of the parish priest of Vieques (1851), CIH, Transcripts of papers pertaining to Vieques.

28. Kenney, *Report*, 12; Kenney to Whittingham, November 25, 1873, MDA, Cuba folder IV; Grace Backhouse to her mother-in-law, March 3, 1854, Backhouse Papers; marriage entry of Carolina Smith and Francisco Javier Molina y García, Book of Marriages no. 2, Iglesia Salvador del Mundo, El Cerro, Havana.

29. Lee, *An Island Grows*, 5, 9; de las Barras y Prado, *Memorias*, 84; Jay, *My Winter*, 128; Marriage records of All Saints Church of St. Thomas, microfilms at Williams Library, St. Croix, U.S. Virgin Islands (hereinafter cited as WL).

30. AGPR, Audiencia Territorial, Acuerdo Real, box 34, file 19; parish priest of Vieques to the bishop of Puerto Rico, March 12, 1857, AHDASJ, Gobierno, Correspondencia Parroquia-Obispo, Vieques, *legajo* G-29; Books of Marriages of the Dutch Reformed Church of Christiansted, St. Croix (microfilms at WL); Ramos, *Prontuario*, 313.

31. D. Ramón Hernández Poggio, *Aclimatación é higiene de los europeos en Cuba* (Cádiz, Spain: Imprenta de la Revista Médica, 1874), 67–70; Marte, *Cuba*, 191; Consul Robertson to William Marcy, July 27, 1854, NA, RG 59, Dispatches from U.S. Consuls in Havana, microfilm roll T20, vol. 28; Ballou, *Due South*, 141; and De Ronceray to William Cass, December 3, 1860, United States, Department of State, *Despachos*, 308.

32. Steele, *Cuban Sketches*, 185; and [Hurlbert], *Gan-Eden*, 136–37.

33. Blythe to Cass, July 20, 1857, NA, Dispatches from U.S. Consuls in Havana, microfilm roll T20, vol. 36; Williams, *Sketches*, 55; and Dana, *To Cuba*, 102–3.

34. Steele, *Sketches*, 174; Philalethes, *Yankee Travels*, 222, 251; Ramos, *Panorama*, 77; and Alexander Jourdan to William Seward, June 2 and July 19, 1866, United States, Department of State, *Despachos consulares*, 707, 719.

35. *El Boletín Eclesiástico de Puerto Rico* 1:19 (October 1, 1859), 219; Roura and Hernández to the bishop of Puerto Rico, April 28, 1887, AHDASJ, Justicia, Procesos Legales, Validación de Matrimonios, *legajo* J-218; Book of Baptisms no. 4, Iglesia Salvador del Mundo, El Cerro; Ramos, *Panorama*, 140; and Books of Defunctions of

Ponce's Roman Catholic Church (microfilms at CIH).
36. AHP, Índice del Cementerio Antiguo, vol. 1, 166; capitán pedáneo de San Lázaro to the captain-general, December 22, 1849, ANC, Gobierno Superior Civil, *legajo* 745, file 25568; and letter of 1853 quoted in Mariano Torrente, *Política ultramarina que abraza todos los puntos referentes a las relaciones de España con los Estados Unidos, con Inglaterra y las Antillas* (Madrid: Compañía General de Impresores y Libreros del Reino, 1854), 198–99.
37. Marrero, *Cuba*, 14: 88; Minutes on Protestant Cemetery, November 8, 1841, AHP; Ángel Cowley of la Junta Superior de Sanidad to the gobernador superior civil, February 17, 1847, and capitán pedáneo de San Lázaro to the capitán general, December 22, 1849, ANC, Gobierno Superior Civil, *legajo* 744, file 25546 and *legajo* 745, file 25568.
38. David Turnbull to the captain-general of Cuba, September 16, 1841, ANC, Gobierno Superior Civil, *legajo* 744, file 25346; and Levis, *Diary*, 108-9.
39. Bishop Young, "Cuba," *Spirit of Missions* 49 (October 1884), 486–87; governor of Matanzas to the parish priest of Matanzas, September 15, 1841, AHPM, Gobierno Provincial, Negociado de Órden Público y Policía, *legajo* 74, file 8349.
40. Blythe to Cass, July 20, 1857; Belot to Charles Helm, April 28, 1860; and Helm to Cass, April 28, 1860, NA, RG 59, Despatches from U.S. Consuls in Havana, microfilm rolls T20, vols. 36, and 40.
41. Acting Consul Jourdan to Seward, July 27, 1854, NA, RG 84, San Juan, vol. 7228; George Coggeshall, *Voyages to Various Parts of the World Made between the Years 1800 and 1831* (New York: D. Appleton, 1853), 144–45; and AHP, *legajo* 35, file 14.
42. Asiento de difuntos protestantes en la isla de Vieques desde 1 de septiembre de 1845, Registro del Gobernador de Vieques, 1838–1845, CIH, vol. 4, copy in AHV; and Budget for the Vieques government, 1879–1880, AGPR, Vieques, box 5, file 41A.

Chapter 5

1. See, for example, Ramos Mattei, *Betances*, 5, 11; Miguel Ángel Monclús, *El caudillismo en la República Dominicana*, 4th ed. (Santo Domingo, DR: Universidad CETEC, 1983), *passim*; William Javier Nelson, "The Haitian Political Situation and Its Effect on the Dominican Republic: 1849–1877," *The Americas* 45:2 (October 1988): 227–35; and Detlev Julio K. Peukert, "Anhelo de dependencia: Las ofertas de anexión de la República Dominicana a los Estados Uni-

dos en el siglo XIX," *Jahrbuch fur Geschichte von Staat, Wirtschaft und Gesellschaft Lateinamerikas* 23 (1986): 305–30.

2. Frank Moya Pons, *Manual de historia dominicana*, 8th ed. (Santiago, DR: Universidad Católica Madre y Maestra, 1984), 268–70.

3. Moya Pons, *Manual*, 276. French consul at Santo Domingo to the French minister of foreign affairs, January 20, 1848, and January 24, 1849, in Emilio Rodríguez Demorizi, ed., *Correspondencia del consul de Francia en Santo Domingo, 1846–1850*, 2 vols. (Santo Domingo, DR: Editora Montalvo, 1944–1947), 2: 34–38, 112–13; text of treaty signed October 22, 1848, in República Dominicana, *Colección de leyes, decretos y resoluciones* (Santo Domingo, DR: Publicaciones ONAP, 1982–), 2: 172–83.

4. Governor of Puerto Rico to Antonio de Benavides, May 18 and October 11, 1847, AHN, Ultramar, *legajo* 3524, files 43, 47; and congressional proclamation in Roberto Marte, *Estadísticas y documentos históricos sobre Santo Domingo (1805–1890)* (Santo Domingo, DR: Museo Nacional de Historia y Geografía, 1984), 115–18.

5. Report of John Hogan to James Buchanan, October 4, 1845, in Alfonso Lockward, ed., *Documentos para la historia de las relaciones dominico americanas (1837–1860)* (Santo Domingo, DR: Editora Corripio, 1987), 1: 54; Charles C. Tansill, *The United States and Santo Domingo, 1798–1873* (Baltimore: Johns Hopkins University Press, 1938), 134; and Secretary John M. Clayton to Benjamin Green, June 13, 1849 (confidential), NA, RG 59, Records of Special Missions, vol. 152.

6. Moya Pons, *Manual*, 289–90.

7. Emilio Rodríguez Demorizi, ed., *Documentos para la historia de la República Dominicana*, 4 vols. (Santo Domingo, DR: Editora Montalvo, 1944–1981), 1: 35–40; and Moya Pons, *Manual*, 291–95.

8. Dominican envoys to the French minister of foreign affairs, March 30, 1848; French consul at Santo Domingo to the French minister of foreign affairs, January 20, 1848; and Dominican envoys to the French minister of foreign affairs, July 23, 1848, all in Rodríguez Demorizi, ed., *Correspondencia* 2: 43–45, 34–38, 94; and Dominican minister of foreign relations to the French consul, October 18, 1849, cited in Vetilio Alfau Durán, ed., *Controversia histórica: polémica de Santana* (Santo Domingo, DR: Editora Montalvo, 1968), 118.

9. See Duff Green and Benjamin Green to the Dominican government, August 26, 1850, in Marte, *Estadísticas*, 61.

10. French consul at Santo Domingo to the French minister of foreign

affairs, April 2, 1850, and French consul at Port-au-Prince to the French minister of foreign affairs, April 30, 1850, both in Rodríguez Demorizi, ed., *Correspondencia* 2: 223–27, 234.

11. Green to Clayton, September 27, 1849, in Lockward, ed., *Documentos*, 1: 92; and Jaime de Jesús Domínguez, *Economía y política: República Dominicana, 1844–1861* (Santo Domingo, DR: Editora de la UASD, 1977), 110.

12. Sumner Welles, *Naboth's Vineyard: The Dominican Republic, 1844–1924*, 2 vols. (New York: Payton and Clarke, 1928), 1: 102.

13. José M. Pando to Valentín Cañedo, August 7, 1852, AHN, Ultramar, *legajo* 3524, file 56bis, document 1; see also document 4, copies at CIH.

14. Communication of the president of the Council of Ministers, November 24, 1852, AHN, Ultramar, *legajo* 3524, file 64, document 1, copy at CIH.

15. Welles, *Naboth's Vineyard* 1: 110.

16. Moya Pons, *Manual*, 304–5.

17. Dominican Council of Ministers to the governor of Puerto Rico, April 4, 1849, AHN, Ultramar, *legajo* 3524, file 52, document 2, copy at CIH; and Báez to the French consul at Santo Domingo, April 19, 1849, in Rodríguez Demorizi, ed., *Correspondencia*, 2: 140.

18. Valentina Peguero and Danilo de los Santos, *Visión general de la historia dominicana*, 10th ed. (Santiago, DR: Universidad Católica Madre y Maestra, 1986), 191–93; French consul at Santo Domingo to the French minister of foreign affairs, June 1 and October 18, 1849, in Rodríguez Demorizi, ed., *Correspondencia*, 2: 153, 187; Alfau Durán, ed., *Controversia histórica*, 94; Jonathan Elliot to the U.S. secretary of state, May 2, 1849, in Lockward, ed., *Documentos*, 1: 82–83; and Lockward, ed., *Documentos* 1: xxiv, 106–7.

19. Emilio Rodríguez Demorizi, *Santana y los poetas de su tiempo* (Santo Domingo, DR: Academia Dominicana de La Historia, 1969), 74.

20. Nelson, "Haitian Political Situation," 232; and Peguero and de los Santos, *Visión general*, 196.

21. Marcy to William Cazneau, November 2, 1853, RG 59, Special Missions, vol. 154. For a discussion of North America's expansionist agenda in the Dominican Republic and the role played by William and Jane Cazneau see Robert E. May, "Lobbyists for Commercial Empire: Jane Cazneau, William Cazneau, and U.S. Caribbean Policy, 1846–1878," *Pacific Historical Review* 48:3 (1979): 383–412, and Robert E. May, "'Plenipotentiary in Petticoats': Jane

M. Cazneau and American Foreign Policy in the Mid-Nineteenth Century," in *Women and American Foreign Policy: Lobbyists, Critics, and Insiders*, ed. Edward P. Crapol (New York: Greenwood, 1987), 19–44.

22. Marcy to Cazneau, June 17, 1854, and Consul Segovia to Santana, January 28, 1856, in Rodríguez Demorizi, ed., *Documentos*, 1: 28, 2: 192–94.

23. Cazneau to Marcy, September 23, 1854, and December 6, 1854, in Lockward, ed., *Documentos* 1: 242–43, 256–59.

24. San Just to Captain-General de la Concha, December 10, 1854, AHN, Ultramar, *legajo* 3524, file 93; Lord Aberdeen to Lord Clarendon, November 5, 1854, and first lord of the admiralty to Lord Clarendon, October 24, 1854, cited in Richard W. van Alstyne, ed., "Anglo-American Relations, 1853–57," *American Historical Review* 42:3 (April 1937), 497–98.

25. Report of Hogan to Buchanan, October 4, 1845, NA, RG 59, Communications from Special Agents, vol. 13; David Dixon Porter, "Diario de una misión secreta a Santo Domingo [1846]," quoted in Lockward, ed., *Documentos* 1: li; Green to Clayton, August 27, 1849, NA, RG 59, Communications from Special Agents, vol. 15; and Green to Clayton, October 14, 1849, cited in Lockward, ed., *Documentos* 1: 111.

26. Cazneau to Marcy, July 24, 1854, in Lockward, ed., *Documentos* 1: 230–32; and May, "'Plenipotentiary,'" 27.

27. Robert Schomburgk to Lord Clarendon, December 18, 1854, quoted in Tansill, *United States*, 197; and Juan de Abril to Fernando de Norzagaray, November 6, 1854, AHN, Ultramar, *legajo* 3524, file 89.

28. Cazneau's letter of October 20, 1854, published in *El Porvenir*, October 22, 1854; Juan N. Tejera to Marcy, December 13, 1854; and Marcy to Elliot, October 9, 1855; in Lockward, ed., *Documentos*, 1: 259–63, 282–83; and San Just to de la Concha, February 13, 1855; and December 7, 1854; AHN, Ultramar, *legajo* 3524, file 101, and *legajo* 3524, file 93.

29. French Consul Pierre Levasseur to the French minister of foreign affairs, April 1848, in Rodríguez Demorizi, ed., *Correspondencia*, 2: 61; Welles, *Naboth's Vineyard*, 1: 156; J. Francisco Pacheco to Manuel Dionisio Cruzat, November 4, 1854, AHN, Ultramar, *legajo* 3524, file 86; and Instructions to San Just, quoted in Luis Álvarez López, "Historia de la anexión de Santo Domingo a España, 1861–1863" (M.A. thesis, Universidad de Puerto Rico, 1977), 56–57.

30. Cazneau to Marcy, December 26, 1854, in Lockward, ed., *Documentos*, 1: 274; Cazneau to Marcy, June 9, 1855, NA, RG 59, Communications, vol. 19; and Cazneau to Quitman, April 25, 1856, in John A. Quitman, *Speech of John A. Quitman, of Mississippi on the Subject of the Neutrality Laws: April 29, 1856* (Washington, DC: Union Office, 1856), 20–21.
31. P. Darasse and Schomburgk to Santana, December 14, 1854, in Lockward, ed., *Documentos*, 1: 275–76.
32. Cazneau to Marcy, June 9, 1855, and Marcy to Cazneau, December 18, 1854, in Lockward, ed., *Documentos*, 1: 280, 264.
33. J. Francisco Pacheco to San Just, September 11, 1854; president of the Spanish Council of Ministers to the Spanish overseas minister, March 16, 1854, AHN, Ultramar, *legajo* 3524, files 77, 72; de Norzagaray to the Spanish minister of state, July 1, 1854, AHN, Ultramar, *legajo* 3524, file 75; and Fernando de Norzagaray, "Diario del gobernador Norzagaray," *Anales de Investigación Histórica* 6:1 (January–June 1979), 109, 112.
34. De Abril to de la Concha, October 7, 1854, AHN, Ultramar, *legajo* 3524, file 81; Carlos F. Pérez, *Historia diplomática de Santo Domingo (1492–1861)* (Santo Domingo, DR: Escuela de Servicios Internacionales, Universidad Nacional Pedro Henríquez Ureña, 1973), 286–88; Spanish minister of state to San Just, September 11, 1854, AHN, Ultramar, *legajo* 3524, file 77; San Just to de la Concha, February 2, 1855, AHN, Ultramar, *legajo* 3524, file 101; and San Just to the governor of Puerto Rico, February 13, 1855, AHN, Ultramar, *legajo* 3524, file 99.
35. Spanish minister of state to Matías Ramón Mella, February 18, 1854, in David G. Yungling, ed., *Highlights in the Debates in the Spanish Chamber of Deputies Relative to the Abandonment of Santo Domingo* (Washington, DC: Murray & Heister, 1941), 146; and Mella to Santana, March 1, 1854, in Rodríguez Demorizi, ed., *Documentos*, 2: 158–60.
36. Welles, *Naboth's Vineyard*, 1: 155.
37. Elliot to Daniel Webster, January 17, 1853, in Lockward, ed., *Documentos*, 1: 206–7 (italics added). Monclús, *Caudillismo*, 21–22.
38. Cazneau to Marcy, June 9, 1855, and Elliot to Marcy, September 10, 1856, in Lockward, ed., *Documentos*, 1: 278–80, 291.
39. Cazneau to Cass, July 2, 1859, in Lockward, ed., *Documentos*, 1: 332; San Just to the governor of Puerto Rico, October 20, 1855, and San Just to the captain-general of Cuba, February 7, 1855, AHN, Ultramar, *legajo* 3524, files 116 and 101 (italics in original).
40. For documents pertaining to the rivalry between Santana and Báez,

see Santana's proclamation of July 3, 1853, and Báez's proclamation of August 1, 1853, in Rodríguez Demorizi, ed., *Documentos*, 1: 272–82, 291–322; and Roberto Cassá, *Historia social y económica de la República Dominicana*, 10th ed., 2 vols. (Santo Domingo, DR: Alfa y Omega, 1991), 2: 58.

41. British consul to the Dominican minister of foreign relations, November 23, 1849, in Rodríguez Demorizi, ed., *Correspondencia*, 2: 196; also see Báez's inaugural speech (1849) quoted in Cassá, *Historia*, 2: 52.

42. Rodríguez Demorizi, ed., *Documentos* 1: 276–79; Emilio Rodríguez Demorizi, ed., *Papeles de Santana* (Rome: Tipografía G. Menaglia, 1952), 107–18; Rodríguez Demorizi, *Santana y los poetas*, 101; and Peguero and de los Santos, *Visión general*, 197–98.

43. Expulsion decrees against Baecistas in, República Dominicana, *Colección de leyes*, 2: 524–27; Elliot to Cass, November 27, 1853, quoted in Tansill, *United States*, 175; Jaime de Jesús Domínguez, *La anexión de la República Dominicana a España* (Santo Domingo, DR: Editora de la UASD, 1979), 45; Domínguez, *Economía y política*, 135; and Rodríguez Demorizi, *Santana y los poetas*, 159.

44. Jacob Pereira (interim U.S. commercial agent) to Marcy, August 7, 1856, in Lockward, ed., *Documentos*, 1: 286–87. See *Gaceta Oficial de Santo Domingo*, January 30, 1855.

45. Spanish commercial agent to the captain-general of Cuba, May 28, 1855, AHN, Ultramar, *legajo* 3524, files 109, 110.

46. Moya Pons, *Manual*, 324–26.

47. Proclamation of Báez, October 9, 1856, in Rodríguez Demorizi, ed., *Documentos*, 1: 353; and Pereira to Marcy, October 30 and November 22, 1856, in Lockward, ed., *Documentos*, 1: 292–301.

48. Báez to the captain-general of Puerto Rico, July 12, 1857, quoted in Pérez, *Historia diplomática*, 335; Félix María del Monte to Cass, May 7, 1857, in Lockward, ed., *Documentos*, 1: 306–8; and del Monte to Cass, May 6, 1857, NA, RG 59, Notes from the Legation of the Dominican Republic in the United States, vol. 1.

49. For peace terms, see República Dominicana, *Colección de leyes* 3: 521–22. Copy of agreement in AHN, Ultramar, *legajo* 3525, file 4, document 2 (copy at CIH); also see *La Crónica de Ambos Mundos*, June 5, 1863, in Emilio Rodríguez Demorizi, ed., *Papeles de Buenaventura Báez* (Santo Domingo, DR: Editora Montalvo, 1969) 169–73; and Elliot to Cass, March 21, 1859, quoted in Tansill, *United States*, 207–8.

50. Perkins, *Monroe Doctrine*, 284–85; and Herminio Portell-Vilá, *Historia de Cuba en sus relaciones con los Estados Unidos y España*, 4

vols. (Havana: Montero, 1938–1941), 2: 153.

51. Charles C. Hauch, "Attitudes of Foreign Governments towards the Spanish Reoccupation of the Dominican Republic," *HAHR* 27:2 (May 1947): 247–68.

52. Report of Mariano Álvarez, April 20, 1860, and report of Antonio Peláez Campomanes, November 8, 1860, in Emilio Rodríguez Demorizi, ed., *Antecedentes de la anexión a España* (Santo Domingo, DR: Academia Dominicana de la Historia, 1955), 100, 113–15.

53. Santana's proclamations of February 15, 1853, and July 16, 1861, in Rodríguez Demorizi, ed., *Documentos*, 1: 267, 2: 393–94.

54. Santana quoted in Rafael Vival, "Prologue," to Pedro María Archambault, *Historia de la Restauración* (Paris: Librairie Technique et Economique, 1938; reprint, Santo Domingo, DR: Biblioteca, Taller, 1973), xiii. See [A. A. Guridi], *Santo Domingo y España* (New York, 1864), reproduced in Rodríguez Demorizi, ed., *Antecedentes*, 355; and Gregorio Luperón, *Notas autobiográficas y apuntes históricos sobre la República Dominicana*, 2d ed., 3 vols. (Santiago, DR: Editorial El Diario, 1939), 1: 81.

55. José de la Gándara y Navarro, *La anexión y guerra de Santo Domingo*, 2 vols. (Madrid: El Correo Militar, 1884), 1: 224; and Report of General Luis J. Golfín, 1861, in Emilio Rodríguez Demorizi, ed., *Samaná, pasado y porvenir* (Santo Domingo, DR: Editora Montalvo, 1945), 162.

56. Report of Captain-General Serrano, September 5, 1861, in Rodríguez Demorizi, ed., *Antecedentes*, 250. See also Archivo General de la Nación, Santo Domingo (hereinafter AGNRD), La Anexión a España (hereinafter Anexión), *legajo* 7, file 2. See Luperón, *Notas autobiográficas* 1: 82; and George A. Lockward, *El protestantismo en Dominicana*, 2d ed. (Santo Domingo, DR: Universidad CETEC, 1982), 129–30.

57. De la Gándara y Navarro, *Anexión* 1: 223–29, 459; [Guridi], *Santo Domingo*, in Rodríguez Demorizi, ed., *Antecedentes*, 356; and orders for the general intendant of the army, February 10, 1863, AGNRD, Anexión, *legajo* 5 and *legajo* 7, document 4.

58. De la Gándara y Navarro, *Anexión*, 1: 223, 228–29; Pedro Santana, "Relación nominal de los eclesiásticos que cooperan con la anexión de Santo Domingo," in Rodríguez Demorizi, ed., *Antecedentes*, 308–9; Father Arturo Meriño to Father Carlos Nouel, September 27, 1902, in Rodríguez Demorizi, ed., *Papeles de Santana*, 262; Domínguez, *Anexión*, 113, 122.

59. Moya Pons, *Manual*, 343.

60. Decree of June 18, 1861, in República Dominicana, *Colección de*

leyes, 4: 155–56.

61. Moya Pons, *Manual*, 350.

62. Proclamation of Geffrard, March 18, 1861, quoted in de la Gándara y Navarro, *Anexión*, 1: 418.

63. *La Crónica de Ambos Mundos*, July 2, 1861; Domínguez, *Anexión*, 151, 264; and Esteban de la Puente García, "1861–1865: anexión y abandono de Santo Domingo," *Revista de Indias* 22:89–90 (1962), 463.

64. Annexation proved particularly detrimental to the interests of the tobacco sector. Marte, *Cuba*, 317, 326–27. See, for example, governor of Santo Domingo to the Spanish overseas minister, September 3, 1863; Gabriel García Tassara to the Spanish minister of state, November 9, 1863; related correspondence, AHN, Ultramar, *legajo* 3525, files 28 and 109, and *legajo* 5088, file 27.

65. For an English translation of the debate, see Yungling, ed., *Highlights*.

66. James D. Richardson, ed., *A Compilation of the Messages and Papers of the Presidents, 1789–1897*, 10 vols. (Washington, DC: Government Printing Office, 1896–1899), 4: 688–89; and Ernest N. Paolino, *The Foundations of the American Empire: William Henry Seward and U.S. Foreign Policy* (Ithaca, NY: Cornell University Press, 1973).

67. Report of January 5, 1867, AHN, Ultramar, *legajo* 5094, file 46; Tansill, *United States*, 241–45; William Seward to Frederick Seward, December 17, 1866, NA, RG 59, Special Missions, vol. 153; and Theodore Clarke Smith, "Expansion after the Civil War, 1865-71," *Political Science Quarterly* 16:3 (1901): 412–36.

68. Tansill, *United States*, 361–63; George N. Robeson to Commander E. K. Owen, July 10, 1869, in Welles, *Naboth's Vineyard*, 1: 370–71; and Admiral Poor to Robeson, March 11, 1870, in Emilio Rodríguez Demorizi, ed., *Proyecto para la incorporación de Santo Domingo a Norte América* (Santo Domingo, DR: Editora Montalvo, 1945), 362.

69. Robeson to Poor, January 29, 1870, and Poor to Saget, February 10, 1870, in Rodríguez Demorizi, ed., *Proyecto*, 356–57.

70. For information on the company's bondholders and a copy of the lease see Luperón, *Notas*, 2: 172–75, 203–5. Rodríguez Demorizi, ed., *Samaná*, 35; Rodríguez Demorizi, ed., *Proyecto*, 298–301.

71. Marte, *Cuba*, 405; Jaime de Jesús Domínguez, *Notas económicas y políticas dominicanas sobre el período julio 1865–julio 1886*, 2 vols. (Santo Domingo, DR: Editora de la UASD, 1983–1984), 2: 494–95; and Cassá, *Historia*, 2: 44.

72. H. Hoetink, *The Dominican People, 1850–1900*, trans. Stephen K. Ault (Baltimore: Johns Hopkins University Press, 1982), 114–19; Moya Pons, *Manual*, 404; Domínguez, *Notas económicas*, 2: 414.

73. Moya Pons, *Manual*, 365; Tansill, *United States*, 228; and Luperón, *Notas autobiográficas*, 1: 371.

74. Domínguez, *Notas económicas*, 2: 431; Rodríguez Demorizi, *Papeles de Báez*, 195–99; and Moya Pons, *Manual*, 367–68.

75. Anti-Cabral leaflet, of December 24, 1867, RG 59, Notes from the Legation of the Dominican Republic in the United States, vol. 1; Luperón to Cabral, April 20, 1868, in Monclús, *Caudillismo*, 68–70; Luperón, *Notas autobiográficas*, 2: 21, 41; and Moya Pons, *Manual*, 372.

76. DeBenneville Randolph Keim, *Pen Pictures and Leaves of Travel, Romance and History, from the Portfolio of a Correspondent in the American Tropics* (Philadelphia: Claxton, Remsen & Haffelfinger, 1870), 71–72; Báez to Fabens, April 2, 1868, in Tansill, *United States*, 260; Báez to President Johnson, NA, Record Group 233, Records of the House of Representatives, file 40-A-F9.13; Domínguez, *Notas económicas*, 2: 508; and Manuel M. Gautier to Hamilton Fish, July 9, 1869, RG 59, Notes from the Legation of the Dominican Republic in the United States, vol. 2.

77. Keim, *Pen Pictures*, 71–72; Báez to Fabens, April 2, 1868, in Tansill, *United States*, 260; Báez to President Johnson, NA, RG 233, Records of the House of Representatives, file 40-A-F9.13; Domínguez, *Notas económicas*, 2: 508; and Manuel M. Gautier to Hamilton Fish, July 9, 1869, NA, RG 59, Notes from the Legation of the Dominican Republic in the United States, vol. 2.

78. Allan Nevins, *Hamilton Fish: The Inner History of the Grant Administration* (New York: Dodd, Mead, and Co., 1936), 315; Mayor Raymond H. Perry to Fish, June 7, 1870, quoted in Welles, *Naboth's Vineyard*, 1: 386; Rodríguez Demorizi, ed., *Proyecto*, 298–301; Moya Pons, *Manual*, 379; and Rodríguez Demorizi, ed., *Samaná*, 35.

79. Captain Bunce to Poor, March 24, 1870, in Rodríguez Demorizi, *Proyecto*, 366–69; and United States, Commission of Inquiry to Santo Domingo, *Report of the Commission of Inquiry* (Washington, DC, 1871), 11–12, 246.

80. Buenaventura Báez to Damián Báez, January 21, 1876, in Rodríguez Demorizi, ed., *Papeles de Báez*, 466–68; Luperón to the governor of Puerto Rico, August 5, 1868, in AHN, Ultramar, *legajo* 5096, file 46.

Chapter 6

1. The term "Spanish-American-Cuban-Filipino War" is used by Thomas G. Paterson in *Major Problems in American Foreign Policy: Documents and Essays*, 3d ed., vol. 1 (to 1914) (Lexington, MA: D. C. Heath, 1989), 381–414. A fine source on the war in Puerto Rico is Ángel Rivero, *Crónica de la Guerra Hispano Americana en Puerto Rico* (1921; reprint, New York: Plus Ultra Educational Publishers, 1973).

2. For previous evaluations of the Puerto Rican historiography on 1898, see Laura Náter Vázquez, "El '98 en la historiografía puertorriqueña: Del político entusiasta al héroe popular," *Op. Cit.: Boletín del Centro de Investigaciones Históricas de la Universidad de Puerto Rico* 4 (1988–1989): 101–22; María de los Ángeles Castro, "El '98 incesante: Su persistencia en la memoria histórica puertorriqueña:" and Carmelo Rosario Natal, "El '98 puertorriqueño en tres tiempos: Ensayo historiográfico," both in Luis González Vales, ed., *1898: enfoques y perspectivas* (San Juan: Academia Puertorriqueña de la Historia, 1997), 17–41, 43–79.

3. Carmelo Rosario Natal, *Puerto Rico y la crisis de la Guerra Hispanoamericana (1895–1898)* (Hato Rey, PR: Ramallo Brothers Printing, 1975), 137–38. In the 1890s, the Autonomist Party split into two factions, one under Luis Muñoz Rivera, another under José Celso Barbosa.

4. Tomás Blanco, *Prontuario histórico de Puerto Rico* (1935; reprint, Río Piedras, PR: Ediciones Huracán, 1981), 56, 81; Antonio S. Pedreira, *Insularismo* (1934; reprint, Río Piedras, PR: Editorial Edil, 1973), 70–74; Luis Muñoz Marín, "The Sad Case of Porto Rico," *American Mercury* 16:62 (February 1929): 136–37.

5. Fernando Picó, "La revolución puertorriqueña de 1898: La necesidad de un nuevo paradigma para entender el '98 puertorriqueño," paper presented at the 28th Annual Meeting of the Association of Caribbean Historians, Barbados, April 14–19, 1996, 27.

6. Edward J. Berbusse, *The United States in Puerto Rico:1898–1900* (Chapel Hill: University of North Carolina Press, 1966), 64.

7. Rosario Natal, *Puerto Rico*, 93–101.

8. Bergad, "Agrarian History," 66–76; Berbusse, *United States*, 150; and Thomas J. Vivian and Ruel P. Smith, *Everything about Our New Possessions* (New York: R. F. Fenno, 1899), 156–60.

9. See for instance, Eugenio María de Hostos, cited in José Luis González, *Puerto Rico the Four-Storeyed Country and Other Essays* (Princeton, NJ: Markus Wiener Publishers, 1993), 4; Salvador

Brau, *Ensayos (disquisiciones sociológicas)* (Río Piedras, PR: Editorial Edil, 1972); and Manuel Zeno Gandía, *La Charca* (1894; reprint, Barcelona: Ediciones Puerto, 1973).

10. Muñoz Marín, "Sad Case," 136–37. Albizu Campos cited in Fernando Picó, *1898: La guerra después de la guerra* (Río Piedras, PR: Ediciones Huracán, 1987), 21–22.

11. Picó, *1898*, 39; Fernando Picó, *Amargo Café (los pequeños y medianos caficultores de Utuado en la segunda mitad del siglo XIX)* (Río Piedras, PR: Ediciones Huracán, 1981); Picó, *Libertad y servidumbre*; Ramos Mattei, *Hacienda*; Scarano, *Sugar and Slavery*, Bergad, *Coffee*; and Guillermo A. Baralt, *Esclavos Rebeldes: Conspiraciones y sublevaciones de esclavos en Puerto Rico (1795–1873)* (Río Piedras, PR: Ediciones Huracán, 1982).

12. Picó, "La revolución," 3–18.

13. Arturo Morales Carrión, "1898: The Hope and the Trauma" in Arturo Morales Carrión, ed., *Puerto Rico: A Political and Cultural History* (New York: W. W. Norton, 1983), 133; Rosario Natal, *Puerto Rico*, 89, 197, 217; Manuel Maldonado Denis, *Puerto Rico: Una interpretación histórico-social* (Mexico City: Siglo Veintiuno Editores, 1973), 52; and Gervasio Luis García, "Strangers in Paradise? Puerto Rico en la correspondencia de los cónsules norteamericanos (1869–1900)," paper presented at the Caribbean between Empires Symposium, Princeton University, May 5–7, 1994, 32.

14. Picó, *1898*, 74; and Rosario Natal, *Puerto Rico*, 227.

15. Picó, *1898*, chaps. 3–5; and Kelvin A. Santiago-Valles, *"Subject People" and Colonial Discourses: Economic Transformation and Social Disorder in Puerto Rico, 1898–1947* (Albany: State University of New York Press, 1994), chap. 4.

16. Maldonado Denis, *Puerto Rico*, 55; García, "Strangers in Paradise?" 32; Picó, *1898*, 155–60; and Rosario Natal, "El '98," 66–68.

17. Luis López Nieves, "Seva: Historia de la primera invasión norteamericana de la isla de Puerto Rico ocurrida en mayo de 1898," *Claridad*, December 23, 1983; Carlos E. Pabón Ortega, "El 98 en el imaginario nacional: Seva o la 'nación soñada,'" in Consuelo Naranjo, Miguel A. Puig-Samper, and Luis Miguel García Mora, eds., *La nación soñada: Cuba, Puerto Rico y Filipinas ante el 98* (Aranjuez, Spain: Ediciones Doce Calles, 1996): 547–57; and García, "Strangers in Paradise?" 33.

18. Muñoz Rivera cited in Morales Carrión, ed., *Puerto Rico*, 142; and Muñoz Rivera cited in Luis E. Agrait, "Puerto Rico en el vórtice del '98: 'A prisa, a toda prisa, formemos la patria,'" in Naranjo, Puig-Samper and García Mora eds., *Nación soñada*, 100.

19. For a summary of the military decrees, see Henry K. Carroll, *Report on the Island of Porto Rico* (1899; reprint, New York: Arno Press, 1975), 53–55.
20. Stuart B. Schwartz, "The Hurricane of San Ciriaco: Disaster, Politics, and Society in Puerto Rico, 1899–1901," *HAHR* 72:3 (August 1992): 303–34.
21. Henna quoted in Raymond Carr, *Puerto Rico: A Colonial Experiment* (New York: Vintage Books, 1984), 33.
22. María Dolores Luque de Sánchez, *La ocupación norteamericana y la ley Foraker (la opinión pública puertorriqueña, 1898–1904)* (Río Piedras: Editorial de la Universidad de Puerto Rico, 1980), 45, 63, 78; and Bergad, "Agrarian History," 75–85.
23. Bergad, "Agrarian History," 75–87; and Ángel G. Quintero Rivera, *Patricios y plebeyos: Burgueses, hacendados, artesanos y obreros* (Río Piedras, PR: Ediciones Huracán, 1988), 103.
24. Santiago-Valles, "*Subject People,*" 59; and Juan A. Giusti Cordero, "En búsqueda de la nación concreta: 'El grupo español' en la industria azucarera de Puerto Rico, 1890–1920," in Naranjo, Puig-Samper, and García Mora, eds. *Nación soñada*, 213.
25. Schwartz, "Hurricane," 333.
26. Picó, *1898*, 137; and Berbusse, *United States*, 119, 122.
27. Santiago-Valles, "*Subject People,*" 46.

Chapter 7

1. Among the few regional or comparative studies that include two or more components of the Hispanic Caribbean, one finds: Marte, *Cuba*; Luis Martínez-Fernández, *Protestantism and Political Conflict in the Nineteenth-Century Hispanic Caribbean* (New Brunswick, NJ: Rutgers University Press, 2002; Martínez-Fernández, *Torn between Empires*; Schmidt-Nowara, *Empire and Antislavery*; and César J. Ayala, *American Sugar Kingdom: The Plantation Economy of the Spanish Caribbean, 1898–1934* (Chapel Hill: University of North Carolina Press, 1999).
2. For a fine discussion of political culture and the literature on the concept's evolution, see Jorge Benítez Nazario, *Reflexiones en torno a la cultura política de los puertorriqueños* (San Juan: Instituto de Cultura Puertorriqeña, 2001), 1–40.
3. Martínez-Fernández, *Torn between Empires*, chaps. 2, 3, and 5.
4. Martínez-Fernández, *Torn between Empires*, chaps. 4, and 6.
5. Louis A. Pérez, Jr., *Cuba under the Platt Amendment, 1902–1934* (Pittsburgh: University of Pittsburgh Press, 1986), 23–25. Also see

Ada Ferrer, *Insurgent Cuba: Race, Nation, and Revolution* (Chapel Hill: University of North Carolina Press, 1999).

6. On el Grito de Lares, see Olga Jiménez de Wagenheim, *El Grito de Lares: Sus causas y sus hombres* (Río Piedras, PR: Ediciones Huracán, 1984); and Bergad, *Coffee*, chap. 3.

7. Quote from Rafael María de Labra y Cadrana, et al., *Los diputados americanos en la cortes españolas* (Madrid: Imprenta Aurelio Alaria, 1880), 159.

8. Jonathan Hartlyn, *The Struggle for Democratic Politics in the Dominican Republic* (Chapel Hill: University of North Carolina Press, 1999), 29.

9. On Heureaux's regime, see Jaime de Jesús Domínguez, *La dictadura de Heureaux* (Santo Domingo, DR: Editora Universitaria, 1986); and Mu-Kien A. Sang, *Ulises Heureaux: Biografía de un dictador* (Santo Domingo, DR: INTEC, 1986).

10. Moya Pons, *Manual*, 414; Emelio Betances, *State and Society in the Dominican Republic* (Boulder, CO: Westview Press, 1995), 47–48; and Sang, *Ulises Heureaux*, 154–57.

11. Moya Pons, *Manual*, 417–18; Sang, *Ulises Heureaux*, 48; and Betances, *State*, 62–74.

12. David P. Healy, *The United States in Cuba, 1898–1902* (Madison: University of Wisconsin Press, 1963), 63; Pérez, *Cuba under the Platt Amendment*, 11; Philip S. Foner, *The Spanish-Cuban-American War and the Birth of American Imperialism, 1895–1902*, 2 vols. (New York: Monthly Review Press, 1972), 1: 105–15; Offner, *Unwanted War*, 71–93, 112; and Portell-Vilá, *Nueva historia de la República de Cuba (1898–1979)* (Miami: La Moderna Poesía, 1986), 70.

13. Joaquín Freire, *Presencia de Puerto Rico en la historia de Cuba* (San Juan: Instituto de Cultura Puertorriqueña, 1966).

14. Eda Burgos-Malavé, *Génesis y práxis de la carta autonómica de 1897 en Puerto Rico* (San Juan: Centro de Estudios Avanzados de Puerto Rico, 1997); Offner, *Unwanted War*, 93; and Rosario Natal, *Puerto Rico*, 57–67.

15. Berbusse, *United States*; and Mario Riera, *Cuba política, 1899–1955* (Havana: n.p., 1955), 27.

16. Berbusse, *United States*; Healy, *United States*, 77–78; and Luis E. Aguilar, *Cuba 1933: Prologue to Revolution* (New York: W. W. Norton, 1974), 17.

17. Robert Whitney, *State and Revolution in Cuba: Mass Mobilization and Political Change, 1920–1940*, (Chapel Hill: University of North Carolina Press, 2001), 18.

18. See Carroll, *Report*, 53–55.
19. Berbusse, *United States*, 119, 122; José Trías Monge, *Puerto Rico: The Trials of the Oldest Colony in the World* (New Haven, CT: Yale University Press, 1997), 52, 57; Morales Carrión "1898," 146; and María Eugenia Estades Font, *La presencia militar de Estados Unidos en Puerto Rico 1898–1918*, 2d ed., (Río Piedras, PR: Ediciones Huracán, 1999), 126.
20. Pérez, *Cuba under the Platt Amendment*, 36–41.
21. David Lockmiller, *Magoon in Cuba: A History of the Second Intervention, 1906–1909* (New York: Greenwood Press, 1969), 36–37; and Jorge Domínguez, *Cuba: Order and Revolution* (Cambridge, MA: Belknap Press, 1978), 15.
22. Lockmiller, *Magoon;* Portell-Vilá, *Nueva historia*, 122; and Riera, *Cuba*, 111–12.
23. Welles, *Naboth's Vineyard*, 1: 127–31; Betances, *State*, 5, 31, 74; Hartlyn, *Struggle*, 31; and Juan Bosch, *Composición social dominicana* (Santo Domingo, DR: La Trinitaria, 1984), 348–58.
24. Welles, *Naboth's Vineyard*, 2: 24–27, 70; and Moya Pons, *Manual*, 436–37.
25. Betances, *State*, 52–55; Welles, *Naboth's Vineyard*, 2: 90–92; Cassá, *Historia*, 2: 195; and Moya Pons, Manual, 440–45.
26. Healy, *United States*, 94.
27. Portell-Vilá, *Nueva historia*, 78, 128; Bergad, "Agrarian History," 75; and Oscar Zanetti Lecuona, *Cautivos de la reciprocidad* (Havana: Ediciones ENPES, 1989).
28. Vivian and Smith, *Everything*, 102–3; and Bergad, "Agrarian History," 74.
29. Pérez, *Cuba under the Platt Amendment*, 72–85; Bergad, "Agrarian History," 83; Whitney, *State*, 23; Jean Stubbs, *Cuba: The Test of Time* (London: Latin America Bureau, 1989); and Zanetti Lecuona and García Álvarez, *Sugar and Railroads*.
30. Nancy Mitchell, *The Danger of Dreams: German and American Imperialism in Latin America* (Chapel Hill, University of North Carolina Press, 1999); and Estades Font, *Presencia militar*, 57.
31. Gónzalo F. Cordova, *Santiago Iglesias: Creador del movimiento obrero de Puerto Rico* (Río Piedras, PR: Editorial Universitaria, 1980).
32. Pérez, *Cuba under the Platt Amendment*, chap. 6; Aguilar, *Cuba*, 33; Domínguez, *Cuba*, 49; and Jorge Ibarra, *Cuba, 1898–1921: Partidos políticos y clases sociales* (Havana: Editorial de Ciencias Sociales, 1992).
33. Aline Helg, *Our Rightful Share: The Afro-Cuban Struggle for Equal-*

ity, 1886–1912 (Chapel Hill: University of North Carolina Press, 1995); and Louis A. Pérez, Jr., "Politics, Peasants and People of Color: The 1912 'Race War' in Cuba Reconsidered," in *HAHR* 66:3 (1986): 509–39.

34. Portell-Vilá, *Nueva historia*, 196–211.
35. Hartlyn, *Struggle*, 37.
36. Estades Font, *Presencia militar*, 202–13.
37. Trías Monge, *Puerto Rico*, 79.
38. Ángel G. Quintero Rivera, *Conflictos de clase y política en Puerto Rico* (Río Piedras, PR: Ediciones Huracán, 1976), 125–32.
39. Juan Manuel García Passalacqua, *Dignidad y jaibería: Temer y ser puertorriqueno* (San Juan: Editorial Cultural, 1993), 66; Silvia Álvarez Curbelo, "La conflictiviad en el discurso político de Luis Muñoz Marín: 1926–1936," in Silvia Álvarez Curbelo and María Elena Rodríguez Castro, eds., *Del nacionalismo al populismo: Cultura y política en Puerto Rico* (Río Piedras, PR: Ediciones Huracán, 1993), 13–36.
40. Pérez, *Cuba under the Platt Amendment*, 118–20.
41. Whitney, *State*, chap. 2.
42. Bruce J. Calder, *The Impact of Intervention: The Dominican Republic during the Occupation of 1916–1924* (Austin: University of Texas Press, 1984).
43. See Calder, *Impact of Intervention*; Bosch, *Composición*, 379; and Cassá, *Historia*, 2: 228–29.
44. Ayala, *American Sugar Kingdom*; Whitney, *State*, 23; and Thomas T. Mathews, *La política puertorriqueña y el Nuevo Trato* (Río Piedras: Editorial de la Universidad de Puerto Rico, 1967), 13.
45. Whitney, *State*, 61–62; and Cassá, *Historia*, 244–47.
46. Domínguez, *Cuba*, 54; Peter H. Smith, *Talons of the Eagle: Dynamics of U.S.–Latin American Relations* (New York: Oxford University Press, 1996), 65; and James Dunkerley, "The United States and Latin America in the Long Run (1800–1945)," in Victor Bulmer-Thomas and James Dunkerley, eds., *The United States and Latin America: The New Agenda* (London: Institute of Latin American Studies, University of London, 1999), 27.
47. Hartlyn, *Struggle*, 39; and Bernard Diederich, *Trujillo: La muerte del dictador* (Santo Domingo, DR: Fundación Cultural Dominicana, 1990).
48. Salient among those who recognized the similarities between Heureaux and Trujillo was Heureaux's son, a Trujillo supporter. He published *Rafael Leónidas Trujillo Molina* (Santo Domingo, DR: Cronos, 1933) where he compared his father and the new dic-

tator. See Hartlyn, *Struggle*, 297–98.

49. Rosario Espinal, *Autoritarismo y democracia en la política domini-cana* (San José, Costa Rica: Editorial Argumentos, 1987), 74; and Cassá, *Historia*, 2: 258–59.

50. See Suzy Castor, *Migración y relaciones internacionales: El caso haitiano dominicano* (Santo Domingo, DR: Editora Universitaria, 1987); Lauren H. Derby, "Haitians, Magic and Money: *Raza* and Society in the Haitian-Dominican Borderlands, 1900–1937," *Comparative Studies in Society and History* 36:3 (July 1994): 488–526; and Ernesto Sagás, *Race and Politics in the Dominican Republic* (Gainesville: University Press of Florida, 2000).

51. Pérez, *Cuba under the Platt Amendment*, 188, 279; Bergad, "Agrarian History," 79–78; Betances, *State*, 29; Piero Gleijeses, *The Dominican Crisis: The 1965 Constitutionalist Revolt and American Intervention*, (Baltimore: Johns Hopkins University Press, 1978), 18; and Santiago-Valles, "*Subject People*," 150. Also see Whitney, *State*.

52. Whitney, *State*, 58; and Riera, *Cuba*, 386–87.

53. Portell-Vilá, *Nueva historia*, 382–97; Whitney, *State*, chap. 5; and Riera, *Cuba*, 412.

54. Aguilar, *Cuba*, 165–78; Whitney, *State*; Barry Carr, "Mill Occupations and Soviets: The Mobilization of Sugar Workers in Cuba, 1917–1933," *Journal of Latin American Studies* 28 (1996): 129–58.

55. Pérez, *Cuba under the Platt Amendment*, 332.

56. Whitney, *State*, 2.

57. Edgardo Meléndez, *Movimiento anexionista en Puerto Rico* (Río Piedras: Editorial de la Universidad de Puerto Rico, 1993), 82.

58. Carr, *Puerto Rico*, 58–61; and Mathews, *Política*, 214, 51.

59. Manuel E. Moraza Ortiz, *La masacre de Ponce* (Hato Rey, PR: Publicaciones Puertorriqueñas, 2001).

60. Hartlyn, *Struggle*, 44.

61. Whitney, *State*, 123.

62. Enrique Lugo Silva, *The Tugwell Administration in Puerto Rico, 1941–1946* (Río Piedras, PR: n.p., 1955.

63. Luis A. Ferrao, *Pedro Albizu Campos y el nacionalismo puertorriqueño* (San Juan: Editorial Cultural, 1990).

Bibliography

Archival Sources

Archives of the Episcopal Church, Austin, TX.
Cuba Scrapbook.

Archivo del Arzobispado de La Habana (AALH).
Matrimonios Ultramarinos.

Archivo del Museo del Cerro (AMC), Havana.
Breve reseña: la Parroquia el Salvador del Mundo del Cerro.
Informe histórico sobre la casa # 256 de la calle Tulipán.

Archivo General de la Nación (AGNRD), Santo Domingo, DR.
La Anexión a España.

Archivo General de Puerto Rico (AGPR), San Juan.
Audiencia Territorial, Acuerdo Real.
Gobernadores Españoles, Ponce.
Vieques.

Archivo Histórico de Ponce (AHP).
Índice del Cementerio Antiguo.
Padrón de productos y capitales, 1869–1870.
Riqueza territorial, 1871–1872.

Archivo Histórico de Vieques (AHV).
Registro del Gobernador de Vieques (copy).
Siegal, Robert Rabin, "Los tortoleños: Obreros de Barlovento
en Vieques: 1864–1874."

Archivo Histórico Diocesano de la Archidiócesis de San Juan
(AHDASJ).
Gobierno, Circulares.
Gobierno, Correspondencia Parroquia-Obispo, Vieques.
Justicia, Procesos Legales, Certificaciones de Soltería.
Justicia, Procesos Legales, Papeles de Extranjeros.
Justicia, Procesos Legales, Validación de Matrimonios.

Archivo Histórico Nacional (AHN), Madrid.
> Ultramar.

Archivo Histórico Provincial de Matanzas (AHPM).
> Negociado de Órden Público y Policía.

Archivo Nacional de Cuba (ANC), Havana.
> Gobierno Superior Civil.

Centro de Investigaciones Históricas de la Universidad de Puerto Rico (CIH), Río Piedras.
> Books of Baptisms of Vieques' Roman Catholic Church (microfilms).
> Books of Deaths of Ponce's Roman Catholic Church (micrfilms).
> Registro central de esclavos (6to. Depto.) (microfilms).
> Transcripts of papers relating to Vieques.

Duke University, Perkins Library, Special Collections.
> John Backhouse Papers.

Iglesia Salvador del Mundo, El Cerro, Havana.
> Book of Baptisms.
> Book of Marriages.

Maryland Diocesan Archives (MDA), Baltimore.
> Cuba.

National Archives (NA), Washington, DC and College Park, MD.
> General Records of the Department of State, Record Group 59.
> Records of Foreign Service Posts, Record Group 84.
> Records of the House of Representatives, Record Group 23.

Public Record Office (PRO), Kew, United Kingdom.
> Foreign Office.

Virginia Historical Society, Richmond.
> Diary of William Norwood, March 24, 1844.

Williams Library (WL), St. Croix, U.S. Virgin Islands.
> Books of Marriages of the Dutch Reformed Church of Christiansted, St. Croix (microfilms).
> Marriage records of All Saints Church of St. Thomas (microfilms).

Newspapers

El Boletín Eclesiástico de Puerto Rico.

La Crónica de Ambos Mundos (Madrid).

La Gaceta de La Habana.

La Gaceta de Puerto Rico.

La Gaceta de Santo Domingo.

El Porvenir (Santo Domingo).

Published Primary Sources

Abbott, John Stevens Cabot. *South and North; or, Impressions Received during a Trip to Cuba and the South.* New York: Abbey & Abbot, 1860.

Ashworth, Henry. *A Tour in the United States, Cuba, and Canada.* London: A. W. Bennett, 1861.

Ballou, Maturin Murray. *Due South; or, Cuba Past and Present.* Boston: Houghton, Mifflin, 1885; reprint, New York: Young People's Missionary Movement, 1910.

Brau, Salvador. *Ensayos (disquisiciones sociológicas).* Río Piedras, PR: Editorial Edil, 1972.

Bremer, Fredrika. *The Homes of the New World; Impressions of America.* 2 vols. New York: Harper and Brothers, 1854.

Bryant, William Cullen. *Letters of William Cullen Bryant.* Edited by William Cullen Bryant II and Thomas G. Voss. 4 vols. New York: Fordham University Press, 1975–1984.

Calderón de la Barca, Frances Erskine. *Life in Mexico.* London: J. M. Dent and Sons, n.d.

Campbell, Reau. *Around the Corner to Cuba.* New York: C. G. Crawford, 1889.

Carroll, Henry K. *Report on the Island of Porto Rico.* 1899; reprint, New York: Arno Press, 1975.

Coggeshall, George. *Voyages to Various Parts of the World Made between the Years 1800 and 1831.* New York: D. Appleton, 1853.

Condesa de Merlín [Mercedes de Santa Cruz y Montalvo]. *Viaje a La Habana*. Havana: Editorial de Arte y Literatura, 1974.

Cuba, Gobierno de. *Cuadro estadístico de la siempre fiel Isla de Cuba, correspondiente al año 1846*. Havana: Imprenta del Gobierno y Capitanía General, 1847.

Cuba, Instituto de Investigaciones Estadísticas. *Los censos de población y viviendas en Cuba*. Vol. 1. Havana: Instituto de Investigaciones Estadísticas, 1988.

Dana, Richard Henry, Jr. *To Cuba and Back: A Vacation Voyage*. Boston: Ticknor and Fields, 1859; reprint, edited by C. Harvey Gardiner, Carbondale: Southern Illinois University Press, 1966.

de Labra y Cadrana, Rafael María. *La cuestión de ultramar*. Madrid: Nogueras, 1871.

de Labra y Cadrana, Rafael María, Joaquín María Sanromá, José Facundo Cintrón, José Antonio Álvarez de Peralta, and Luis Ricardo Padial. *Los diputados americanos en la cortes españolas*. Madrid: Imprenta Aurelio Alaria, 1880.

de la Gándara y Navarro, José. *La anexión y guerra de Santo Domingo*. 2 vols. Madrid: El Correo Militar, 1884.

de la Sagra, Ramón. *Cuba, 1860: Selección de artículos sobre agricultura cubana*. Havana: Comisión Nacional Cubana de la UNESCO, 1963.

de las Barras y Prado, Antonio. *Memorias, La Habana a mediados del siglo XIX*. Madrid: Ciudad Lineal, 1925.

de Norzagaray, Fernando. "Diario del Gobernador Norzagaray." *Anales de Investigación Histórica*. 6:1–2 (January–December 1979): 70–132.

de Roches, V. *Cuba under Spanish Rule*. New York: Great American Engraving and Printing, [1869?].

España, Ministerio de Ultramar. *Cuba desde 1850 a 1873*. Madrid: Imprenta Nacional, 1873.

Fisher, Richard S., ed. *The Spanish West Indies: Cuba and Porto Rico*. New York: J. H. Colton, 1861.

Gallenga, Antonio C. N. *The Pearl of the Antilles*. London: Chapman and Hall, 1873; reprint, New York: Negro Universities Press, 1970.

García de Arboleya, José. *Manual de la isla de Cuba*. Havana: Imprenta del Tiempo, 1859.

Gibbes, Robert W. *Cuba for Invalids*. New York: W. A. Townsend & Co., 1860.

Gómez Colón, José María. *Memoria sobre la utilidad del trabajo de la muger pobre en la isla de Cuba y medios para conseguirlo*. Havana: Imprenta de Manuel Soler, 1857.

Great Britain, Parliament, House of Commons. *British Parliamentary Papers [Slave Trade]*. 95 vols. Shannon, Ireland: Irish University Press, 1968–1971.

Gurney, Joseph John. *A Winter in the West Indies*. London: J. Murray, 1840.

Hacendado, Un [Cristóbal F. Madan]. *Llamamiento de la isla de Cuba a la nación española*. New York: E. Hallet, 1854.

Hazard, Samuel. *Cuba with Pen and Pencil*. Hartford, CT: Hartford Publishing, 1871.

Hernández Poggio, D. Ramón. *Aclimatación é higiene de los europeos en Cuba*. Cádiz, Spain: Imprenta de la Revista Médica, 1874.

Howe, Julia Ward. *A Trip to Cuba*. Boston: Ticknor and Fields, 1860; reprint, New York: Negro Universities Press, 1969.

Hulse, Hiram H. "The History of the Church in Cuba." *Historical Magazine of the Protestant Episcopal Church* 6:2 (June 1937): 249–70.

Humboldt, Alexander. *The Island of Cuba. Translated from Spanish, with Notes and a Preliminary Essay by J. S. Trasher*. New York: Derby & Jackson, 1856.

[Hurlbert, William Henry]. *Gan-Eden; or, Pictures of Cuba*. Boston: J. P. Jewett, 1854.

Jay, W.M.L. [Julia Louisa M. Woodruff] *My Winter in Cuba*. New York: E. P. Dutton, 1871.

Keim, DeBenneville Randolph. *Pen Pictures and Leaves of Travel, Romance and History, from the Portfolio of a Correspondent in the American Tropics*. Philadelphia: Claxton, Remsen & Haffelfinger, 1870.

Kenney, Edward. *Report of Our Mission in Cuba: October 1874–October 1877*. Detroit: Diocesan Printing Office, 1878.

[Kimball, Richard Burleigh]. *Cuba and the Cubans; Comprising a History of the Island of Cuba, Its Present Social, Political and Domestic Conditions, etc*. New York: Samuel Hueston, 1850.

Lee, Albert E. *An Island Grows: Memoirs of Albert E. Lee, Puerto Rico, 1872–1942*. San Juan: Lee and Son, 1963.

Levis, Richard J. *Diary of a Spring Holiday in Cuba*. Philadelphia: Porter and Coates, 1872.

Luperón, Gregorio. *Notas autobiográficas y apuntes históricos sobre la República Dominicana*. 2d ed. 3 vols. Santiago: Editorial El Diario, 1939.

Madden, Richard Robert. *The Island of Cuba: Its Resources, Progress, and Prospects*. London: Partridge & Oakey, 1853.

Mark, John. *Diary of My Trip to America and Havana*. Manchester, UK: J. E. Cornish, 1885.

Moore, Rachel Wilson. *Journal of Rachel Moore, Kept during a Tour to the West Indies and South America, in 1863–64*. Philadelphia: T. E. Zell, 1867.

Murray, Amelia Matilda. *Letters from the United States, Cuba and Canada*. New York: Putnam, 1857.

Murray, Henry Anthony. *Lands of the Slave and the Free; or, Cuba, the United States, and Canada*. 2 vols. London: J. W. Parker and Son, 1855.

Norman, Benjamin Moore. *Rambles by Land and Water; or, Notes to Travel in Cuba and Mexico*. New York: Paine & Burgess, 1845.

O'Kelly, James J. *The Mambi-Land; or, Adventures of a Herald Correspondent in Cuba*. Philadelphia: J. B. Lippincott, 1874.

O'Neil, J. T. "Porto Rico." In *The Spanish West Indies: Cuba and Porto Rico*, edited by Richard S. Fisher. New York: J. H. Colton, 1861.

Philalethes, Demoticus. *Yankee Travels through the Island of Cuba; or, The Men, Government, the Laws and Customs of Cuba, as Seen by American Eyes*. New York: D. A. Appleton, 1856.

Phillippo, James Mursell. *The United States and Cuba*. London: Pewtress, 1857.

Quitman, John A. *Speech of John A. Quitman, of Mississippi on the Subject of the Neutrality Laws: April 29, 1856*. Washington, DC: Union Office, 1856.

Ramos, Francisco. *Prontuario de disposiciones oficiales: Disposiciones más notables del Gobierno Superior desde 1824 a 1865*. San Juan: Imprenta de González, 1866.

Rawson, James. *Cuba*. New York: Lane & Tippet, 1847.

República Dominicana. *Colección de leyes, decretos y resoluciones*. 52 vols. Santo Domingo, DR: Publicaciones ONAP, 1982–.

[Rogers, Carlton H.]. *Incidents of Travel in the Southern States and Cuba*. New York: R. Craighead, 1862.

Sala, George Augustus Henry. *Under the Sun: Essays Mainly Written in Hot Countries*. London: Tinsley Brothers, 1872.

Shufeldt, Robert Wilson. "Secret History of the Slave Trade to Cuba." Edited by Frederick C. Drake. *Journal of Negro History* 55:3 (July 1970): 218–35.

Steele, James William. *Cuban Sketches*. New York: Putnam's Sons, 1881.

Tanco Armero, Nicolás. "La Isla de Cuba." In *La Isla de Cuba en el siglo XIX vista por los extranjeros,* edited by Juan Pérez de la Riva, 107–39. Havana: Editorial de Ciencias Sociales, 1981.

Thrasher, John S. *A Preliminary Essay on the Purchase of Cuba*. New York: Derby & Jackson, 1859.

Torrente, Mariano. *Bosquejo económico político de la isla de Cuba*. 2 vols. Madrid and Havana: M. Pita-Barcina, 1852–1853.

_____. *Política ultramarina que abraza todos los puntos referentes a las relaciones de España con los Estados Unidos, con Inglaterra y las Antillas*. (Madrid: Compañía General de Impresores y Libreros del Reino, 1854).

Trollope, Anthony. *The West Indies and the Spanish Main*. Reprint, London: Frank Cass, 1968.

Tudor, Henry. *Narrative of a Tour in North America, Comprising Mexico, the Mines of Real del Monte, the United States, and the British Colonies with an Excursion to the Island of Cuba.* 2 vols. London: James Duncan, 1834.

Turnbull, David. *Travels in the West: Cuba with Notices of Porto Rico and the Slave Trade.* London: 1840; reprint, New York: Negro Universities Press, 1968.

United States, Commission of Inquiry to Santo Domingo. *Report of the Commission of Inquiry.* Washington, DC: Government Printing Office, 1871.

United States, Department of State, San Juan Consulate. *Despachos de los cónsules norteamericanos en Puerto Rico (1818–1868).* Edited by CIH. Río Piedras: Editorial de la Universidad de Puerto Rico, 1982.

La Verdad, editors. *Cuestión negrera de la isla de Cuba.* New York: La Verdad, 1851.

Williams, George W. *Sketches of Travel in the Old and New World.* Charleston: Walker, Evans & Cogswell, 1871.

Wilson, Thomas William. *The Island of Cuba in 1850; Being a Description of the Island, Its Resources, Productions, Commerce & Co.* New Orleans: La Patria, 1850.

[Wurdemann, John George F]. *Notes on Cuba.* Boston: J. Munro and Co., 1844; reprint, New York: Arno Press, 1971.

Young, Bishop. "Cuba." *Spirit of Missions* 49 (October 1884): 486–87.

Zaragoza, Justo. *Isla de Cuba, suspensión de conventos y contribución extraordinaria de guerra.* Madrid: n.p., 1837.

Secondary Sources

Agrait, Luis E. "Puerto Rico en el vórtice del '98: 'A prisa, a toda prisa, formemos la patria.'" In *La nación soñada: Cuba, Puerto Rico y Filipinas ante el 98,* edited by Consuelo Naranjo, Miguel A. Puig-Samper, and Luis Miguel García Mora, 97–108. Aranjuez, Spain: Ediciones Doce Calles, 1996.

Aguilar, Luis E. *Cuba 1933: Prologue to Revolution.* New York: W. W. Norton, 1974.

Alfau Durán, Vetilio, ed. *Controversia histórica: Polémica de Santana.* Santo Domingo, DR: Editora Montalvo, 1968.

Álvarez Curbelo, Silvia. "La conflictividad en el discurso político de Luis Muñoz Marín: 1926–1936." In *Del nacionalismo al populismo: Cultura y política en Puerto Rico*, edited by Silvia Álvarez Curbelo and María Elena Rodríguez Castro, 13–36. Río Piedras, PR: Ediciones Huracán, 1993.

Álvarez López, Luis. "Historia de la anexión de Santo Domingo a España, 1861–1863." M.A. thesis, Universidad de Puerto Rico, 1977.

Archambault, Pedro María. *Historia de la Restauración.* Paris: Librairie Technique et Economique, 1938; reprint, Santo Domingo, DR: Biblioteca Taller 20, 1973.

Arróm, Silvia. *The Women of Mexico City.* Stanford, CA: Stanford University Press, 1985.

Ayala, César J. *American Sugar Kingdom: The Plantation Economy of the Spanish Caribbean, 1898–1934.* Chapel Hill: University of North Carolina Press, 1999.

Aykroyd, W. R. *The Sweet Malefactor.* London: Heinemann, 1967.

Baralt, Guillermo A. *Esclavos Rebeldes: Conspiraciones y sublevaciones de esclavos en Puerto Rico (1795–1873).* Río Piedras, PR: Ediciones Huracán, 1982.

Barnet, Miguel. "The Culture That Sugar Created." *Latin American Literary Review* 8:16 (Spring–Summer 1980): 38–46.

Beckford, George. *Persistent Poverty: Underdevelopment in Plantation Economies of the Third World.* New York: Oxford University Press, 1972.

Benítez Nazario, Jorge. *Reflexiones en torno a la cultura política de los puertorriqueños.* San Juan: Instituto de Cultura Puertorriqeña, 2001.

Benítez Rojo, Antonio. "La cultura caribeña en Cuba: Continuidad *versus* ruptura." *Cuban Studies/Estudios Cubanos* 14:1 (Winter 1984): 1–16.

_____ . *The Repeating Island: The Caribbean and the Postmodern Perspective*. Durham, NC: Duke University Press, 1992.

Berbusse, Edward J. *The United States in Puerto Rico: 1898–1900*. Chapel Hill: University of North Carolina Press, 1966.

Bergad, Laird W. "Agrarian History of Puerto Rico, 1870–1930." *Latin American Research Review* 13:3 (1978): 63–94.

_____ . *Coffee and the Growth of Agrarian Capitalism in Nineteenth-Century Puerto Rico*. Princeton, NJ: Princeton University Press, 1983.

_____ . *Cuban Rural Society in the Nineteenth Century: The Social and Economic History of Monoculture in Matanzas*. Princeton, NJ: Princeton University Press, 1990.

_____ . "¿Dos alas del mismo pájaro? Notas sobre la historia socioeconómica comparativa de Cuba y Puerto Rico." *Historia y Sociedad* 1 (1988): 143–54.

_____ . "The Economic Viability of Sugar Production Based on Slave Labor in Cuba, 1859–1878." *Latin American Research Review* 24:1 (1989): 95–113.

Betances, Emelio. *State and Society in the Dominican Republic*. Boulder, CO: Westview Press, 1995.

Blanco, Tomás. *Prontuario histórico de Puerto Rico*. 1935; reprint, Río Piedras, PR: Ediciones Huracán, 1981.

Bolland, O. Nigel. "Creolization and Creole Societies." In *Struggles for Freedom: Essays on Slavery, Colonialism and Culture in the Caribbean and Central America*, edited by O. Nigel Bolland, 7–10. Belize City: Angelus Press, 1997.

Bonnet Benítez, Juan Amédée. *Vieques en la historia de Puerto Rico*. 2d ed. San Juan: F. Ortiz Nieves, 1977.

Bosch, Juan. *Composición social dominicana*. Santo Domingo, DR: La Trinitaria, 1984.

Burgos-Malavé, Eda. *Génesis y práxis de la carta autonómica de 1897 en Puerto Rico*. San Juan: Centro de Estudios Avanzados de Puerto Rico, 1997.

Calder, Bruce J. *The Impact of Intervention: The Dominican Republic during the Occupation of 1916–1924*. Austin: University of Texas Press, 1984.

Carr, Barry. "Mill Occupations and Soviets: The Mobilization of Sugar Workers in Cuba, 1917–1933." *Journal of Latin American Studies* 28 (1996): 129–58.

Carr, Raymond. *Puerto Rico: A Colonial Experiment*. New York: Vintage Books, 1984.

Casanovas, Joan. *Bread, or Bullets! Urban Labor and Spanish Colonialism in Cuba, 1850–1898*. Pittsburgh: University of Pittsburgh Press, 1998.

Cassá, Roberto. *Historia social y económica de la República Dominicana*. 10th ed. 2 vols. Santo Domingo, DR: Alfa y Omega, 1991.

Castor, Suzy. *Migración y relaciones internacionales: El caso haitiano dominicano*. Santo Domingo, DR: Editora Universitaria, 1987.

Castro, María de los Ángeles. "El '98 incesante: Su persistencia en la memoria histórica puertorriqueña." In *1898: Enfoques y perspectivas*, edited by Luis González Vales, 17–41. San Juan: Academia Puertorriqueña de la Historia, 1997.

Centro de Investigaciones Históricas, Universidad de Puerto Rico. *El proceso abolicionista en Puerto Rico: Documentos para su estudio*. 2 vols. San Juan: Instituto de Cultura Puertorriqueña, 1974–1978.

Cepero Bonilla, Raúl. *Azúcar y abolición*. Havana: Cenit, 1948.

Coll y Toste, Cayetano, ed. *Boletín histórico de Puerto Rico*. 14 vols. San Juan: Tipografía Cantero Fernández, 1914–1927.

Cordova, Gónzalo F. *Santiago Iglesias: Creador del movimiento obrero de Puerto Rico*. Río Piedras, PR: Editorial Universitaria, 1980.

Corwin, Arthur F. *Spain and the Abolition of Slavery in Cuba, 1817–1886*. Austin: University of Texas Press, 1967.

Cruz Monclova, Lidio. *Historia de Puerto Rico (siglo XIX)*. 3 vols. Río Piedras, PR: Editorial Universitaria, 1952–1964.

Curet, José A. "De la esclavitud a la abolición: Transiciones económicas en las haciendas azucareras de Ponce, 1845–1873." In *Azúcar y esclavitud*, edited by Andrés A. Ramos Mattei, 59–86. San Juan: privately printed, 1982.

Curtin, Philip D. *The Atlantic Slave Trade: A Census*. Madison: University of Wisconsin Press, 1969.

de la Puente García, Esteban. "1861–1865: Anexión y abandono de Santo Domingo." *Revista de Indias* 22:89–90 (1962): 411–72.

Derby, Lauren H. "Haitians, Magic and Money: *Raza* and Society in the Haitian-Dominican Borderlands, 1900–1937." *Comparative Studies in Society and History* 36:3 (July 1994): 488–526.

Díaz Quiñones, Arcadio. "De cómo y cuándo bregar." In *El arte de bregar*, 19–87. San Juan: Ediciones Callejón, 2000.

Díaz Soler, Luis Manuel. *Historia de la esclavitud negra en Puerto Rico*. Río Piedras, PR: Editorial Universitaria, 1967.

Diederich, Bernard. *Trujillo: La muerte del dictador*. Santo Domingo, DR: Fundación Cultural Dominicana, 1990.

Domínguez, Jaime de Jesús. *La anexión de la República Dominicana a España*. Santo Domingo, DR: Editora de la UASD, 1979.

_____. *La dictadura de Heureaux*. Santo Domingo, DR: Editora Universitaria, 1986.

_____. *Economía y política: República Dominicana, 1844–1861*. Santo Domingo, DR: Editora de la UASD, 1977.

_____. *Notas económicas y políticas dominicanas sobre el período julio 1865–julio 1886*. 2 vols. Santo Domingo, DR: Editora de la UASD, 1983–1984.

Domínguez, Jorge. *Cuba: Order and Revolution*. Cambridge, MA: Belknap Press, 1978.

_____. *Insurrection or Loyalty: The Breakdown of the Spanish American Empire*. Cambridge, MA: Harvard University Press, 1980.

Dunkerley, James "The United States and Latin America in the Long Run (1800–1945)." In *The United States and Latin America: The New Agenda*, edited by Victor Bulmer-Thomas and James Dunkerley, 3–32. London: Institute of Latin American Studies, University of London, 1999.

Eltis, David. "The Nineteenth-Century Transatlantic Slave Trade: An Annual Time Series of Imports into the Americas Broken Down by Region." *HAHR* 67:1 (February 1987): 109–38.

Eltis, David, Stephen Behrendt, David Richardson, and Herbert S. Klein, eds. *The Trans-Atlantic Slave Trade: A Database on CD-ROM*. New York: Cambridge University Press, 2000.

Ely, Roland T. *Cuando reinaba su majestad el azúcar: Estudio histórico-sociológico de una tragedia latinoamericana*. Buenos Aires: Editorial Sudamericana, 1963.

Espinal, Rosario. *Autoritarismo y democracia en la política dominicana*. San José, Costa Rica: Editorial Argumentos, 1987.

Estades Font, María Eugenia. *La presencia militar de Estados Unidos en Puerto Rico 1898–1918*. 2d ed. Río Piedras, PR: Ediciones Huracán, 1999.

Ferrao, Luis A. *Pedro Albizu Campos y el nacionalismo puertorriqueño*. San Juan: Editorial Cultural, 1990.

Ferrer, Ada. *Insurgent Cuba: Race, Nation, and Revolution*. Chapel Hill: University of North Carolina Press, 1999.

Foner, Philip S. *The Spanish-Cuban-American War and the Birth of American Imperialism, 1895–1902*. 2 vols. New York: Monthly Review Press, 1972.

Franqui, Carlos. *Diary of the Cuban Revolution*. New York: Seaver Books, 1980.

Freire, Joaquín. *Presencia de Puerto Rico en la historia de Cuba*. San Juan: Instituto de Cultura Puertorriqueña, 1966.

García, Gervasio Luis. "Strangers in Paradise? Puerto Rico en la correspondencia de los cónsules norteamericanos (1869–1900)." Paper presented at the Caribbean between Empires Symposium, Princeton University, May 5–7, 1994.

García Passalacqua, Juan Manuel. *Dignidad y jaibería: Temer y ser puertorriqueno* (San Juan: Editorial Cultural, 1993.

Giusti Cordero, Juan A. "En búsqueda de la nación concreta: 'El grupo español' en la industria azucarera de Puerto Rico, 1890–1920." In *La nación soñada: Cuba, Puerto Rico y Filipinas ante el 98*, edited by Consuelo Naranjo, Miguel A. Puig-Samper, and Luis Miguel García Mora, 211–24. Aranjuez, Spain: Ediciones Doce Calles, 1996.

Gleijeses, Piero. *The Dominican Crisis: The 1965 Constitutionalist Revolt and American Intervention.* Baltimore: Johns Hopkins University Press, 1978.

González, José Luis. *El país de los cuatro pisos y otros ensayos.* Río Piedras, PR: Ediciones Huracán, 1980.

———. *Puerto Rico the Four-Storeyed Country and Other Essays.* Princeton, NJ: Markus Wiener Publishers, 1993.

González, Justo L. *The Development of Christianity in the Latin Caribbean.* Grand Rapids, MI: Wm. B. Eerdmans, 1969.

Greer, Harold. "Baptists in Western Cuba." *Cuban Studies* 19 (1989): 61–77.

Guerra y Sánchez, Ramiro. *Azúcar y población en las Antillas.* Havana: Cultural, S.A., 1927.

Guillén, Nicolás. "Balada de los dos abuelos." In *Nueva Antología,* 43–45. 4th ed. Mexico City: Editores Mexicanos Unidos, 1986.

Hahner, June E. "The Nineteenth-Century Feminist Press and Women's Rights in Brazil." In *Latin American Women: Historical Perspectives,* edited by Asunción Lavrin, 253–85. Westport, CT: Greenwood Press, 1978.

Hartlyn, Jonathan. *The Struggle for Democratic Politics in the Dominican Republic.* Chapel Hill: University of North Carolina Press, 1999.

Hauch, Charles C. "Attitudes of Foreign Governments towards the Spanish Reoccupation of the Dominican Republic." *HAHR* 27:2 (May 1947): 247–68.

Healy, David P. *The United States in Cuba, 1898–1902.* Madison: University of Wisconsin Press, 1963.

Helg, Aline. *Our Rightful Share: The Afro-Cuban Struggle for Equality, 1886–1912.* Chapel Hill: University of North Carolina Press, 1995.

Heureaux, Ulises. *Rafael Leónidas Trujillo Molina.* Santo Domingo, DR: Cronos, 1933.

Hoetink, H. *The Dominican People, 1850–1900.* Translated by Stephen K. Ault. Baltimore: Johns Hopkins University Press, 1982.

_____ . "'Race' and Color in the Caribbean." In *Caribbean Contours,* *edited by* Sidney W. Mintz and Sally Price, 55–84. Baltimore: Johns Hopkins University Press, 1995.

Ibarra, Jorge. *Cuba, 1898–1921: Partidos políticos y clases sociales.* Havana: Editorial de Ciencias Sociales, 1992.

Ichazo, León, director. *Azúcar amarga.* First Look Films/Overseas Film Group, 1996.

Iglesias García, Fe. "The Development of Capitalism in Cuban Sugar Production Based on Slave Labor in Cuba, 1860–1900." In *Between Slavery and Free Labor,* edited by Manuel Moreno Fraginals, Frank Moya Pons, and Stanley L. Engerman, 54–76. Baltimore: Johns Hopkins University Press, 1985.

Instituto Cubano del Libro and Instituto de Cooperación Iberoamericana, eds. *Nuestra común historia: Poblamiento y nacionalidad.* Havana: Editorial de Ciencias Sociales, 1993.

Jiménez de Wagenheim, Olga. *El Grito de Lares: Sus causas y sus hombres.* Río Piedras, PR: Ediciones Huracán, 1984.

Kinsbruner, Jay. *Not of Pure Blood: The Free People of Color and Racial Prejudice in Nineteenth-Century Puerto Rico.* Durham, NC: Duke University Press, 1996.

Knight, Franklin W. *The Caribbean: The Genesis of a Fragmented Nationalism.* 2d ed. New York: Oxford University Press, 1990.

_____ . "Origins of Wealth and the Sugar Revolution in Cuba, 1750–1850." *HAHR* 57:2 (May 1977): 231–53.

_____ . *Slave Society in Cuba during the Nineteenth Century.* Madison: University of Wisconsin Press, 1970.

Lemoine, Maurice. *Sucre amer.* Paris: Eucre, 1981.

Lockmiller, David. *Magoon in Cuba: A History of the Second Intervention, 1906–1909.* New York: Greenwood Press, 1969.

Lockward, Alfonso, ed. *Documentos para la historia de las relaciones dominico americanas (1837–1860).* Santo Domingo, DR: Editora Corripio, 1987.

Lockward, George A. *El Protestantismo en Dominicana.* 2d ed. Santo Domingo, DR: Universidad CETEC, 1982.

López Nieves, Luis. "Seva: Historia de la primera invasión norteamericana de la isla de Puerto Rico ocurrida en mayo de 1898." *Claridad*, December 23, 1983.

López Segrera, Francisco. *Cuba: Capitalismo dependiente y subdesarrollo (1510–1959)*. 2d ed. Mexico City: Editorial Diógenes, 1979.

Lugo Silva, Enrique. *The Tugwell Administration in Puerto Rico, 1941–1946*. Río Piedras, PR: n.p., 1955.

Luque de Sánchez, María Dolores. *La ocupación norteamericana y la ley Foraker (La opinión pública puertorriqueña, 1898–1904)*. Río Piedras: Editorial de la Universidad de Puerto Rico, 1980.

Maldonado Denis, Manuel. *Puerto Rico: Una interpretación histórico-social*. Mexico City: Siglo Veintiuno Editores, 1973.

Marrero, Leví. *Cuba: Economía y sociedad*. 15 vols. Madrid: Editorial Playor, 1971–1992.

Marte, Roberto. *Cuba y la República Dominicana: Transición económica en el Caribe del siglo XIX*. Santo Domingo, DR: Universidad APEC, [1988].

_____ . *Estadísticas y documentos históricos sobre Santo Domingo (1805–1890)*. Santo Domingo, DR: Museo Nacional de Historia y Geografía, 1984.

Martínez-Alier, Verena. *Marriage, Class and Colour in Nineteenth-Century Cuba*. Ann Arbor: University of Michigan Press, 1989.

Martínez-Fernández, Luis. "'Don't Die Here': The Death and Burial of Protestants in the Hispanic Caribbean, 1840–1885." *The Americas* 49:1 (July 1992): 23–47.

_____ . *Fighting Slavery in the Caribbean: The Life and Times of a British Family in Nineteenth-Century Havana*. Armonk, NY: M. E. Sharpe, 1998.

_____ . *Protestantism and Political Conflict in the Nineteenth-Century Hispanic Caribbean*. New Brunswick, NJ: Rutgers University Press, 2002.

_____ . *Torn between Empires: Economy, Society, and Patterns of Political Thought in the Hispanic Caribbean, 1840–1878*. Athens: University of Georgia Press, 1994.

Mathews, Thomas T. *La política puertorriqueña y el Nuevo Trato.* Río Piedras, PR: Editorial de la Universidad de Puerto Rico, 1967.

May, Robert E. "Lobbyists for Commercial Empire: Jane Cazneau, William Cazneau, and U.S. Caribbean Policy, 1846–1878." *Pacific Historical Review* 48:3 (1979): 383–412.

_____. "'Plenipotentiary in Petticoats': Jane M. Cazneau and American Foreign Policy in the Mid-Nineteenth Century." In *Women and American Foreign Policy,* edited by Edward P. Crapol, 19–44. New York: Greenwood Press, 1987.

Meléndez, Edgardo. *Movimiento anexionista en Puerto Rico.* Río Piedras: Editorial de la Universidad de Puerto Rico, 1993.

Mendelson, Johanna S. R. "The Feminine Press: The View of Women in Colonial Journals of Spanish America, 1790–1810." In *Latin American Women: Historical Perspectives,* edited by Asunción Lavrin, 198–218. Westport, CT: Greenwood Press, 1978.

Miller, Beth K. "Avellaneda, Nineteenth-Century Feminist." *Revista/ Review Interamericana* 4 (Summer 1974): 177–83.

Mintz, Sidney W. "The Caribbean as a Socio-cultural Area." *Journal of World History* 9:4 (1966): 912–37.

_____. "The Caribbean Region." In *Readings in Caribbean History and Economics: An Introduction to the Region,* edited by Roberta Marx Delson, 6–11. New York: Gordon and Breach, 1981.

_____. *Caribbean Transformations.* New York: Columbia University Press, 1989.

_____. "Enduring Substances, Trying Theories: The Caribbean Region As OIKOUMENÊ." *Journal of the Royal Anthropological Institute* 2:2 (June 1996): 289–311.

_____. *Sweetness and Power: The Place of Sugar in Modern History.* New York: Viking Press, 1985.

Mintz, Sidney W., and Richard Price. *The Birth of African-American Culture: An Anthropological Perspective.* Boston: Beacon Press, 1992.

Mitchell, Nancy. *The Danger of Dreams: German and American Imperialism in Latin America.* Chapel Hill: University of North Carolina Press, 1999.

Monclús, Miguel Ángel. *El caudillismo en la República Dominicana*. 4th ed. Santo Domingo, DR: Universidad CETEC, 1983.

Morales Carrión, Arturo. "1898: The Hope and the Trauma." In *Puerto Rico: A Political and Cultural History*, edited by Arturo Morales Carrión, 121–59.. New York: W. W. Norton, 1983.

_____ . *Auge y decadencia de la trata negrera en Puerto Rico (1820–1860)*. San Juan: Instituto de Cultura Puertorriqueña, 1978.

_____ , ed., *Puerto Rico: A Political and Cultural History*. New York: W. W. Norton, 1983.

Moraza Ortiz, Manuel E. *La masacre de Ponce*. Hato Rey, PR: Publicaciones Puertorriqueñas, 2001.

Moreno Fraginals, Manuel. *Cuba/España España/Cuba: Historia común*. Barcelona: Editorial Crítica, 1995.

_____ . *El ingenio: El complejo económico social del azúcar*. 3 vols. Havana: Editorial de Ciencias Sociales, 1978.

_____ . "Plantations in the Caribbean: Cuba, Puerto Rico, and the Dominican Republic in the Late Nineteenth Century." In *Between Slavery and Free Labor,* edited by Manuel

Moreno Fraginals, Frank Moya Pons, and Stanley L. Engerman, 3–21. Baltimore: Johns Hopkins University Press, 1985.

Moreno Fraginals, Manuel, Frank Moya Pons, and Stanley L. Engerman, eds. *Between Slavery and Free Labor: The Spanish-Speaking Caribbean in the Nineteenth Century*. Baltimore: Johns Hopkins University Press, 1985.

Moya Pons, Frank. *Manual de historia dominicana*. 8th ed. Santiago, DR: Universidad Católica Madre y Maestra, 1984.

Muñoz Marín, Luis. "The Sad Case of Porto Rico." *American Mercury* 16:62 (February 1929): 136–41.

Murray, David. *Odious Commerce: Britain, Spain, and the Abolition of the Cuban Slave Trade*. Cambridge: Cambridge University Press, 1980.

Naipaul, V. S. *The Middle Passage*. New York: Vintage Books, 1990.

Naranjo Orovio, Consuelo. "La emigración española a Iberoámerica desde 1880 a 1930: Análisis cuantitativo." In *Nuestra común historia*, edited by Instituto Cubano del Libro and Instituto de Cooperación Iberoamericana,116–55. Havana: Editorial de Ciencias Sociales, 1993.

Naranjo, Consuelo, Miguel A. Puig-Samper, and Luis Miguel García Mora, eds. *La nación soñada: Cuba, Puerto Rico y Filipinas ante el 98*. Aranjuez, Spain: Ediciones Doce Calles, 1996.

Náter Vázquez, Laura. "El '98 en la historiografía puertorriqueña: Del político entusiasta al héroe popular." *Op. Cit.: Boletín del Centro de Investigaciones Históricas de la Universidad de Puerto Rico* 4 (1988–1989): 101–22.

Nelson, William Javier. "The Haitian Political Situation and Its Effect on the Dominican Republic: 1849–1871." *The Americas* 45:2 (October 1988): 227–35.

Neumann Gandía, Eduardo. *Verdadera y auténtica historia de la ciudad de Ponce desde sus primitivos tiempos hasta la época contemporánea.* San Juan: n.p., 1913.

Nevins, Allan. *Hamilton Fish: The Inner History of the Grant Administration.* New York: Dodd, Mead, 1936.

Offner, John L. *An Unwanted War: The Diplomacy of the United States and Spain over Cuba, 1895–1898.* Chapel Hill: University of North Carolina Press, 1992.

Oostindie, Gert J. "Cuban Railroads, 1803–1868: Origins and Effects of Progressive Entrepreneurialism." *Caribbean Studies* 20:3–4 (1988): 24–45.

———. "España y el resurgimiento desigual del Caribe Hispánico, 1760–1860." In *Europa e Iberoamérica, cinco siglos de intercambios*, coordinated by María Justina Saravia Viejo, 2:705–24. Proceedings of the 9th International Congress of the History of the Americas. Seville: AHILA, 1992.

Ortiz, Fernando. *Contrapunteo cubano del tabaco y el azúcar.* Havana: Jesús Montero, 1940.

———. "Los factores humanos de la cubanidad." Havana: Molina y Compañía, n.d. Originally published in *Revista Bimestre Cubana* 45:2 (1940).

Pabón Ortega, Carlos E. "El 98 en el imaginario nacional: Seva o la 'nación soñada.'" In *La nación soñada: Cuba, Puerto Rico y Filipinas ante el 98*, edited by Consuelo Naranjo, Miguel A. Puig-Samper, and Luis Miguel García Mora, 547–57. Aranjuez, Spain: Ediciones Doce Calles, 1996.

Paolino, Ernest N. *The Foundations of the American Empire: William Henry Seward and U.S. Foreign Policy*. Ithaca, NY: Cornell University Press, 1973.

Paquette, Robert Louis. *Sugar Is Made with Blood: The Conspiracy of La Escalera and the Conflict between Empires over Slavery in Cuba*. Middletown, CT: Wesleyan University Press, 1988.

Paterson, Thomas G. *Major Problems in American Foreign Policy: Documents and Essays*. 3d ed. Vol. 1. Lexington, MA: D. C. Heath, 1989.

Pedreira, Antonio S. *Insularismo*. 1934; reprint, Río Piedras, PR: Editorial Edil, 1973.

Peguero, Valentina, and Danilo de los Santos. *Visión general de la historia dominicana*. 10th ed. Santiago, DR: Universidad Católica Madre y Maestra, 1986.

Pérez, Carlos F. *Historia diplomática de Santo Domingo (1492–1862)*. Santo Domingo, DR: Escuela de Servicios Internacionales, Universidad Nacional Pedro Henríquez Ureña, 1973.

Pérez, Louis A., Jr. *Cuba: An Annotated Bibliography*. New York: Greenwood Press, 1988.

_____. *Cuba: Between Reform and Revolution*. 3rd ed. New York: Oxford University Press, 2006.

_____. *Cuba between Empires, 1878–1902*. Pittsburgh: University of Pittsburgh Press, 1983.

_____. *Cuba under the Platt Amendment, 1902–1934*. Pittsburgh: University of Pittsburgh Press, 1986.

_____. "North American Protestant Missionaries in Cuba and the Culture of Hegemony, 1898–1920." In *Essays on Cuban History: Historiography and Research*, edited by Louis A. Pérez, Jr., 53–72. Gainesville: University Press of Florida, 1995.

_____ . *On Becoming Cuban: Identity, Nationality, and Culture.* Chapel Hill: University of North Carolina Press, 1999.

_____ . "Politics, Peasants and People of Color: The 1912 'Race War' in Cuba Reconsidered." *HAHR* 66:3 (1986): 509–39.

_____ . *Winds of Change: Hurricanes and the Transformation of Nineteenth-Century Cuba.* Chapel Hill: University of North Carolina Press, 2001.

Pérez de la Riva, Juan. "Demografía de los culíes. Chinos en Cuba (1853–1874)." In *El Barracón: Esclavitud y capitalismo en Cuba*, edited by Juan Pérez de la Riva, 55–87. Barcelona: Editorial Crítica, 1978.

_____ . "Desaparición de la población indígena cubana." *Universidad de La Habana* 196–197 (1972): 61–84.

Pérez Vega, Ivette. "Las oleadas de inmigración sobre el sur de Puerto Rico: El caso de las sociedades mercantiles creadas en Ponce (1816–1830)." *Revista del Centro de Estudios Avanzados de Puerto Rico y el Caribe* 9 (January–June 1987): 114–23.

Peukert, Detlev Julio K. "Anhelo de dependencia: Las ofertas de anexión de la República Dominicana a los Estados Unidos en el siglo XIX." *Jarbuch fur Geschichte von Staat, Wirtschaft und Gesellschaft Lateinamerikas* 23 (1986): 305–50.

Picó, Fernando. *1898: La guerra después de la guerra.* Río Piedras, PR: Ediciones Huracán, 1987.

_____ . *Amargo Café (Los pequeños y medianos caficultores de Utuado en la segunda mitad del siglo XIX).* Río Piedras, PR: Ediciones Huracán, 1981.

_____ . *Libertad y servidumbre en el Puerto Rico del siglo XIX (Los jornaleros utuadeños en vísperas del auge del café.* 2d ed. Río Piedras, PR: Ediciones Huracán, 1982.

_____ . "La revolución puertorriqueña de 1898: La necesidad de un nuevo paradigma para entender el '98 puertorriqueño." Paper presented at the 28th annual meeting of the Association of Caribbean Historians, Barbados, April 14–19, 1996.

Portell-Vilá, Herminio. *Historia de Cuba en sus relaciones con los Estados Unidos y España*. 4 vols. Havana: Montero, 1938–1941.

_____ . *Nueva historia de la República de Cuba (1898–1979)*. Miami: La Moderna Poesía, 1986.

Quintero Rivera, Ángel G. *Conflictos de clase y política en Puerto Rico*. Río Piedras, PR: Ediciones Huracán, 1976.

_____ . *Patricios y plebeyos: Burgueses, hacendados, artesanos y obreros*. Río Piedras: Ediciones Huracán, 1988.

_____ . *¡Salsa, sabor y control! Sociología de la música "tropical."* Mexico City: Siglo XXI Editores, 1998.

Ramos, Marcos Antonio. *Panorama del protestantismo en Cuba*. San José, Costa Rica: Editorial Caribe, 1986.

Ramos Mattei, Andrés A., ed. *Azúcar y esclavitud*. San Juan: privately printed, 1982.

_____ . *Betances en el ciclo revolucionario antillano, 1867–1875*. San Juan: Instituto de Cultura Puertorriqueña, 1987.

_____ . *La hacienda azucarera: Su crecimiento y crisis en Puerto Rico (siglo XIX)*. San Juan: CEREP, 1981.

_____ . "La importación de trabajadores contratados para la industria azucarera puertorriqueña: 1860–1880." In *Inmigración y clases sociales en el Puerto Rico del siglo XIX*, edited by Francisco A. Scarano, 125–42. Río Piedras, PR: Ediciones Huracán, 1981.

_____ . "El liberto en el régimen de trabajo azucarero de Puerto Rico, 1870–1880." In

Azúcar y esclavitud, edited by Andrés A. Ramos Mattei, 91–124. San Juan: privately printed, 1982.

Rauch, Basil. *American Interest in Cuba: 1848–1855*. New York: Columbia University Press, 1948.

Richardson, James D. *A Compilation of the Messages and Papers of the Presidents, 1789–1897*. 10 vols. Washington, DC: Government Printing Office, 1896–1899.

Rico, Gumersindo. "Prólogo." In *Nuestra común historia*, edited by Instituto Cubano del Libro and Instituto de Cooperación Iberoamericana, vii–x. Havana: Editorial de Ciencias Sociales, 1993.

Riera, Mario. *Cuba política, 1899–1955*. Havana: n.p., 1955.

Rivera Martínez, Antonio. *Así empezó Vieques*. Río Piedras: Universidad de Puerto Rico, 1963.

Rivero, Ángel. *Crónica de la Guerra Hispano Americana en Puerto Rico*. 1921; reprint, New York: Plus Ultra Educational Publishers, 1973.

Rodríguez Demorizi, Emilio, ed. *Antecedentes de la anexión a España*. Santo Domingo, DR: Academia Dominicana de la Historia, 1955.

_____ , ed. *Correspondencia del consul de Francia en Santo Domingo, 1846–1850*. 2 vols. Santo Domingo, DR: Editora Montalvo, 1944–1947.

_____ , ed. *Documentos para la historia de la República Dominicana*. 4 vols. Santo Domingo, DR: Editora Montalvo–Academia Dominicana de la Historia, 1944–1981.

_____ , ed. *Papeles de Buenaventura Báez*. Santo Domingo, DR: Editora Montalvo, 1969.

_____ , ed. *Papeles de Pedro Bonó, para la historia de las ideas políticas en Santo Domingo*. Santo Domingo, DR: Editora del Caribe, 1964.

_____ , ed. *Papeles de Santana*. Rome: Tipografía G. Menaglia, 1952.

_____ , ed. *Proyecto para la incorporación de Santo Domingo a Norte América*. Santo Domingo, DR: Editora Montalvo, 1945.

_____ , ed. *Samaná, pasado y porvenir*. Santo Domingo, DR: Editora Montalvo, 1945.

_____ , ed. *Santana y los poetas de su tiempo*. Santo Domingo, DR: Academia Dominicana de la Historia, 1969.

Rosario Natal, Carmelo. "El '98 puertorriqueño en tres tiempos: Ensayo historiográfico." In *1898: Enfoques y perspectivas*, edited by Luis González Vales, 43–79. San Juan: Academia Puertorriqueña de la Historia, 1997.

_____ . *Puerto Rico y la crisis de la Guerra Hispanoamericana (1895–1898)*. Hato Rey, PR: Ramallo Brothers Printing, 1975.

Sagás, Ernesto. *Race and Politics in the Dominican Republic*. Gainesville: University Press of Florida, 2000.

Sánchez-Boudy, José. *Filosofía del cubano . . . y de lo cubano*. Miami: Ediciones Universal, 1996.

Sang, Mu-Kien A. *Buenaventura Báez: El caudillo del sur (1844–1878)*. Santo Domingo, DR: Ediciones Taller, 1991.

_____. Ulises Heureaux: Biografía de un dictador. Santo Domingo, DR: INTEC, 1986.

Santiago-Valles, Kelvin A. *"Subject People" and Colonial Discourses: Economic Transformation and Social Disorder in Puerto Rico, 1898–1947*. Albany: State University of New York Press, 1994.

Scarano, Francisco A. "Inmigración y estructura de clases: Los hacendados de Ponce, 1815–1845." In *Inmigración y clases sociales en el Puerto Rico del siglo XIX*, edited by Francico A. Scarano, 21–66. Río Piedras, PR: Ediciones Huracán, 1981.

_____. *Sugar and Slavery in Puerto Rico: The Plantation Economy of Ponce, 1800–1850*. Madison: University of Wisconsin Press, 1984.

Schmidt-Nowara, Christopher. *Empire and Antislavery: Spain, Cuba, and Puerto Rico, 1833–1874*. Pittsburgh: University of Pittsburgh Press, 1999.

Schroeder, Susan. *Cuba: A Handbook of Historical Statistics*. Boston: G. K. Hall, 1982.

Schwartz, Stuart B. "The Hurricane of San Ciriaco: Disaster, Politics, and Society in Puerto Rico, 1899–1901." *HAHR* 72:3 (August 1992): 303–34.

Scott, Rebecca J. *Slave Emancipation in Cuba: The Transition to Free Labor, 1860–1899*. Princeton, NJ: Princeton University Press, 1985.

Smith, Peter H. *Talons of the Eagle: Dynamics of U.S.–Latin American Relations*. New York: Oxford University Press, 1996.

Smith, Theodore Clarke. "Expansion after the Civil War, 1865–71." Political Science Quarterly 16:3 (1901): 412–36.

Stubbs, Jean. *Cuba: The Test of Time*. London: Latin America Bureau, 1989.

Tansill, Charles C. *The United States and Santo Domingo, 1798–1873*. Baltimore: Johns Hopkins University Press, 1938.

Torres-Cuevas, Eduardo. "Patria, pueblo y revolución." In *Nuestra común historia*, edited by Instituto Cubano del Libro and Instituto de Cooperación Iberoamericana, 1–22. Havana: Editorial de Ciencias Sociales, 1993.

Trías Monge, José. *Puerto Rico: The Trials of the Oldest Colony in the World*. New Haven, CT: Yale University Press, 1997.

Van Alstyne, Richard W., ed. "Anglo-American Relations, 1853–57." *American Historical Review* 42:3 (April 1937): 491–500.

Vivian, Thomas J., and Ruel P. Smith. *Everything about Our New Possessions*. New York: R. F. Fenno, 1899.

Welles, Sumner. *Naboth's Vineyard: The Dominican Republic, 1844–1924*. 2 vols. New York: Payson and Clarke, 1928.

Whitney, Robert. *State and Revolution in Cuba: Mass Mobilization and Political Change, 1920–1940*. Chapel Hill: University of North Carolina Press, 2001.

Williams, Eric. *From Columbus to Castro: The History of the Caribbean*. New York: Vintage Books, 1984.

Yungling, David G., ed. *Highlights in the Debates in the Spanish Chamber of Deputies Relative to the Abandonment of Santo Domingo*. Washington, DC: Murray & Heister, 1941.

Zanetti Lecuona, Oscar. *Cautivos de la reciprocidad*. Havana: Ediciones ENPES, 1989.

Zanetti Lecuona, Oscar, and Alejandro García Álvarez. *Sugar and Railroads: A Cuban History, 1837–1959*. Chapel Hill: University of North Carolina Press, 1998.

Zeno Gandía, Manuel. *La Charca*. 1894; reprint, Barcelona: Ediciones Puerto, 1973.

CPSIA information can be obtained
at www.ICGtesting.com
Printed in the USA
FFOW02n2057040215
10793FF